Wagner's *Meistersinger*

Wagner's *Meistersinger*
Performance, History, Representation

Edited by
Nicholas Vazsonyi

University of Rochester Press

Copyright © 2002 Nicholas Vazsonyi

All Rights Reserved. Except as permitted under current legislation, no part of this work may be photocopied, stored in a retrieval system, published, performed in public, adapted, broadcast, transmitted, recorded, or reproduced in any form or by any means, without the prior permission of the copyright owner.

First published 2003
Soft cover edition published 2004

The University of Rochester Press
668 Mt. Hope Avenue, Rochester, NY 14620, USA
Boydell & Brewer, Ltd.
P.O. Box 9, Woodbridge, Suffolk IP12 3DF, UK
www.urpress.com

ISBN 1–58046–131–X (hard cover)
ISBN 1–58046–168–9 (soft cover)

Library of Congress Cataloging-in-Publication Data

Wagner's Meistersinger : performance, history, representation / edited by Nicholas Vazsonyi.
   p. cm.
   Includes bibliographical references (p.) and index.
   Contents: Climbing Mount Everest : on conducting Die Meistersinger / P. Schneider — We must finally stop apologizing for Die Meistersinger : a conversation with Harry Kupfer / H. Kupfer — Richard Wagner's cobbler poet / D. Fischer-Dieskau — The dangers of satisfaction : on songs, rehearsals, and repetition in Die Meistersinger / L. Goehr — Stereoscopic vision : sight and community in Die Meistersinger / . Koepnick — The most German of all German operas : Die Meistersinger through the lens of third Reich / D.B. Dennis — http://worldwidewagner.richard.de : an interview with the composer concerning history, nation, and Die Meistersinger / P. Höyng — Die Meistersinger as comedy : the performative and social signification of genre / K. van den Berg —Masters and their critics : Wagner, Hanslick, Beckmesser, and Die Meistersinger / T.S. Grey — Du warst mein Feind von je : the Beckmesser controversy revisited / H.R. Vaget — I married Eva : gender construction and Die Meistersinger / E. Rieger.
   ISBN 1-58046-131-X
   1. Wagner, Richard, 1813–1883. Meistersinger von Nërnberg. I. Vazsonyi, Nicholas, 1963–
ML410.W1 A286 2002
781.1—dc21   2002035762

British Library Cataloguing-in-Publication Data
A catalogue record for this book is available from the British Library

Designed and typeset by Straight Creek Bookmakers
Printed in the United States of America
This publication is printed on acid-free paper

Contents

List of Illustrations   vii

Introduction. *Die Meistersinger*: Performance, History, Representation   1
NICHOLAS VAZSONYI

I. Performing (in) *Die Meistersinger*   21

   1. "Climbing Mount Everest": On Conducting *Die Meistersinger*   23
       PETER SCHNEIDER
   2. "We Must Finally Stop Apologizing for *Die Meistersinger*!": A Conversation with Harry Kupfer   39
       HARRY KUPFER
   3. Richard Wagner's Cobbler Poet   51
       DIETRICH FISCHER-DIESKAU
   4. The Dangers of Satisfaction: On Songs, Rehearsals, and Repetition in *Die Meistersinger*   56
       LYDIA GOEHR

II. History in/of *Die Meistersinger*   71

   5. Stereoscopic Vision: Sight and Community in *Die Meistersinger*   73
       LUTZ KOEPNICK
   6. "The Most German of All German Operas": *Die Meistersinger* through the Lens of the Third Reich   98
       DAVID B. DENNIS
   7. http://*worldwidewagner*.richard.de: An Interview with the Composer concerning History, Nation, and *Die Meistersinger*   120
       PETER HÖYNG

III. Representation and/in *Die Meistersinger*   143

   8. *Die Meistersinger* as Comedy: The Performative and Social Signification of Genre   145
       KLAUS VAN DEN BERG
   9. Masters and Their Critics: Wagner, Hanslick, Beckmesser, and *Die Meistersinger*   165
       THOMAS S. GREY

10. "Du warst mein Feind von je": The Beckmesser Controversy
    Revisited   190
    HANS RUDOLF VAGET
11. "I Married Eva": Gender Construction and
    Die Meistersinger   209
    EVA RIEGER

Works Cited   226
Contributors   239
Index   242

Illustrations

Figure 2.1.	Act III—Sachs's workshop	43
Figure 2.2.	Act II—Beckmesser's Serenade	44
Figure 2.3.	Act III—Sachs's workshop	45
Figure 2.4.	Act I—St. Catherine's Church	47
Figure 2.5.	Act II—Riot scene	48
Figure 2.6.	Act III—Festival meadow	50
Figure 5.1.	Heinrich Döll's 1869 set for Act III of *Die Meistersinger*: Meadow on the banks of the Pegnitz	83
Figure 5.2.	Wheatsone's original stereoscope	86
Figure 5.3.	The ordinary stereoscope of Brewster	87

Introduction
Die Meistersinger: Performance, History, Representation

Nicholas Vazsonyi

Few personalities in cultural memory provide such ideal ground for interdisciplinary, or at least multidisciplinary, consideration as Richard Wagner, arguably the most significant composer this side of Beethoven. There is Wagner the musical innovator with a genius for evocative and sensuous sounds, Wagner the avant-garde dramatist with conservative tastes, Wagner the anti-Semite with Jewish friends, the nationalist political pamphleteer who associated with Marx and Bakhunin, the transcendent romanticist with a keen eye for business, the womanizing egotist, chased by creditors but with a king in the palm of his hands, worshipped and loathed by Nietzsche, Wagner the founder of the longest-standing theatrical tradition in German history. All these and more have been studied in what annually becomes an ever more unwieldy array of publications. And yet there is still work to be done, primarily in overcoming what may be the most stubborn of disciplinary divides, the one between music and what I will broadly call the "other" humanities. The problem with music is that its constituent components reach in several directions and require an assemblage of different skills and expertise not ordinarily associated with any other discipline that readily comes to mind. While music history and literature—for want of a better term—certainly do belong to the "humanities," music theory combines not only the study of musical structures and a "grammar" that is almost mathematical in its conceptual complexity, but demands also the development of an acoustic sensitivity that includes the ability to "visualize" sound. The physics and physicality of this ear-brain training has much to do with what I would call the third branch of "music": performance. This branch adds to the intellectual and auditory requirements additional physical and mental skills, including the capability of remembering large amounts of data, often under intense pressure. Talking about music in any reasonable way requires sensitivity to, if not actual experience with all of these. In the meantime, what we generally call the humanities are a long way off. Traditional scholars of the humanities—even the music lovers among them—thus understandably shy away from addressing musical issues in their scholarship.

There have more recently been notable—though not uncontroversial—exceptions to this divide. Lawrence Kramer[1] has made significant contributions to our understanding of eighteenth- and nineteenth-century music as a culturally coded referent; Carolyn Abbate and Roger Parker[2] have also sought to expand the dimensions of operatic analysis beyond what has traditionally constituted the disciplinary limits of music history and musicology. Specifically in the case of Wagner, these exceptions include Marc Weiner's admittedly problematic indictment of Wagner which is nevertheless supported by extensive and close attention to musical detail.[3] There have also been musicological studies that conversely demonstrate a keen sensitivity to the text and dramatic development. Specifically in the case of *Die Meistersinger von Nürnberg*, these have recently included Ray Komow's analysis of the mastersingers' guild scene in Act I, including Walther's two arias, which demonstrates in minute detail how Wagner uses musical and textual structures to augment dramatic characterization.[4] Despite lingering rejection by traditional Germanists of what they have deemed Wagner's inferior poetic and linguistic skills, Komow shows instead how Wagner is the consummate master of using all means—textual, musical, and dramatic—to create convincing characterizations that are successful precisely because even apparently insignificant formal details have been carefully honed to contribute to the overall effect. Looking instead at large-scale forms and relationships, William Kinderman analyzes musical and textual references connecting Acts II and III of *Die Meistersinger* to develop our understanding of Hans Sachs's relationship with Eva and to show just how deep the musical connections are to *Tristan und Isolde*.[5] But I would submit that these excep-

---

1. Lawrence Kramer, *Music and Poetry: The Nineteenth Century and After* (Berkeley: U of California P, 1984), and *Music as Cultural Practice, 1800–1900* (Berkeley: U of California P, 1990). Others involved in aspects of this project, like Peter Kivy, John Neubauer, and Susan McClary, not to mention Lydia Goehr (who is a contributor to this volume) also come readily to mind.

2. Carolyn Abbate and Roger Parker, eds., *Analyzing Opera: Verdi and Wagner* (Berkeley: U of California P, 1989), and Carolyn Abbate, *Unsung Voices: Opera and Musical Narrative in the Nineteenth Century* (Princeton, N.J.: Princeton UP, 1991).

3. Marc A. Weiner, *Richard Wagner and the Anti-Semitic Imagination* (Lincoln: U of Nebraska P, 1995).

4. Ray Komow, "The Structure of Wagner's 'Assembly of the Mastersingers' Guild,'" *Journal of Musicological Research* 13 (1993): 185–206. See also Paul Buck's exhaustive study of the leitmotivs in *Die Meistersinger* and their relationship to dramatic development, and in particular at the intersections of text and music, see Paul Buck, *Richard Wagners 'Meistersinger': Eine Führung durch das Werk*, (Frankfurt/M: Lang, 1990).

5. William Kinderman, "Hans Sachs's 'Cobbler Song,' *Tristan*, and the 'Bitter Cry of the Resigned Man,'" *Journal of Musicological Research* 13 (1993): 161–84.

tions only prove the rule, and it is rare indeed to find books and articles where discussion of the music rests comfortably beside textual or cultural critique. I will return to the notion of "comfort" later on.

In his thought-provoking introduction to a set of innovative critical readings of opera libretti, David Levin complained that, historically, opera criticism has simultaneously placed music at the center and suppressed or banalized the text.[6] But ironically, in the case of Wagner, the reverse is also true, a phenomenon which Levin's volume on operatic analysis, from which music is conspicuously absent, reflects. The frequent avoidance of the musical dimension, or separation of the musical and non-musical, in Wagner scholarship can be explained on two grounds. First, Wagner was one of the few composers whose non-musical activities are arguably as significant as the musical ones. Second, as I already suggested, the specific theoretical knowledge of musical structures and terminology necessary for any analysis is not as easily grasped and appropriated as the methodologies of one discipline in the "other" humanities that can be transferred to another. Thus, while literary critics often avail themselves of models from psychoanalysis or political theory, it would be more extraordinary for that same literary critic to incorporate discussions of modulations and orchestration. The standard institutional division that comfortably places political science, language, and literature alongside departments of psychology within the same "college," while separating music into its own "school" merely confirms these seemingly entrenched limits of interdisciplinarity.

While the two most prominent Wagner handbooks[7] make every effort to integrate the music with the "other" humanities, monographs and volumes of collected essays are less apt to do so.[8] This disciplinary *manqué* accounts in part for the chronic problem of distorted emphasis that continues to plague Wagner scholarship and fuels the ongoing acrimony evident in so many exchanges.[9] The problem is a complex one which I do not wish

---

6. David J. Levin, ed., *Opera through Other Eyes* (Stanford: Stanford UP, 1993), 2.

7. Ulrich Müller and Peter Wapnewski, eds., *Richard-Wagner-Handbuch* (Stuttgart: Alfred Kröner, 1986), English translation, *Wagner Handbook,* trans. John Deathridge (Cambridge, Mass.: Harvard UP, 1992); and Barry Millington, ed., *The Wagner Compendium: A Guide to Wagner's Life and Music* (London: Thames & Hudson, 1992 and New York: Schirmer, 1992).

8. Two recent collections of significant essays, which, however, entirely bypass musical questions, illustrate the point: Saul Friedländer and Jörg Rüsen, eds., *Richard Wagner im Dritten Reich* (Munich: Beck, 2000), and Dieter Borchmeyer, Ami Maayani, and Susanne Vill, eds., *Richard Wagner und die Juden* (Stuttgart: Metzler, 2000).

9. On a national level, the ongoing though unofficial ban in Israel of performing Wagner's music and the controversy surrounding Daniel Barenboim's recent (2001) performance of a portion of *Tristan und Isolde* in Jerusalem serve to illustrate the point. I will refrain from mentioning examples of individual scholars engaged in what occasionally deteriorate into insultingly personal attacks.

to oversimplify by pointing solely to insufficient cooperation between academic fields, or by insinuating that some studies are published by scholars lacking sufficient or appropriate breadth of knowledge. Wagner himself can in part be held responsible for taking on tasks normally split between composer and librettist, for (mis)using his notoriety to make public declarations about history, linguistics, politics, philosophy, and race for which he lacked any formal training or expertise, declarations which, because of his notoriety, remain accessible and relevant long after such pronouncements would normally have sunk into oblivion. Then there is the long and ever-lengthening history of the representation and appropriation of Richard Wagner by his family and others which further complicates the issue. By necessity, everyone is compelled to create his or her own particular Wagner, a Wagner who then becomes an object to be defended or attacked relentlessly.

The state that characterizes Wagner scholarship in general is no different for the particular subject of this volume: *Die Meistersinger von Nürnberg*. Here, too, there are two handbooks that attempt to address the broad issues and thus necessarily attend to both the technically musical and musical-humanistic dimensions.[10] In the absence of any volume of collected essays on *Die Meistersinger*, individual articles and studies almost of necessity focus on specific aspects of the work and their significance. The problem with many such studies is that they nevertheless attempt a holistic grasp. Thus, depending on whom one reads, Richard Wagner's *Die Meistersinger* is either about "the medium in which it is written,"[11] about "art, tradition and authority,"[12] about "correct and false art,"[13] about art

---

10. Attila Csampai and Dietmar Holland, eds., *"Die Meistersinger von Nürnberg": Texte, Materialien, Kommentare*, (Reinbek b. Hamburg: Rowohlt, 1981), and John Hamilton Warrack, ed., *Richard Wagner, "Die Meistersinger von Nürnberg,"* Cambridge Opera Handbooks (Cambridge: Cambridge UP, 1994). For an excellent, though brief, overview of the significant musicological issues in *Die Meistersinger*, see John Warrack's chapter "'Wahn,' Words and Music," in his *Richard Wagner, "Die Meistersinger,"* 111–34.

11. Lucy Beckett, "*Die Meistersinger*: Naïve or Sentimental Art?" in *Richard Wagner, "Die Meistersinger,"* ed. John Warrack, 98–110, here 98.

12. Michael Tanner, *Wagner* (Princeton, N.J.: Princeton UP, 1996), 156. Later: "*Die Meistersinger* is, more that anything else, about the connections between life and art, between individuals' lives and the art they produce, and between the life of a community and its attitude to art" (160). In fairness to Tanner, see also his essay "Richard Wagner and Hans Sachs" in *Richard Wagner, "Die Meistersinger,"* ed. John Warrack, 83–97, where, among other nuanced observations, he writes: "It is an achievement of *Die Meistersinger* that one's focus on it keeps moving from the outside . . . to areas within it, and this process never stops" (97).

13. Peter Wapnewski, *Richard Wagner: Die Szene und ihr Meister*, 2nd ed. (Munich: Beck, 1983), 62: "Denn endlich geht es . . . um *rechte und falsche Kunst*: das Wagnersche Lebensproblem" (emphasis in original).

as "the only thing that justifies life,"[14] or about the dialectic between "improvisation and expertise,"[15] about "masters who paradoxically teach by not teaching,"[16] about "romantic sacrifice"[17] about "Wahn und Witz" (delusion and wit)[18] or, less charitably, about "hardly enough to fill even a modest two-act Singspiel."[19] More narrowly, the work has been interpreted as an exercise in failed reading,[20] more ominously as a blueprint for the type of German state orchestrated by Adolf Hitler.[21]

That Wagner's music drama continues to provide such fertile ground is hardly surprising, especially given ongoing controversies. But that such a diverse collection of readings, however selective, provocative, or objectionable for those who disagree, can in some measure at least be sustained by textual examination is a testament to *Meistersinger*'s complexity and subtlety—a word not often used to describe the work or its composer. Nevertheless, when read carefully, *Die Meistersinger* often seems to undermine or at least question the arguments it so boldly and emphatically presents. For example, on one level, Beckmesser is guilty of too zealously clinging to outmoded rules of song and composition. However, after his final humiliation cunningly orchestrated by Hans Sachs and accompanied by the jeers of all Nürnberg, it is none other than Sachs who turns to the opera's hero, Walther, as well as to townsfolk and audience with the injunction that the mastersingers and their tradition—precisely what Beckmesser had represented—must be upheld and respected. This

---

14. Carl Dahlhaus, *Richard Wagner's Music Dramas,* trans. Mary Whittall (Cambridge: Cambridge UP, 1979), 68.

15. Dieter Borchmeyer, *Das Theater Richard Wagners: Idee—Dichtung—Wirkung* (Stuttgart: Reclam, 1982), 206–30, especially 212. The subtitle of the *Meistersinger* chapter and its main thrust centers on "Improvisation und Metier—Die Poetik der *Meistersinger.*"

16. Lydia Goehr, *The Quest for Voice: On Music, Politics, and the Limits of Philosophy: The 1997 Ernest Bloch Lectures* (Oxford: Clarendon, 1998), which includes a chapter on *Die Meistersinger,* 48–87, here 74.

17. Paul Robinson, *Opera and Ideas: From Mozart to Strauss* (New York: Harper & Row, 1985), 211.

18. Nike Wagner, "Wahn und Witz in den *Meistersingern,*" *Wagner Theater* (Frankfurt/M: Insel, 1998), 126–63. She asserts that "Wahn und Witz" constitute the "secret center of the opera" (das geheime Zentrum dieser Oper), 126.

19. Eduard Hanslick, "Die Meistersinger von Richard Wagner," in his *Die moderne Oper: Kritiken und Studien* (Berlin: Hoffman, 1875, reprint Westmead: Gregg International, 1971), 293: "und kaum hinreichenden Stoff für ein bescheidenes, zweiactiges Singspiel bietet."

20. David J. Levin, "Reading Beckmesser Reading: Antisemitism and Aesthetic Practice in *The Mastersingers of Nuremberg,*" *New German Critique* 69 (1996): 127–46, esp. 138.

21. Joachim Köhler, "Der Meistersinger-Staat," in his *Wagners Hitler: Der Prophet und sein Vollstrecker* (Munich: Karl Blessing Verlag, 1997), 347–81.

complex and highly problematic operation, which involves creating and casting out a devil, only to reinstate him (or at least that which he represents) later as a necessary part of the whole, clearly requires unpacking to an extent I will not attempt here. My point is that the work, for all its apparently bombastic, dare I say Faustian, self-confidence and unwieldy length, is often delicate, decidedly uncertain, and, to borrow a term from Cultural Studies, polyvalently coded. By offering the reader so many possibilities, it, like Goethe's magnum opus, resists definitive interpretation.

To say that *Die Meistersinger* is exclusively "about" anything thus probably misses the mark. Nevertheless, a book must have its focus, and the unifying principle for this collection of essays on *Die Meistersinger von Nürnberg* is that, reduced to its essence, Wagner's music drama is concerned with performance, history, and representation. These three categories are not only interconnected within the work but become the modalities through which the story of its existence as an integral component of German culture can be traced since its premiere on June 21, 1868. What I mean by this is that, if we wish to think about *Die Meistersinger von Nürnberg*, we must also consider its performance, history, and representation, meaning also its history of performance as well as how it has performed in history. Perhaps even more importantly, however, and in response to what I have argued remains the greatest impediment to a new and more inclusive form of Wagner scholarship, these three categories establish a context in which specifically musical and more broadly cultural (humanistic) issues can be addressed side by side. Having made this claim, however, I would hasten to add that, while this volume has endeavored to mediate between a number of different voices and even open up a space for types of discourse not often seen in a more traditional academic publication, its focus remains more pronounced towards issues of text and culture than those which would be considered purely musicological.

Performance is a category both extrinsic and intrisic to *Die Meistersinger*. It is a work to be performed and, as such, I have included the voices of performers in this volume, even though their contributions do not conform to the more scholarly discourse of the remainder. The possibilities and limitations inherent in performance are important to consider, even for more theoretically oriented academic discussions. Within the work, performance is intimately bound up with the drama's central poetic dilemma, which probes the essential question posed by (musical) aesthetics as a philosophical discipline, namely "what is beautiful?" In his consideration of this question, Wagner departs from German philosophical tradition by refusing to answer in theoretical terms alone, but rather attempting to answer in practice, through performance. So pervasive is the imperative to perform that other major categories, such as good and evil, success and failure, acceptance and rejection—in sum, the aesthetic, cultural, and even political stakes of the drama—are determined by and reflected in Walther von Stolzing's and Sixtus Beckmesser's ability or inability to perform. The sexual metaphor represents overtones which abound in and interfere with the aesthetic dilemma and are hardly coincidental, a (con)fusion which Walther himself thematizes in the climax of his Act III Prize Song, where Eva becomes the literal embodiment of the aesthetic (the muse of Parnassus) and the erotic (Eva in Paradise).[22] Within the terms of the drama, the "ability to perform" necessarily means both winning the song competition (aesthetic) and getting the girl (erotic). Given "performance" as the criterion of analysis, it turns out that Veit Pogner's idea of offering his daughter as the prize for the winner of the song contest, however troubling and inappropriate in terms of even nineteenth-century gender politics and human rights, seems entirely appropriate within the discursive modality of the drama.[23]

Beginning as early as Hanslick's review, critical scholarship has made much of the fact that *Die Meistersinger* is the most "realistic" of Wagner's works,[24] or the only one that presents historical figures in an existing location rather than reinscribing a medieval or Germanic myth.[25] Nevertheless, by idealizing Nürnberg, its culture, and its albeit historical residents, *Die Meistersinger* formalizes a process of myth-making and mystification which preempts the most sophisticated political and corporate propaganda machines of the twentieth century and their multimedia capabilities. The fact that it is grounded in history has only served to render the myth more powerful. One of the devices making *Die Meistersinger* "the most German of all German operas"[26] is that

---

22. I disagree with Jeremy Tambling's assertion that there is a "repression of the sexual in Eva and *Die Meistersinger* generally," (42). While the point might be sustained in the case of Eva, though Harry Kupfer would certainly object (see his interview in this volume), even a cursory look at the music and text of Walther's Trial Song ("Fanget an") reveals that it is loaded with the acoustics and sentiments of unbounded sexuality. See Jeremy Tambling, *Opera and the Culture of Fascism* (Oxford: Clarendon, 1996).
23. On the gendered conflation of the sexual and the aesthetic within the feminine, see Eva Rieger's essay in this volume.
24. Hanslick, "Meistersinger," 299: "Er [Wagner] wendet endlich seinen Zwergen, Riesen und Walkyren den Rücken, stellt sich mitten in die reale Welt und gibt uns lebensvolle Bilder aus dem deutschen Volks- und Bürgerleben."
25. Recently, musicologist Martin Geck has even discussed *Die Meistersinger* as the example of Wagner's "musical realism," see *Zwischen Romantik und Restauration: Musik im Realismus-Diskurs 1848–1871* (Stuttgart: Metzler, 2001): especially 164–65, arguing in part that much of what the characters in *Die Meistersinger* "naturally" would be doing involves singing, thereby making the opera acceptable "even for opera skeptics."
26. Joseph Goebbels, "Richard Wagner und das Kunstempfinden unserer Zeit: Rundfunkrede von Reichsminister Dr. Goebbels," partially reprinted in *Die Meistersinger von Nürnberg: Texte, Materialien, Kommentare*, ed. Attila Csampai and Dietmar Holland, 194–99, here 196: "Unter all seinen Musikdramen ragen die *Meistersinger* als das deutscheste immerdar hervor."

it is rooted in, perpetuates, and intensifies a historical myth already three centuries old by the time Wagner conceived the work. The "real" mastersingers of the sixteenth-century and earlier had already created their own idealized lineage back to the so-called "twelve great masters," mostly actual poets of the Medieval period, including Walther von der Vogelweide, who represented the first flowering of German literature and culture early in the thirteenth century. The number twelve with its clearly biblical allusion served already then to characterize German art as a noumenal messiah around whom the living Masters were gathered. It is entirely fitting then that, in *Die Meistersinger,* there are also twelve masters. Fitting also that the opera's hero, the fictitious sixteenth-century Walther von Stolzing, names the historical thirteenth-century Walther von der Vogelweide as the master—though dead—from whom he learned his craft. Wagner's nineteenth-century fusion, or blurring, of fact and fiction adds yet another historical layer. When character Hans Sachs implores his townsfolk to "honor your German masters," Wagner presents a historical Sachs who would quite plausibly have been referring to the original masters of the 1200s and their successors, meaning Sachs himself. In addition, Wagner transforms his historical figure into a graven image, making Sachs a nineteenth-century mouthpiece through whom Wagner the composer addresses his contemporary audience. The lineage stretching back to the thirteenth century now includes not only the sixteenth-century Sachs, but the full roster of German "masters" up to and including Wagner. Wagner thus inscribes himself into an admittedly constructed, but successfully unified, "imagined" German cultural history for which he becomes the latest incarnation and disciple (read: Master). This "invented tradition," to borrow a concept from Eric Hobsbawm, is what, for better or worse, makes *Die Meistersinger* an enduring representation of the German national culture, German cultural history, or, in the words of Goebbels, "the most German of German operas."[27] It was this "invented tradition" that the Nazis appropriated and in turn extended by inscribing their own program and pageantry into the existing model constructed by Wagner, thereby also legitimizing National Socialism as an organic outgrowth of a deeply rooted German culture, rather than as an upstart political clique.

The literary-cultural lineage is complemented by Wagner's self-proclaimed use of a musical idiom reminiscent of Johann Sebastian Bach, generally evident in the work's richly contrapuntal style—which the prelude so proudly announces, and especially in the opening chorale.[28] Wagner was not alone

---

27. Eric Hobsbawm and Terence Ranger, eds, *The Invention of Tradition* (Cambridge: Cambridge UP, 1983). In a similar argument, Lydia Goehr also invokes Hobsbawm's concept of "invented tradition" in her *Quest for Voice,* 51–52.

28. See Arthur Groos, "Constructing Nuremberg: Typological and Proleptic Communities in *Die Meistersinger,*" *19th-Century Music* 16, 1 (1992): 18–34, esp. 22, 26, as well as Peter Schneider's essay in this volume.

among composers and musicians of the nineteenth century in ceding Bach a unique place in music history: the first coherent exponent of Western tonal music, and hence the first great German composer.[29] By incorporating allusions to Bach's musical style, Wagner not only creates a parallel to the literary-cultural narrative, but continues the type of codification of German musical history already found in utterances like Franz Grillparzer's speech delivered at the funeral of Ludwig van Beethoven in 1827, where Beethoven is declared the successor to "Händel, Bach, Haydn, and Mozart."[30] When compared with its literary counterpart, this musical continuum may be shorter in duration, but the sheer quantity and brilliance of the output matches and arguably exceeds what authors using the German language produced. Wagner rehearses this continuum, a historical tradition he did not invent, but one which he once again appropriates, and where he again places himself at its head.

As with the literary-cultural lineage, there was Nazi appropriation of this musical line as well, perhaps most evident in the musicological analyses of Alfred Lorenz, as Stephen McClatchie argued recently in his cogently written book.[31] Lorenz's main project, to discern coherent structure and form in Wagner's works, played "an important role in remaking Wagner into a monument to the great German tradition rhapsodized by the Nazis by removing the 'taint of decadence' that still clung to Wagner."[32] As it happens, *Die Meistersinger* figured prominently in Lorenz's "remaking" of Wagner, because, next to the "German" element of Beethoven, it was the so-called Bar form, which Lorenz maintained was the unifying structural principle of Wagner's operas.[33] The Bar form is rooted in German medieval tradition and thus becomes the centerpiece of the formal aesthetic lesson imparted to Walther and the audience via the *Tabulatur* in Act I and in Sachs's lecture of Act III. It is the "German" Bar form which gives shape to Walther's unbounded genius or, alternately, the genius of Walther's apparently spontaneous improvisations is reflected in their "natural" organization in Bar form.[34]

---

29. See for instance Wagner's glorification of Bach in "Was ist deutsch?" 47–48, in his *Gesammelte Schriften und Dichtungen,* vol. 10, ed. Wolfgang Golther (Berlin and Leipzig: Bong & Co., 1913), 36–53.

30. Franz Grillparzer, "Grillparzers Grabrede, 29. März 1827," in *Ludwig van Beethoven: In Briefen und Lebensdokumenten,* ed. Reinhold Schimkat (Stuttgart: Reclam, 1961), 212.

31. Stephen McClatchie, *Analyzing Wagner's Operas: Alfred Lorenz and German Nationalist Ideology,* Eastman Studies in Music (Rochester: U of Rochester P, 1998).

32. Ibid., 207.

33. Alfred Lorenz, *Das Geheimnis der Form bei Richard Wagner,* vol. 3 of 4, *Der musikalische Aufbau von Richard Wagners "Die Meistersinger von Nürnberg"* (Berlin: Max Hesse, 1924–33; reprint, Tutzing: Hans Schneider, 1966.)

34. On the notion of "spontaneity" in *Die Meistersinger,* see Dahlhaus, *Richard Wagner's Music Dramas,* 69–70.

Clearly, the blatant representation of "German" culture, especially music, is the centerpiece of the drama, but it is through the representation of types and ideas that *Die Meistersinger* becomes infused with contour and nuance. For instance, the major characters—Hans Sachs, Walther von Stolzing, Eva Pogner, Sixtus Beckmesser, David, even Veit Pogner—constitute allusions to long-standing literary and cultural archetypes as well as being possibly contentious representations of race and gender. Of these, the debate concerning Beckmesser as Wagner's representation of the Jew has been the most intense in recent years, originating, it seems, from a brief passage in Theodor W. Adorno's book-length essay "Versuch über Wagner."[35] A satisfactory resolution to this debate seems unlikely, as the disagreement centers not so much on Richard Wagner—who was unquestionably an anti-Semite—but on the ways in which a work of art should be read. An extreme example of this problem, reproduced in a number of studies, is illustrated in a statement made by pianist-conductor Daniel Barenboim and the subsequent response by Marc Weiner. Since there are no overt references to Jews in *Die Meistersinger,* Daniel Barenboim—himself Jewish—argues against an anti-Semitic reading of the work, on the grounds that Wagner "would have called a spade a spade."[36] Marc Weiner, who insists on a more complex reading which understands the work as a polyvalently coded text embedded in a specific cultural context, accuses Barenboim and other "apologists" of naively reducing Wagner's "contradictory complexity . . . to straightforward mimesis."[37]

The more enduring and ultimately less contentious focus of discussion has been on Sachs, or in some cases on the combination of Sachs and Walther, as conduits for Wagner's poetics. But some characters have been ignored almost completely. William McDonald's careful analysis of the musical and textual characterization of Sachs, Walther, and even David is a case in point because, like so many others, he pays no attention to the figure of Eva or to the issue of gender, specifically the nexus of gender and music that turn out to be central concerns in the work.[38] Eva Rieger's essay in this volume attempts to fill this particular lacuna.

---

35. Theodor W. Adorno, "Versuch über Wagner," in his *Gesammelte Schriften,* vol. 13 (Frankfurt/M: Suhrkamp, 1971), 7–148, here: 21: "der impotente intellektuelle Kritiker Hanslick-Beckmesser, all die Zurückgewiesenen in Wagners Werk sind Judenkarikaturen." English version: *In Search of Wagner,* trans. Rodney Livingstone (London: New Left Books, 1981).

36. "Daniel Barenboim and Edward Said: A Conversation," *Raritan* 18.1 (1998): 1–31, here 18.

37. Marc Weiner, "Reading the Ideal," *New German Critique* 69 (1996): 53–83, here 55 and 83.

38. William E. McDonald, "Words, Music and Dramatic Development in *Die Meistersinger,*" *19th-Century Music* 1, 3 (1978): 246–60. For an essay dealing with Eva, see Mary A. Cicora, "'Eva im Paradies': An Approach to Wagner's *Meistersinger,*" *German Studies Review* 10.2 (1987): 321–33.

Wagner did not initiate the gendered discourse of music. Instead he again reinscribes one this time developed by German music critics during the eighteenth century, which sought to create a distinctly German musical paradigm, separate from that of the French and Italians.[39] In the process of doing so, German music critics identified "German" music as being harmonically more complex, contrapuntal, predominantly instrumental, intellectually and emotionally more demanding, and hence more "manly" than French and Italian music, which were characterized as vocal, melodic, using simple harmonies, and thus superficial and "effeminate." Whereas Germans wrote music increasingly understood *per se* as the "universal" language, all others wrote in easily identifiable "national" styles. Wagner was committed to the notion of perpetuating a distinctly "German" style and developing a uniquely "German" form of opera, a lifelong project announced at length in his famous theoretical works written between 1849 and 1851—*Die Kunst und die Revolution* (1849; Art and Revolution), *Das Kunstwerk der Zukunft* (1849; Artwork of the Future); *Oper und Drama* (1851; Opera and Drama) and *Eine Mitteilung an meine Freunde* (1851; A Communication to my Friends). Wagner's emphatic affirmation and representation of a national "German" musical style is evident in the demonstratedly symphonic and contrapuntal prelude to *Die Meistersinger* as has been frequently noted, perhaps most succinctly by Friedrich Nietzsche and by musicologists ever since.[40] Less discussed, and perhaps more difficult to explain, is Wagner's possibly hypocritical incorporation in *Die Meistersinger* of French and Italianate musical dramatic elements most commonly associated with the genre of grand opera.[41] These include the use of large chorus, grand finales, as well as the prominence, uncharacteristic for Wagner, of melody, principally in Walther's arias which, considering Wagner's theoretical dismissal of Italianate opera, are surprisingly florid, passionate, dare I say "effeminate."[42] In the context, these elements are reinscribed as manly and virile, since Walther uses them successfully not only to woo Eva but to convince the masters and townsfolk of his own mastery. Barry Millington has noted Wagner's inclusion of these "foreign"

---

39. On this topic, see the excellent study by Mary Sue Morrow, *German Music Criticism in the Late Eighteenth Century: Aesthetic Issues in Instrumental Music* (Cambridge: Cambridge UP, 1997).

40. See Friedrich Nietzsche, "Achtes Hauptstück: Völker und Vaterländer," in his *Jenseits von Gut und Böse, Nietzsche Werke, Kritische Gesamtausgabe*, 6 Abt., Bd. 2, ed. Giorgio Colli and Mazzino Montinari (Berlin: Walter de Gruyter, 1968), §240: "Diese Art von Musik drückt am besten aus, was ich von den Deutschen halte: sie sind von Vorgestern und von Übermorgen—*sie haben noch kein Heute*" (188).

41. On this point, see also Dahlhaus, *Richard Wagner's Music Dramas*, 75.

42. Cf. Robert W. Gutman, *Richard Wagner: The Man, His Mind, and His Music* (New York: Harcourt Brace, 1968), 292.

elements, arguing that Wagner here is not returning to the principles of grand opera, "rather he has found a way of integrating these elements into his music drama."[43] I would go a step further than Millington, however, and suggest that in *Die Meistersinger,* Wagner accomplishes multiple objectives by affirming the century-old discourse of German music and, in addition, seizing and thereby legitimizing (i.e., making "German") the above-mentioned "foreign" elements. This supports a supposed characteristic of "the Germans" who, according to Wagner, have the capacity to absorb "foreign" elements and make them their own.[44] The habit of taking from other cultures, by the way, is one which Wagner also repeatedly associates with Jews, though, importantly, Jews fail at the process of "making it their own," revealing the extent to which they are spiritually as well as culturally foreign and homeless.[45]

Beyond the representational dimension of individual characters, Wagner also transforms social groups and conventions such as the guild system and its rites, musical devices like the chorale and counterpoint, not to mention the city of Nürnberg into coded signifiers. Perhaps the most loaded of these is Nürnberg, supplied even with its own musical call sign. It is possible, even advisable, to read Nürnberg on several levels.[46] There is the historical city whose heyday recalls the economic success of semi-independent German towns, particularly in the early modern period preceding the Thirty Years' War. For Wagner's contemporaries, the utopian image of a pre-industrial and ultimately harmonious community in the geographical and thus spiritual heart of Germany served as a marker against the encroachment of a modernity that had been so steadfastly resisted since Schiller and the Romantic generation.[47] This reading of Nürnberg as a bulwark against modernity and a symbol of the truly German had already been articulated

---

43. Barry Millington, *Wagner,* rev. ed. (Princeton, N.J.: Princeton UP, 1992): 250.

44. Richard Wagner, "Was ist deutsch?" "es [war] dem deutschen Geiste bestimmt, das Fremde, ursprünglich ihm Fernliegende . . . zu erfassen und sich anzueignen" (40). "Er [der Deutsche] will aber nicht nur das Fremde, als solches, als rein Fremdes, anstarren, sondern er will es 'deutsch' verstehen" (44). "Von den Italienern hatte der Deutsche sich auch die Musik angeeignet" (46).

45. Richard Wagner, "Das Judentum in der Musik," in his *Gesammelte Schriften und Dichtungen,* vol. 5, ed. Wolfgang Golther (Berlin and Leipzig: Bong & Co, 1913): "Der Jude hat nie eine eigene Kunst gehabt, . . . daß er unmöglich den Mut zur Mitwirkung bei unserem Kunstschaffen sich erhalten könnte . . . er [horcht] daher auf unser Kunstwesen und dessen lebengebenden inneren Organismus nur ganz oberflächlich hin" (76–78).

46. See Peter Uwe Hohendahl, "Reworking History: Wagner's German Myth of Nuremberg," *Re-Reading Wagner,* ed. Reinhold Grimm and Jost Hermand (Madison: U of Wisconsin P, 1993): 39–60.

47. *Cf.* Millington, *Wagner,* 252.

during the earliest phase of Romanticism, in which this city of Albrecht Dürer and Hans Sachs was revived and thus promoted along with its most significant residents in such works as Wackenroder's *Herzensergießungen eines kunstliebenden Klosterbruders* (ca. 1796). The utopian element is juxtaposed with the notion of decadence both within *Meistersinger* and in the nineteenth-century context of its composition and performance. Sixtus Beckmesser and Hans Sachs are engaged in a struggle over how best to save and maintain a tradition that seems to have fallen into disrepair. The corrupt state of the art is addressed by Veit Pogner in his lengthy presentation to the Guild during their meeting in Act I. By offering his only daughter Eva as the "prize" for a worthy Lied, he hopes to inject new life into a dying art. Wagner's contemporary and mentor, Franz Liszt, was equally concerned with musical stagnation in nineteenth-century Europe and sought a rejuvenation of musical aesthetics and form, declaring that "new wine demands new bottles."[48] *Tristan und Isolde* was perhaps Wagner's most daring formal answer to this call, but the musically more traditional *Meistersinger*, which followed immediately thereafter, also addresses the question of aesthetic innovation and its urgency.[49] Thus, aesthetically and despite the superficial differences in their "sound," *Tristan* and *Meistersinger* actually present two sides of the same coin by pursuing, albeit differently, the loosely defined goals of the New German School. Even structurally, both works are built on the idea of musical or melodic transformation, an idea Liszt and Wagner pioneered, though again with differing results and, despite its reputation for diatonicism, *Meistersinger* is filled with chromaticism more reminiscent of *Tristan*. Dramatically, Nürnberg becomes the contested ground where these issues of stagnation and utopian redemption meet. The key role Wagner gives to this city above and beyond the homage to Sachs and the mastersinger tradition quite literally prepared the ground for the even more significant and problematic prominence of Nürnberg in the twentieth century.

Thus it is perhaps through Nürnberg that we make the smoothest transition to "performance, history, and representation" as categories through which we can best explore and understand the importance of *Die Meistersinger* within German culture. The historical and political meaning of Nürnberg over the last century and a half, and especially for the Nazi regime, can in large measure be attributed to the city's glorification in

---

48. Quoted in Alan Walker, *Franz Liszt*, vol. 2: *The Weimar Years, 1848–1861* (New York: Knopf, 1989), 309. The quote is attributed to Liszt by his pupil August Stradal in the latter's *Erinnerungen an Franz Liszt* (Bern: P. Haupt, 1929); the quote in German: "Neuer Wein bedarf neuer Schlaeuche." My thanks to Alan Walker for the additional insight.

49. On the relationship between *Die Meistersinger* and *Tristan,* see Kinderman, "Hans Sachs's Cobbler Song," as well as Lydia Goehr's essay in this volume.

Wagner's work. Moreover, the history of the work's performance, the manner in which the work has itself been (re)presented to the public, is closely linked to the contemporaneous politics of German culture. While a performance can always be read in terms of a given cultural context, *Die Meistersinger* has a special place. Indeed, one can possibly even speak of a symbiotic relationship between the story of the work's performance and political/cultural developments in Germany. Beyond merely reflecting a certain climate, the performance history of *Die Meistersinger* reveals moments when the theatrical experience preceded political reality.

The first of these uncanny coincidences are the years surrounding the work's completion and first performance. One explanation for the instant success of *Die Meistersinger* and its ascension to unofficial German national opera (*Nationaloper*) lies in its aesthetic and textual unification of a people and a nation in anticipation of a long-awaited political unification, which, as it turned out, took place three years later: the founding of the Second Reich in 1871 under Otto von Bismarck. The link between the opera and the German nation was thus forged, which makes the notorious spontaneous singing of the *Deutschlandlied* at the close of the 1924 Bayreuth production understandable, though, again, this political gesture can be read as a preview: the politicization and nationalization of German culture in general and *Die Meistersinger* in particular during the Nazi period after 1933. Considering the degree to which *Die Meistersinger* was appropriated as the signature opera of the Third Reich,[50] it is perhaps counterintuitive that Hitler would forbid the habit of singing the national anthem at the work's conclusion: almost as if the *Deutschlandlied* were no longer necessary since the opera *in toto* had itself become a part of Germany's national music.

Given the vexing association between the work and the Hitler regime, it is noteworthy that one of the operas selected for the reopening season of the Bayreuth festival after the war was again *Die Meistersinger*. Even more problematic, considering the role of the work between 1933 and 1945, and the Wagner clan's embrace of Hitler and his regime, was the highly publicized slogan which accompanied that 1951 season: "Hier gilt's der Kunst."[51]

---

50. See David Dennis's essay in this volume.
51. Translated at the time as "Art is our aim!"; see Hartmut Zelinsky, *Richard Wagner—ein deutsches Thema: Eine Dokumentation zur Wirkungsgeschichte Richard Wagners 1876–1976* (Frankfurt/M: Zweitausendeins, 1976). The full text of the plea reads: "Im Interesse einer reibungslosen Durchführung der Festspiele bitten wir von Gesprächen und Debatten politischer Art auf dem Festspielhügel freundlichst absehen zu wollen." "Hier gilt's der Kunst" had already been used as a slogan during performances of *Die Meistersinger* at the 1925 Bayreuth Festival, along with the plea not to sing the German national anthem. On this and other details of *Die Meistersinger* at Bayreuth, see Frederic Spotts, *Bayreuth: A Concise History of the Wagner Festival* (New Haven, Conn.: Yale UP, 1994), here esp. 142–43.

The choice of words was doubly insidious because it is actually a quote taken from a line spoken by Eva in Act II of *Die Meistersinger*. The innocent and virginal Eva was thus appropriated in order to cleanse a tarnished Bayreuth and, by extension, Richard Wagner. However, this arguably disingenuous and rather hypocritical attempt at depoliticization represented only the first of many phases of *Vergangenheitsbewältigung* (overcoming the past), or more accurately, the absence of it. Nevertheless, if we look at the entire context, the choice of *Die Meistersinger* was both conservative and daring. It was a gesture of stubborn denial but also of a stubborn determination to carry on and "reclaim" that which had been seized and transformed. The combination of timeless and archaic setting in Wieland Wagner's 1956 production signified yet another stage in the process: a depoliticization on stage to match the rhetoric of 1951, where "overcoming" seemed more like avoidance.[52] But Wieland Wagner's bare sets, his "Mastersingers without Nuremberg" as some complained, suggested also Germany as an empty space waiting to be filled, once again.[53] Whatever way we choose to read these highly contested moments in the history of the work's performance, the important point is that *Die Meistersinger* and the manner it, and thus Germany, was represented in performance is intimately bound up with questions of German historical and political identity and self-representation.

Given the broad range of issues that the categories "performance, history, and representation" raise, a single book devoted to their exploration cannot hope to be comprehensive. This volume brings together a diverse group of contributors to discuss aspects of the issues raised above. The diversity becomes readily apparent in terms of academic disciplines represented—philosophy, history, musicology, theater studies, German studies—as well as the inclusion of active performers. By inviting the kinds of contributions presented, I wanted to open up a space for discourse at multiple levels of complexity and for fresh, even unconventional, modes of writing. Rather than streamline or homogenize the sound and language of the individual chapters, I decided to let the authors speak with their own disciplinary voices, however much their vocabularies or methodologies seem strange or off-putting to the reader not initiated into the peculiarities of a particular discipline.

While the deliberately eclectic mixture of chapters brings music and the "other" humanities into closer proximity, thus encouraging a broader, more

---

52. For details on this and other stagings of *Die Meistersinger*, see *Die Meistersinger und Richard Wagner: Die Rezeptionsgeschichte einer Oper von 1868 bis heute,* Eine Ausstellung des Germanischen Nationalmuseums in Nürnberg (Cologne: Kopp, 1981), as well as Patrick Carnegy, "Stage History," in *Richard Wagner, "Die Meistersinger,"* 135–52.

53. See Spotts, *Bayreuth,* 218–21, and also Hans Mayer, *Richard Wagner in Bayreuth 1876–1976,* trans. Jack Zipes (New York: Rizzoli, 1976), 189–91.

inclusive way of thinking about Richard Wagner and his works, this same eclecticism carries with it both the benefits and difficulties associated with interdisciplinary or, better said, multidisciplinary ventures. Though each of the essays reflects the approach, style, methodology, and language consistent with the conventions of a specific discipline, these may rest "uncomfortably" beside the essay directly preceding or following it. Nowhere is this difference more acute than between Dietrich Fischer-Dieskau's succinct, almost tersely worded essay on performing Hans Sachs and the following chapter by philosopher Lydia Goehr on the stakes of performance in *Die Meistersinger*, which approaches the question via the often impenetrable language and thought—for lay readers—of Wittgenstein and Theodor W. Adorno. As a consequence, this volume offers no continuing narrative, but rather a presentation of often contradictory vignettes, grouped within the three main categories, and concerning the same object: *Die Meistersinger von Nürnberg*. There are, of course, points of intersection between the essays, but in many instances the differences or disagreements between them may be even more stimulating than the similarities. For the reader, the multidisciplinary multiperspectivism should result in a truly interdisciplinary experience.

With this in mind, it was a priority in the conception to include the voices of artists actively engaged in the work's performance. As I suggested earlier, it is important that the issue of actual performance be part of any broader consideration of a musical or dramatic work. Although many artists wish their performance to speak for itself, I was delighted that a conductor, at least one stage director,[54] and a singer were prepared to share their performatory insights and experiences. From the vantage point of anyone involved in the performance of this or any other major work by Wagner, the undertaking is a major feat on three fronts: intellectual, emotional, and physical.

This in the first place is true for the conductor, who not only is responsible for questions of global conceptualization like the stage director, but who must also withstand the unremitting physical and emotional demands of actual performance. Conductor Peter Schneider likens the task to a mountain climb—indeed a climb of the highest mountain on earth. His essay leads us through a performance of the work by examining how Wagner has constructed his monumental work using the utmost economy of means: the intervals of a third and fourth, and the scale. His musical analysis owes much to the work of Alfred Lorenz and, in light of McClatchie's book mentioned earlier, demonstrates nicely the divide between academic discussions—which are often concerned with and (involuntarily) perpetuate the politicization of aesthetics—and the imperatives of interpretation for

---

54. I report with deep regret that Götz Friedrich, who had agreed to supply a chapter on staging *Die Meistersinger*, passed away before completing his essay.

the purpose of performance, which continue to bring to the foreground the notion of music unencumbered. Interestingly, it is often the sections discussed less from a textual or dramatic perspective that prove the most formidable for the conductor.

Harry Kupfer's provocative call to "finally stop apologizing for *Die Meistersinger*" reflects his perhaps shocking vision of the opera's role in a new post-Wall Germany, to dispel lingering shadows of the Third Reich and, instead, to think about issues of identity in the context of a unified Europe. The bulk of the interview with Kupfer concerns general questions of characterization and interpretation within the context of his new 1998 staging of *Die Meistersinger* at the Staatsoper in Berlin, including careful and revealing comments about Hans Sachs, Walther von Stolzing, and Eva and Veit Pogner. He also confronts the perennial problem of Beckmesser, and responds to the issue of the town clerk as representation or caricature of the Jew. By setting the opera to play in "history, today, and nowhere" he does seem to suggest a way out of the highly charged role *Die Meistersinger* has played in German cultural history.

Dietrich Fischer-Dieskau's essay on performing the role of Hans Sachs combines an examination of its technical requirements with important insights into characterization, demonstrating the degree to which the physicality of vocal technique is inseparable from the intellectual and emotional dimensions of performing the role, which, he argues, may well be the most demanding of all the roles Wagner created for the singer-actor.

Philosopher of music Lydia Goehr turns our attention from performing *Die Meistersinger* to performance in the work. By examining the sequence of drafts, or what might be considered rehearsals, preceding Walther's final presentation of the *Preislied*, Goehr argues that the audiences on stage and in the theater are being primed to accept Walther's song as the "only" and "correct" version, a song that thus leaves us satisfied, a metaphor for the opera's own success. In terms of the aesthetic innovation that the text of the opera preaches, however, the *Preislied*—like the opera itself—is a failure because it takes no risks. It is a failure, Goehr argues, which actually primes the theater audience to accept Wagner's truly innovative work: *Tristan und Isolde*.

The next section, *Meistersinger* and German history, addresses from the vantage point of three different centuries the manner in which the work is situated in history, represents history, and is laden with unique burdens of its own history of and in performance. Lutz Koepnick investigates the nineteenth-century optical origins of Adorno's concept of "phantasmagoria"—often used as a tool for understanding Wagner's compositional technique. The "phantasmagorias" of vision and visuality in *Die Meistersinger,* which locate the drama in "neither past nor present," connect nicely with the underlying concept of Harry Kupfer's production, but also reflect and participate in the transformation of visual culture during the nineteenth century. Koepnick uses his findings to argue against the legitimacy of Heinz Tietjen's 1933 Bayreuth staging of *Die Meistersinger* as a Nazi rally. Similarly flawed, he submits, are the arguments proposed by postwar critics who have accepted the Nazi appropriation of the work as somehow prefigured in Wagner's mis-en-scene.

Historian David Dennis continues where Koepnick leaves off by looking closely at the perennial and troubling issue of the ways in which the work was appropriated and read by the leadership of the Third Reich. While he does not confront the contested issue of the work's embedded anti-Semitism per se, his analysis proposes a new approach to resolving the debate. Dennis's careful and exhaustive archival research reveals the many ways in which the opera became emblematic for the kind of Germanness promoted by the Nazi regime. From 1933 on, *Die Meistersinger* was used on every imaginable occasion for purposes of political exigency to create an inviolable link between it and the Nazis, between it and Germany. Surprisingly, none of the leading Nazi voices ever made mention of anti-Semitic elements, nor was Beckmesser ridiculed as representative of the Jew or, as Adorno suggested, as embodiment of Grimm's notorious "Der Jude im Dorn" (Jew in the brambles). Dennis suggests provocatively that we reconsider to what extent claims of anti-Semitic coding in current academic discourse are legitimate if even the Nazis did not think to use the opera for their anti-Semitic propaganda, especially since they used it so freely for demonstrations of pro-Germanness.

Peter Höyng's twenty-first-century interview with Richard Wagner is a lighthearted but nevertheless serious encounter with Wagner's published utterances and positions, viewed retrospectively through the twists and turns of German history since his death in 1883. The conversation covers aspects of German history and identity connected with the opera, and imagines Wagner's response to the issue of anti-Semitism in the wake of Hitler and the Holocaust. This *jeu d'esprit* or Goethean "ernster Scherz" using current technology to create a cyber-reality can be legitimated by pointing to the common practice since the Nazi period of judging Wagner in light of historical developments of which he had no knowledge and over whose occurrence he may or may not have had any influence and therefore responsibility. Is it any more of a stretch to postulate Wagner's responses to an interrogation which presumes his own opportunity to witness post-Wagnerian German history?

The last section of the volume, devoted to "representation" in its widest context, deals with several questions either insufficiently examined to date or whose contentiousness demands continued reflection. Theater historian Klaus van den Berg begins by revisiting the problematic issue of *Die Meistersinger*'s genre designation as "comedy." Too often in studies the question is dismissed with facile remarks about Wagner's "cruel"[55] or "un-

---

55. Gutman, *Richard Wagner*, 220.

trustworthy"[56] sense of humor. Van den Berg approaches genre from the perspective of theatrical traditions and tropes to show unexpected ways in which *Die Meistersinger* conforms to and deviates from conventions stretching back to antiquity. Linking the use of comedic structures to the question of anti-Semitic coding, van den Berg adds a dimension to Marc Weiner's oft-cited study by showing how comedy and anti-Semitism function reciprocally in the opera. In order for the anti-Semitism to deliver its punch, the drama needs to provoke laughter at its highly determined target. By the same token, audience laughter is enabled by creating in Beckmesser a character and a situation which couple grotesque anti-Semitic stereotypes with long-standing comic tropes.

Musicologist Thomas Grey revisits the Wagner–Hanslick–Beckmesser nexus by looking once again at the 1869 republication of Wagner's infamous essay, "Judaism in Music." Reminding us that, while the original and anonymously published 1850 version was directed against fellow composers—specifically Mendelssohn and Meyerbeer—the 1869 version, and the "afterword" Wagner wrote for the occasion, is directed against a Jewish-led conspiracy of critics. Grey reconstructs in some detail the relationship between Wagner and Hanslick, showing how they traded insults and provocations over several decades, leading ultimately to Wagner's representation in Beckmesser of the music critic (Hanslick), Hanslick's repost in his "Beckmesserian" review of *Die Meistersinger*, which, in turn, prompted Wagner's republication of the "Judaism" essay with its new focus.

The focus on Beckmesser is rounded off with an essay by Germanist Hans Vaget, which takes a comprehensive look at the controversy, sparked, it seems, by Theodor Adorno, but fueled by an interest in the Holocaust which has become especially intense since the 1970s. Vaget distills the existing and rather wide-ranging debate to four salient aspects, which he analyzes in detail. Many of the points he addresses have already been touched on by others in this volume, creating an interesting and productive intersection of approaches to this currently most vexing issue. Vaget argues that the possibility of anti-Semitic coding as well as the clearly political inscription of the work cannot be overlooked, despite its own plea to be valued solely in terms of aesthetics and culture. However, Vaget also stresses that these are but elements in a complex work which, ultimately, must be judged in its entirety.

Playing off a most revealing quote of Wagner's ("I married Eva"), musicologist Eva Rieger examines the issue of *Die Meistersinger* and gender construction, in particular the representation of the feminine through Eva Pogner. By looking on the one hand at musical structures, phrases, and so-called leitmotifs, and on the other at Wagner's correspondence with the

---

56. Dahlhaus, *Richard Wagner's Music Dramas*, 65.

assorted women in his life during composition of the work, Rieger reveals the deep ambiguity of Wagner's position. While he projected and sublimated onto Sachs the renunciation and resignation he was compelled to endure in his own life—for instance in the case of Mathilde Wesendonck—he was unable to achieve the kind of nobility in life for which Sachs is emblematic. In terms of gender roles, however, Wagner in real life was most interested in intelligent women with independent minds, with whom he would discuss matters of importance, yet in his dramatic representation of the feminine—e.g., Eva Pogner—he remained imprisoned in nineteenth-century bourgeois norms where the woman was a "natural" being, objectified by and subservient to male interests.

Eva Rieger's bold challenge to current academic convention, by reinvesting biographical detail into textual analysis while nevertheless insisting on a precise and careful reading of a fictional work, nicely captures the spirit of this volume. While the techniques of what is considered legitimate or appropriate scholarship change with time, the essays in this volume take their cue from the advice Hans Sachs gives to the young Walther von Stolzing, when asked: "How shall I begin according to the rule?" (Wie fang' ich nach der Regel an?). Sachs responds: "Ihr stellt sie selbst, und folgt ihr dann" (You set it yourself, and then follow it). Based on the notion that no approach to writing about *Die Meistersinger* should be rejected simply on grounds of form, the "rule" guiding this volume is that, on the contrary, a work as complex and with as layered a life as *Die Meistersinger* necessitates a certain openness to different forms of analysis, especially to those that break with established convention. As the editor, I can only hope that the reader shares in this vision.

N.B. The following system is used to denote pitch octaves: CC C c c' c" ... where c' is middle C.

Part I

Performing (in) Die Meistersinger

1

Climbing Mount Everest: On Conducting *Die Meistersinger*

Peter Schneider

Wie fang' ich nach der Regel an?
Ihr stellt sie selbst und folgt ihr dann.
—*Die Meistersinger*, Act III[1]

Following this advice from Act III of *Die Meistersinger von Nürnberg*, I would like to propose the following "rule": to portray as uncomplicatedly and clearly as possible the thoughts, feelings, observations, and experiences of a conductor in his work with Wagner's *Meistersinger* before and during a performance of the work. The feelings that dominate one right before the performance can, in my opinion, be no better described and compared than with those of a mountain climber who, standing at the foot of one of the Himalayan peaks, sets out on his climb. A great deal of preparation is necessary to get to this moment, whether in planning the route (knowledge of the work), organization of the team (rehearsals with all the participants), and, last but not least, being mentally and physically fit so that one can endure such a challenge. It is a long way to the summit, perhaps the longest in the entire operatic landscape, often very arduous but, at least in the case of *Die Meistersinger*, adorned by the most beautiful wonders of music, which compensate amply for the difficulties that must be overcome.

The Prelude

Already at the beginning of the prelude, Richard Wagner shows us that he is a composer who does not follow well-worn paths. Upon hearing the first measure, one might think of a rather pompous march played by all the members of the orchestra, and carried by a majestically triumphant melody. But it strikes one immediately that the instruments that classically convey

---

1. "How shall I begin according to the rule? / You set it yourself, and then follow it."

melody, the violins, pause in the first measure and yield first place to their colleagues in the wind section, only to take charge with even more vigor from the second measure onwards (see example 1.1).

One could conceivably write this off as a small delicacy of instrumentation, were this detail not an indication of a pattern that persists throughout

Example 1.1

the entire four hours of music: the particularity of the first intervallic leap of a fourth in the trumpets, oboes, and clarinets, as shown in example 1.2.[2]

Example 1.2

It becomes evident as the work unfolds that this interval of a fourth is the most important compositional building block for the vast majority of the motifs in the work. The fourth as an interval denotes uprightness—straightness, if one so wishes—of the right angle, which holds everything tightly together: symbol for the handworker guilds of the historical mastersingers and even of their petty bourgeois stodginess. But this is not all. The entrance of the violins as the main voice introduces us to two further compositional elements, the third and the scale (see example 1.3).

Example 1.3

With these three building blocks: the fourth, the third, and the scale—all present in the opening measures of the prelude—Wagner constructs the entire musical edifice of this colossal work. Even where these elements are intentionally avoided, circumvented, or not used, they indicate by their absence the dramaturgical significance of otherness, novelty, or unusualness, as I will demonstrate.

One would certainly do an injustice to a genius of Richard Wagner's stature if one were to believe that he was using this musical material according to some lifeless, largely cerebral, schema. Rather the opposite is the case: the construction is never an end in itself, and is never blatantly obvious, or rather audible, but instead is concealed in a refined manner. Indeed, occasionally one might think that these three building blocks serve only as a source, as the impulse that inspires the most beautiful ideas, true musical wonders. One is involuntarily reminded of the compositional style of Johann Sebastian Bach, to whom, aside from Beethoven, Wagner of course felt particularly indebted. Nowhere is he closer to Bach than in *Die Meistersinger,* which is structurally his most polyphonic score. This circumstance, however, often causes problems for the conductor concerning the orchestra's volume, even though this work, together with *Der fliegende Holländer,* calls for the smallest ensemble among Wagner's operatic works. The quandary is that the polyphonic voice-

---

2. In these examples the intervals are indicated as follows: a fourth: solid line; a third: dashed line; a scale: dotted line.

leading continually seduces each instrumentalist into believing that the beauty of his particular musical line deserves in that moment to be especially emphasized. This is a problem which sometimes creates difficulties even in the famously favorable acoustics of the Bayreuth Festival Theater.

Even the second subject—according to Alfred Lorenz the "lyrical theme"—consists exclusively of the material established by the first theme, as shown in example 1.4, and becomes the germ for many other motifs in the course of the work, as I will demonstrate later at the appropriate place.

Example 1.4

The third theme in this prelude, which supposedly originates from an actual fanfare from the historical period of the mastersingers—often referred to as the "King David" motif—can be appropriately characterized as one which clings to old, perhaps even outmoded, traditions, as shown in example 1.5. Even if Wagner did indeed borrow this theme, it nevertheless fits his concept perfectly with the exception of the penultimate note, the "a." I will show later that this note takes on a special significance with the construction of an new motif (see example 1.16).

Example 1.5

Eighteen measures later (m. 40), an emphatic song is adjoined—according to the rules of the mastersingers, an "Abgesang"—which contains a multitude of examples to demonstrate how artistically and yet discreetly Wagner works with his material. To those who are particularly interested, I would point out the bass line in the double basses and the bass tuba (example 1.3).

A little later, after the *poco rall.* and the move to E major (m. 97), something completely new happens: this melody, which is actually the "Abgesang" from Walther's Prize Song in Act III, does not follow the already established criteria; quite the opposite, it begins with the intervals of the fifth and sixth, until now mostly ignored (see example 1.6). It thus sets itself apart from the old mastersinger rules and instead presents itself as something individual, personified through the figure of Walther von Stolzing.

Example 1.6

That this was conceived all along as the counterpart to the mastersingers is evident from the finale of the prelude (and from Sachs's closing monologue in Act III), where the first violins play it as counterpoint (literally, the opposing voice) to the mastersinger motif, which is played in the bass. As if this were not enough, in addition to these two themes, the second violins, violas, and several winds play the King David motif (example 1.5) with jocular quickness, almost hopping, and in a compressed form (see example 1.7). This whole episode is unique amongst all of Wagner's work and signifies the greatest nod to Johann Sebastian Bach, who had spent the most important years of his career in Leipzig, the city of Wagner's birth.

Example 1.7

Though there is such an abundance of interesting, noteworthy and beautiful moments in the prelude, I wish to point to only two more. There is a rhythmic compression already described of a motif which sounds earlier, as shown in example 1.8, and is clearly conceived as a parody of the petty-bourgeois mastersinger organization.

Example 1.8

Set in contrast to it is the caricature of another motif (see example 1.9), which Alfred Lorenz describes as the "Youth Motif" in his excellent and highly recommended book[3] as far as the formal structure of the work is concerned. Once again, this motif also consists of fourths, thirds, and scales.

---

3. Alfred Lorenz, *Der musikalische Aufbau von Richard Wagners "Die Meistersinger von Nürnberg"* (Tutzing: Hans Schneider, 1966).

Example 1.9

One cannot conclude the discussion of the prelude without referring to Wagner's theoretical treatise *Über das Dirigieren* (On Conducting), where, using the prelude as his example, he speaks to the issue of tempo, and warns against an overly slow and inflexible interpretation. I am aware of one orchestral score in which Wagner's tempo marking for the prelude, *Sehr mässig bewegt,* is translated verbatim and substituted with *molto moderato animato.* But, in his essay, Wagner himself describes the tempo as *allegro maestoso,* and these two are worlds apart. While *mässig* is one of the tempo markings Wagner used most frequently and has been regarded by many conductors of the past, the present, and probably also the future as a slow tempo, in my opinion it marks a mid-point between "fast" and "slow."

Act One

"Genug der Wort!" (Act III). Enough about the prelude, and now onwards on the way to the summit.

The curtain rises and we hear a chorale in the spirit of Luther, which is another perfect example of Wagner's economy in his use of material—fourth and scale (see example 1.10). Wagner deftly uses the pauses (*fermata*), which are standard for the structure of such chorales, for dramatic purposes in order depict the flirtation between Eva and Walther in a musically quasi improvisational way.

Example 1.10

The following conversation scene between Eva, Magdalene, Walther, and, later, David presents for me one of the earliest and most successful examples of through-composed dialogues that lack any hint of arioso or recitative—a seed for the later operatic style of Richard Strauss. Even the typically Straussian "portraiture" of individual terms in the text is already employed, as, for instance, at the mention of David and Goliath and of the sling with which David sends the stone, or of the "light locks" that shimmer about his head (see example 1.11).

Climbing Mount Everest: On Conducting Die Meistersinger

Example 1.11

A particularly good, but rather concealed, example for Wagner's ingenious application of his musical building blocks is the theme for the apprentice David, which sounds punctually at the first mention of his name (see example 1.12). In the upper voice is the scale, under which at the distance of a fourth is the second voice, and again below that the third.

One could interpret it as representing the future master, which David will surely become at one point, who still finds himself in the vertical growth of an apprentice and who is not yet able to unfold himself into a horizontal blossoming.

Example 1.12

The following instructions, which Walther receives from David, are first characterized by David's description of his studies with his master and teacher Hans Sachs, meaning that of the shoemaker in 6/8 time and that of the poet in 2/4 time. Because of this circumstance, one sees very soon that David, in his eagerness to learn, ends up confusing everything. At this point we recall, in addition to Bach, one of his contemporaries, to whom Wagner owes much for the poetry of *Die Meistersinger*: Johann Christoph Wagenseil, who published a book in 1697 entitled *Der Meister-Singer Holdseligen Kunst* (Concerning the Beautiful Art of the Mastersingers). David then recounts by name, using the most colorful musical depiction, every detail of the varied songs of the masters. Next to Beckmesser's serenade in Act II, this episode is technically the most difficult to conduct in the work. Indeed, all of the apprentice scenes belong to this category, since the musical pitfalls, which can result in mistakes of precision, are numerous. The song of the "Blumenkränzlein" forms the end of the entire first part of Act I, and is again constructed by Wagner with an utmost economy of means, which we have already discussed. This song contains what in my opinion has traditionally been a faulty interpretation at the following point (see example 1.13). Wagner's two strokes (//) are usually taken as a sign for a caesura in the musical flow between the two words "Seiden" and "fein," which actually belong together, a point which may be quite justified as far as other composers are concerned. For Wagner, however, the sign is simply an exact indication from which point in the bar the *"molto riten."* is supposed to begin. He had already used this sign earlier in the same sense without any kind of caesura being in the least possible or called for. Later repetitions of this song (e.g., in Act II) dispense with this senseless interpretational nuance.

Example 1.13

Finally, the title characters of the opera appear in person one after the other, individually or in groups, and Wagner bathes the entire scene in a dense symphonic-polyphonic tapestry of voices, which requires the conductor to exercise extreme caution in orchestral dynamics, especially during the roll call of the individual masters. Of all the motifs that come to bear, we will mention only the "Johannistag" motif from Veit Pogner's speech as representative, because it also appears in very exposed places in Acts II and III (see figure 1.14). Even though it begins with a sixth, it is really only a loving paraphrase of a fourth and an indication that analysis of construction should not be done too schematically.

Example 1.14

All the more bewildering is example 1.15; as the knight Walther von Stolzing is introduced, he appears before the masters with a sequence of notes (melody) which is characteristic for him: young, elegant, dynamic and fit, almost in a modern sense, open, and free.

Example 1.15

The masters immediately sense danger, since this knight represents in many respects the opposite of their own staid tradition-bound society, for which, as already mentioned, the King David motif is representative. And indeed, juxtaposed, we recognize that Stolzing's motif is almost the opposite of the "tradition" theme, its inverse (see example 1.16). In musical terminology, this occurrence is of course called "retrograde."

Example 1.16

Interestingly, a little later, the "marker" Beckmesser, Stolzing's rival, is characterized with a rhythmically very similarly constructed notational series, a descending scale (see example 1.17), which, through its harmonization, gives off the impression of a narrow-minded and untrusting person, and has nothing left of von Stolzing's openness.

Example 1.17

This carefree openness is all the more evident in Stolzing's attempt, after the litany-like and starkly funny reading of the Tabulatur, to improvise a Meisterlied which is carried by the impetuous Youth motif (see example 1.9) and by a new musical idea (example 1.18) in the horns using the notes of a chord which consists of three thirds.

Example 1.18

But this bliss of thirds does not lead to the hoped for success; quite the opposite, the whole act ends with a tonal chaos in which the problem for the conductor is to convince the singers that they do not have to defend their "master" status by singing as loudly as possible, but rather that Walther, despite the turbulent ensemble, is still the main voice and should be audible.

Act Two

And with that—staying with the Himalayan imagery—one arrives at the second base camp, and can plunge oneself after a little recuperation into the next assault on the summit.

Climbing Mount Everest: On Conducting Die Meistersinger   33

Act II begins with a spectacular achievement in instrumentation, the whole orchestra trilling and jubilant, painting a bright eve of St. John's Day in early summer, and a scene for the apprentices, which, for all concerned, presents a delicate challenge in precision. In the Pogner-Eva dialogue, one hears next to enchanting birdsong-imitations in the clarinet a seemingly new motif, which clearly refers to the city of Nuremberg with its walls and battlements. By now one is almost tempted to say, "of course" it consists of thirds and fourths. Upon closer examination, one sees the origin of this theme from the prelude, the relationship to which is veiled only by a strongly dotted rhythm. There follow several examples (from earlier but also later) of what Alfred Lorenz called this motif, namely the "lyrical motif" (see example 1.19), which I have partly transposed to make them more recognizable.

Example 1.19

We now come to one of the core moments of the entire work, the *Fliedermonolog*, in which we meet Hans Sachs alone for the first time, here more as poet than as shoemaker. Musically, this scene is mainly carried by two motifs which we already heard in Act I: first, the stormy youthful motif (see example 1.9) now expanded, enlarged, without any impetuosity, only pensive and thoughtful (see example 1.20); and second, the horn thirds from example 1.18, which, with the violin tremolo underneath, conjure up a unique early-summer aura, in which one could believe that one was breathing the scent of the elderberry (*Fliederbeere*), as the elder (*Hollunder*) was earlier called (see example 1.21). (The real lilac [*Flieder*] is no longer in blossom on June 24, St. John's Day.) This monologue closes with the words: "Lenzes Gebot, die süsse Not, die legt es ihm in die Brust."

Example 1.20

Example 1.21

We see that example 1.21 is only another expansion of example 1.20. In the dialogue that follows between Eva and Sachs, the conductor often has to struggle with the problem that Eva's part is written very low and, because of this, the audibility of the singer often suffers.

On the subject of being low: a humorous little idea of Wagner's concerns the night watchman in his two appearances. Everything in the music points to the fact that his "call" should be sung in F-sharp Major: his night watchman's horn is also tuned to this note. But the apparently already quite elderly man sings out of tune and begins a half tone below, only to then be corrected by his own horn at the end of his song.

In order not to exceed the bounds of this essay, I will concern myself with only a few specific points from now on. But I do hope that the interested reader has by now perhaps become inquisitive enough to want to examine the score himself or herself in search of fourths, thirds, scales, and their combinations. For instance, immediately after the night watchman's song, the sound of a lute cuts through the darkness, with a sound of strummed open strings, which are tuned like a guitar, and consisting of fourths and one third. And thus this fits in perfectly with Wagner's intentions, except that a player in this kind of a prelude would probably not necessarily strum only the open strings. By the way, this part is in reality not played by a lute, but rather by a small specially designed harp, the Beckmesser harp played by a harpist.

Sachs's cobbling song is indeed rather earthy and rather noisily orchestrated, made even more dense in the third strophe by the addition of a contrapuntal opposing voice (see example 1.22). At this point, both Sachs and conductor are particularly challenged to create a balance of sound, since it is not only the singer's voice which should be heard, but also the opposing voice in the orchestra, which, in the development of the opera, becomes a pivotal point and should be consciously heard by the listener. Characteristic for this motif is the almost complete absence of our well-known building blocks, and thus it indirectly indicates a fundamental shift in Sachs's thinking, namely the realization of his own powerlessness to be able to steer events.

Example 1.22

But before this idea becomes conscious in the Wahn monologue of Act III, we have to get through yet another hike along a ridge which is unique in all of Wagner's work: Beckmesser's serenade and the so-called "fight fugue" (see example 1.23).

Example 1.23

For the most part, the serenade melody again follows the three compositional elements and is accompanied by Sachs's marker beats on Beckmesser's shoes. These beats seem to be arbitrary, but if one examines them carefully, one sees that Sachs really hits only when Beckmesser breaks the rules, i.e., Sachs must really produce every strike exactly as written in the score, which requires of the singer unbelievable concentration and the most detailed knowledge. The conductor is caught in the middle here and must hold all the participants together, in the truest sense of the word, during this scene, which Wagner did not make particularly user-friendly. From the perspective of conducting technique, this is the most difficult passage Wagner composed. It gives way to the street brawl of all against all and is, strictly speaking, not a fugue, but rather more like a fugally conceived toccata. Beside the serenade melody as a *cantus firmus* (see example 1.23), it is the "fight" motif which carries the music (see example 1.24) and, as we see, it consists almost entirely of a sequence of fourths.

Example 1.24

When Act II has ended, and if this scene has come off precisely, every conductor, probably without exception, is relieved, and can go off satisfied to a well-earned intermission break, only to brace himself for one of the longest acts in operatic history, which is about to follow.

Act Three

As if released from the lowlands, our journey takes us to a place of the most quiet meditation. Turned inward, we hear the Wahn motif, which we already know as the counterpoint to the cobbler's song and which is structured so differently from the other motifs (see example 1.22). But quite new in this prelude to Act III is the first appearance of the ceremonial and peaceful Reformation hymn "Wach auf" (see example 1.25), which, later, is sung loudly by the whole chorus and all the soloists with the exception of Hans Sachs, in whose honor it is being performed. This melody is again in keeping with the most beautiful of contrapuntal criteria—a fourth and scales, and gives the entire prelude a sublime character of noble resignation.

Example 1.25

To be allowed to conduct this introduction, given all that has gone before and all that is about to happen, belongs to one of the most beautiful moments of my profession. After a brief episode with David, the mood of the prelude returns with Sachs's Wahn monologue, which begins with a bass trombone solo (see example 1.22) and which is to be played *sehr zart und gebunden,* a test for every instrumentalist. Another test is for the person singing Sachs, namely, how to give shape to the monologue. I would like to point to a place that is unheard and also overlooked in this monologue because it is difficult to recognize in a piano reduction. When Sachs sings "doch eines Abends spat, ein Unglück zu verhüten bei jungendheissen Gemüten," etc., the bass tuba plays an extremely extended (augmented) version of the Wahn motif as the basis (see example 1.26).

Example 1.26

In addition, one of the most beautifully sounding moments in all of Wagner is to be found in this scene, when Sachs sings the words: "ein Kobold half wohl da, ein Glühwurm fand sein Weibchen nicht. . . ." The whole magical sound of musical impressionism, still a long way off, is here already preempted with extreme delicacy. As regards the dialogue between Sachs and Stolzing (see example 1.27), which is carried by a melody rhythmically connected to Veit Pogner's Johannistag motif (see example 1.14) and, in terms of interval structure, is connected to the Wahn motif, one may confidently assert that the German language cannot be better set to a Belcanto line than Wagner does here.

Example 1.27

In the Preislied itself (see example 1.28), which is, of course, written and composed in this scene, we recognize Stolzing's efforts to obey the rules of the mastersingers, symbolized by the consistent effort to follow their basic principles; only with the "Abgesang" does Walther find his own voice (see example 1.6).

Example 1.28

The next scene between Sachs and Beckmesser is filled with reminders and, for the conductor, is characterized above all by the many changes in time signature, which is rather rare for Wagner (*Götterdämmerung*, Act II, *Tristan und Isolde,* Act III). Equally unusual for Wagner's work is an equivalent to the heavenly quintet at the end of Act III, scene 4, which is very difficult for the conductor in terms of tempo choice so as not to make it too hard for the person singing Eva. Although it is not of real musical relevance, may I be permitted a small remark concerning the text: Eva composes the baptismal words for the "selige Morgentraum-Deutweise" in that she uses one word from the title given by Sachs as the beginning of each of the verses she sings:

> *Selig,* wie die Sonne meines Glückes lacht
> *Morgen* voller Wonne, selig mir erwacht
> *Traum* der höchsten Hulden, himmlisch Morgenglühn !
> *Deutung* euch zu schulden, selig süss Bemühn !
> Eine *Weise,* mild und hehr . . . etc.

The following music, which connects to the Festwiese scene, is once again filled with all sorts of musical reminiscences and is to my knowledge the only occasion in the operatic literature where the noise generated by the actual scene change is not at all a disturbance, but is almost needed. As the curtain rises, the sight delivers the requisite "jolt" for the conductor to be able to continue and hold together all the masses of guilds, each with its own theme (fourths!). The "Wach auf" fourth brings us then to a kind of pre-summit with a clear and optimistic view of the final summit, which, however, for the conductor, leads across many a dangerous path (Chorus: "scheint mir nicht der Rechte," Beckmesser's departure, etc.) until one has finally reached the summit with the cymbal crash and the high C in the sopranos of the choir on the word "Kunst" (art).

A long journey filled with many unbelievable panoramas and beautiful gems, which to describe in words must remain an illusion ("Wahn"). For that there remains only, to quote Hugo von Hofmannsthal, "die heilige Musik."

—Translated by Nicholas Vazsonyi

2

"We Must Finally Stop Apologizing for *Die Meistersinger!*": A Conversation with Harry Kupfer

HARRY KUPFER

Mr. Kupfer, you have staged Wagner's works from Der fliegende Holländer *to* Parsifal. *Where do you think* Die Meistersinger *fits into Wagner's oeuvre?*

The great political and philosophical dimension, which the *Ring* opens up, is portrayed on a very individual level in *Tristan*. The destruction of people by people themselves takes shape in *Tristan* through lies, untruths, and social convention. By contrast, in the miraculous work of *Die Meistersinger* one finds these problems overcome. This is especially the case in the wonderful figure of Hans Sachs who is truly a democratic personality. After an intense internal struggle he comes to the realization that in order for people to live together successfully, reason and the renunciation which is associated with it are a vital necessity. In this sense, *Die Meistersinger* is the most utopian and optimistic of Wagner's works, where, in contrast to the pessimistic endings of all his other works, the possibility is shown of how people actually could live democratically with one another if they take responsibility by renouncing the idea that self-realization must be achieved at all costs.

It is common knowledge that in the past Die Meistersinger *was often and repeatedly used and misused not only for purposes of specific representation, but also that performances especially before 1945 were laden with a markedly nationalistic accent. What is your position concerning the nationalistic element, and Sachs's formulation of "Was deutsch und echt" (what is German and true) in the final speech?*

The possibility for misuse and falsification is contained throughout Wagner's oeuvre. The contradictions of the nineteenth century, all of which Wagner synthesizes and takes to the extreme, also render his work open for misuse.

It is well known that the final speech, complete with its national overemphasis, is essentially Cosima's fault. Originally, Wagner did not want to write it *quite* like that. Immediately after the Nazi period, these words caused a shiver to run up our spine. But today we can also perceive them differently. What has now become of "German and true" and of German culture in general, given the shadow of Americanization, makes the work explosive in an entirely new way, without us having to read it nationalistically. As we struggle today for a united Europe, it is constantly stressed that the particularity of each nation should not be lost. Whenever I pass by a McDonalds, whenever I turn on the TV in the evenings and immediately switch it off because of a program that follows an American model, whenever I hear the disregard of the German language (why do we never say "Kinder" anymore, but instead "kids"?), Hans Sachs's words seem like music to my ears. We should not see them as being nationalistic, but rather as a wake-up call. One can also explain this in terms of the period when *Die Meistersinger* was conceived and written: an appeal to respect the best traditions that every nation possesses. In this case, one does not even need to overemphasize the word "deutsch" (German). Wagner never uses the word alone, but always supplements it with the term "echt" (true). This entails something positive, which goes to the heart of *Die Meistersinger*. The point here is the balance between good traditions and the development of new ones, while simultaneously rejecting bad traditions. Neither the anarchic-new, however inspired, nor the time-honored but sterile tradition have much of a future. Hans Sachs mediates between the two, and the solution to the problem lies only in the dialectic tension between them. This way of looking at it rules out the possibility of any nationalistic or even fascistic interpretation. We must finally stop apologizing for *Die Meistersinger.* I will mount every barricade to defend this work against the non-culture (*Unkultur*) which confronts us today.

Beside to the connection to Tristan *do you also see one between* Die Meistersinger *and* Tannhäuser? *After all, the work was originally conceived by Wagner as a sort of satyr of the "Sängerkrieg auf dem Wartburg" (song contest on the Wartburg). Did something remain from this conception?*

Well, most certainly both works have something to do with one another. Both are dramas about the artist. At the center of *Tannhäuser* stands the artist who finds himself torn between opportunism and anarchism. By contrast, *Die Meistersinger* offers a rational solution not found in *Tannhäuser.* *Tannhäuser* ends tragically with the death and canonization of the artist, who only in death becomes subject to misuse for the existing staid society. In *Die Meistersinger,* on the other hand, Hans Sachs educates a young genius who learns to understand that there are rules in art, rules that the artist must learn to master and that can be gleaned only from the great masters of the past, but without getting stuck in one's ways. It is surely Sachs's great achievement that, while he recognizes Stolzing's contravention of the rules, he understands that alternative paths are also possible. In addition, Sachs makes it clear to Stolzing that, if he wants to succeed in life, he must also behave according to rational principles in terms of mundane existence, in love, and in marriage.

How does Stolzing's future actually look?

Stolzing has the best teacher in the world, and I hope that he understands something of what he has learned. Most likely he will still break free, but at the same time he will find the middle way which leads to mastery if he still wants to create art.

Will he become a more significant Mastersinger than Hans Sachs?

I would say that he has already surpassed Hans Sachs in many respects. Sachs's great problem consists not only in the human renunciation of his love for Evchen, but he realizes in the *Fliedermonolog* that Stolzing towers over him: "Dem Vogel, der heut' sang, dem war der Schnabel hold gewachsen. . . . Es klang so alt, und war doch so neu, Wie Vogelgesang im süßen Mai!" (A lovely beak has grown on the bird who sang today. . . . It sounded so old—yet was so new, like birdsong in sweet May!) It is here that Sachs bids farewell to the knowledge that he is the greatest. He comes to the realization that he is a mere artisan poet, and recognizes that Stolzing is a genius. It is a sign of his greatness that he does not let it tear him apart, like some rabid wolf, but instead helps the young man.

How old is Sachs?

Mid-forties, at most. He needs to be old enough for Eva to conceivably be his daughter, but young enough so that it is entirely possible for him to be a suitable partner for her; he is still in the full bloom of life and sexually potent, and there is a strong mutual attraction between them. But he notices the spontaneous connection between Eva and Stolzing. He could destroy it, but through tremendous self-restraint, he helps the young couple. One should think only of the end of the scene in the shoemaker's home (Act III, scene 4), when Sachs explodes on the verge of a nervous breakdown. For me, Sachs is a character who fights unflinchingly. One should just follow the sequence in Act I from the way he meets Stolzing, how he declares himself to Stolzing in the Song School (*Singschule*), how initially he, too, is consternated and astonished but nevertheless makes an effort to grasp the novelty which confronts him. For me, Sachs is a strong man who is in conflict with himself, but who finds the path to humanity.[1]

One of the many clichés of "Meistersinger" interpretation is the idea that Beckmesser is a ridiculous character, or even that he is a caricature of a Jew, a "Jew in the brambles" ("Jude im Dorn") taken freely from Grimm's fairy tale.

One must not isolate Beckmesser from the rest of society. He is the town clerk and, as Wolfgang Wagner explained to me, is thus also the highest police authority. The whole point of the story is that it is he of all people who causes the nighttime scandal on the streets in Act II. It is also important to understand that he is a serious candidate to become Pogner's son-in-law, and that Pogner indeed favors him. Beckmesser is admittedly not wealthy, but enjoys prestige in the city. He is an intellectual, and is certainly a genuine authority when it comes to the rules of the Mastersinger-Tabulatur. But he is not creative and has no imagination. This person, who is not talented but who has taught himself the whole rule-business, finds himself in a situation which makes him go mad. What happens with the courtship song on the fair grounds (*Festwiese*) is frightening and borders on insanity. After all, those are images of death he comes up with—it is not only absurd, it is shocking. He is a petit bourgeois intellectual, pedantic, narrow-minded, precise, but not stupid. He is by all means able to get Sachs unhinged in the Song School. Nevertheless, one should not ignore the fact that Wagner used this figure to get revenge on the Viennese critic Eduard Hanslick. In many places one almost cannot avoid degrading Beckmesser. Master Wagner also poured out all his venom on him in the composition.

In Act I, Pogner clearly favors Beckmesser as Evchen's suitor. In Act II, he seeks a conversation with Hans Sachs. Does he perhaps hope for Sachs to become his son-in-law?

No, the reason lies much deeper. Pogner is intellectually somewhat limited, but is rich and loves art. He has now come up with the most immoral idea in the world by offering his daughter Eva as the prize in a singing competition, to the greater glory—or so he thinks—of himself, Nürnberg, and art. But he has his doubts nevertheless: he says, "War's nicht vielleicht nur Eitelkeit?" (Was it perhaps not just vanity?). Step by step, Pogner falls apart and degenerates into total confusion. Sachs has a special role in this process. Still, Pogner at least agrees that Eva's vote should decide the issue. But she may take none other to be her husband; it must be a Mastersinger.

---

1. The photographs in this chapter are production photos from a staging of *Die Meistersinger von Nürnberg* in 1998 at the Staatsoper Berlin (Unter den Linden). Director: Harry Kupfer; Sets: Hans Schavernoch; Costumes: Buki Shiff; Conductor: Daniel Barenboim.

A Conversation with Harry Kupfer

Figure 2.1. Act III—Sachs's workshop. Eva: Carola Höhn; Sachs: Falk Struckmann. Photograph by Monika Rittershaus. Reprinted by permission.

Figure 2.2. Act II—Beckmesser's Serenade. Beckmesser: Andreas Schmidt. Photograph by Monika Rittershaus. Reprinted by permission.

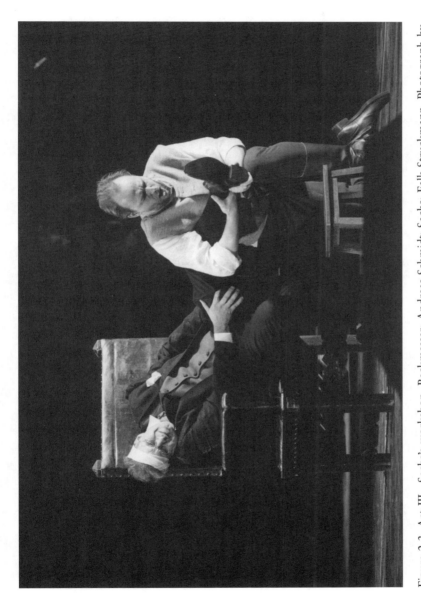

Figure 2.3. Act III—Sachs's workshop. Beckmesser: Andreas Schmidt; Sachs: Falk Struckmann. Photograph by Monika Rittershaus. Reprinted by permission.

Pogner now discovers that he has set a bomb which explodes in his hands.[2] This is why he wants to talk to Sachs, but he shies away from it because they had had an argument about the whole matter in Act I, and Sachs had tried to make the immorality of his intentions clear to him.

How does Evchen behave in the face of her imposed subordination within the patriarchy? What should one think of a sentence like: "Ein artig Kind gefragt nur spricht!" (A well-behaved child only speaks when spoken to!)

This is pure hypocrisy. She is an unabashed hussy—of course "hussy" is expressing it too negatively. She is a thoroughly healthy woman, full of vitality. The way she behaves towards Stolzing in the church—"Euch oder keinen!" (You or no one at all!)—she literally flings herself at him and is prepared to break with every convention. She also does not really understand what the whole hullabaloo is with the Mastersingers. If a guy is good looking and attracts her sexually, and if she loves him, then he must surely be a Mastersinger. And then there is her relationship to Sachs! This snake of a woman! The way she lures him out of his hesitation, until she finds out what she wants to know: how her knight had made out at the song trial—this bears all the markings of infinite brazenness.

The historical Nürnberg and Wagner's rendition of it are not identical. What is the Nürnberg one sees in Wagner's Die Meistersinger?

It's something we find the world over. This conflict is after all not just a conflict about art, but also a social conflict, a conflict between young and old, between the generations, between inspiration and tradition. Nürnberg is wherever this conflict takes place. Such a conflict could be played out as much in small town America of today as in Munich or Berlin. Actually, this conflict is latently present always and everywhere.

Can the confrontation between Stolzing and the Mastersinger guild be simply reduced to the antagonism between avant-garde and convention? The rules of the guild are clearly derided by Wagner. Does Stolzing actually get off scot-free? Phrased differently, why does Sachs—who after all reveals a thoroughly critical attitude to the formalism of the Tabulatur—nevertheless conclude by singing the praises of German art and, with that, clearly also the praises of the art of his fellow guild members?

Stolzing's creations, especially in Act I, are thoroughly amateurish. He is talented, but if one examines the rhymes in his trial song "Fanget an!" (Let it begin!), one ascertains that, while inspired, it is also pubescent. Sachs makes wicked fun of him in his home when he says to Stolzing: "Eu'r Lied, das hat ihnen (nämlich den Meistern) bang gemacht; und das mit Recht"

---

2. The original reads: "Pogner kommt nun dahinter, daß er eine Bombe gelegt hat, die ein Rohrkrepierer wird." "Rohrkrepierer" is a shot that explodes prematurely in the barrel or muzzle during firing.

A Conversation with Harry Kupfer

Figure 2.4. Act I—St. Catherine's Church. Eva: Carola Höhn; Stolzing: Francisco Araiza. Photograph by Monika Rittershaus. Reprinted by permission.

48   *Performing (in)* Die Meistersinger

Figure 2.5. Act II—Riot scene. Photograph by Monika Rittershaus. Reprinted by permission.

(Your song made them [meaning the Masters] anxious; and rightly so), because the song from front to back really makes no sense. Stolzing is the typical Storm and Stress daredevil, but as yet he is unable to accomplish anything. He must learn to control himself, to organize his thoughts and to bring them into proper form so that they are effective. Sachs continually points out to Stolzing that form and content must be in synch. Stolzing has yet to comprehend all of this. When people are accepted to an art academy, though they must have talent, they aren't immediately declared to be geniuses, rather they must learn something at the hands of a master. The danger in Act I is to make the Masters seem ridiculous and degrade them, which then makes Stolzing seem correct from the very beginning. On the contrary, one should show that his artistic claims may be well founded, but that it is equally justified for the Masters to contest him.

Aren't there also very personal interests involved in the case of Beckmesser?

Of course, he wants to eliminate his rival. But he is no falsifier, rather everything that he marks as a mistake is one that Stolzing clearly makes. Only Sachs thinks further ahead by realizing that while the song was not conceived according to the rules, it is perhaps necessary to reconsider the rules. Beckmesser is simply unable to grasp this step. He would still not be able to do so, even if there were no personal interests involved.

When and where does Harry Kupfer's Meistersinger *take place? What do the stage sets and costumes represent?*

In history, today, and nowhere. More concretely: between the quotation marks of historical development. We have interwoven various cultural achievements in an inlay-floor which is destroyed and which could stem from various epochs. In addition, there is a tower which could be from any age between Roman and Medieval times, like in a museum. It is open at the top for whatever future generations want to add to it; in other words it leaves the door open for any and all forms of development. All of this lies in front of a backdrop which suggests that Nürnberg could be temporally and geographically anywhere and everywhere.

What entices you to bring this work anew to the stage, given your productions at the Komische Oper (Berlin) and in Amsterdam?

The work is of such inspiration and perfection as no other work of Wagner's. At the same time, it has a simplicity which, unlike the *Ring* which conveys everything indirectly, brings everything clearly to the point. I enormously look forward to staging the work once again.

—Interview conducted by Manfred Haedler and Walter Rösler
—Translated by Nicholas Vazsonyi

50   *Performing (in)* Die Meistersinger

Figure 2.6. Act III—Festival meadow. Sachs: Falk Struckmann; Stolzing: Francisco Araiza. Photograph by Monika Rittershaus. Reprinted by permission.

3

Richard Wagner's Cobbler Poet

Dietrich Fischer-Dieskau

Hans Sachs in *Die Meistersinger von Nürnberg* may well be considered the most demanding and extensive among the roles Richard Wagner assigns the singer-actor—and not only those for baritones. According to international stage convention, the cobbler poet from Nürnberg belongs to the same voice type as Wotan, in other words that of the *Heldenbariton*. But when the two roles are compared with regard to vocal requirements, an essential difference soon becomes apparent.

Some singers might ascribe little significance to the slight difference in voice type that Wagner identifies in the *dramatis personae*, where Wotan is classified as "High Bass" and Sachs as "Bass." Indeed, such a decision seems to be supported by the fact that in *Die Meistersinger* all parts written in the bass clef are characterized as "Bass." Moreover, the vocal range of the two parts—Sachs and Wotan—are almost identical, since the former sings from A to f^1 and the latter from F to f^1–*sharp* although the deep F only appears once, *parlando* and *pianissimo* (*Die Walküre*, Act II).

In keeping with the totally divergent characteristics of the two roles, Wotan requires primarily a robust chest voice and, in the dramatic outbursts, fluctuates in wide accented *fortissimo* intervals which, as far as register is concerned, should not pose too great a problem for basses with a well-rounded chest voice and an elastic-slender high range. Thus basses with light high ends like Michael Bohnen, Georg Hann, or Paul Bender could sing Wotan successfully.

The situation is somewhat different with Sachs. He too requires above-average vocal amplitude and seamless control throughout the entire vocal range. But in contrast to the imperiously irate and vivaciously quarrelsome God, the benevolent Sachs affirms life, and thus his vocal line tends to move about in the higher and brighter resonances. Wagner has placed a few contemplative passages in the lower regions, and those seldom as fully projected tones. However, when Sachs interjects himself into the story line and becomes "active," when he grows passionate, raising his powerful voice, then he also moves vocally into a higher register, usually in the upper middle range.

In this respect, I am thinking above all of the lively exchange with Stolzing in Act III, which proceeds mostly in a fluid tempo. There, it is insufficient to want to pit a light *parlando* against the polyphonic and ample orchestra as one is wont to do with Mozart or some of the Italians. On the contrary, here it is necessary to bring a bright, sonorous resonance of the strengthened middle voice to bear, never without employing an open larynx, and never succumbing to a mere recitative (*Sprechgesang*), which over time certainly exhausts the vocal chords.

Admittedly, a baritone who tends to favor the upper register will be hard-pressed to guarantee that, even with maximum vocal economy with overdependence on a "chest tone of conviction," the constant additional use of the bass register will not render him prematurely (before the final curtain, that is) fatigued or even crippled, as I have seen with colleagues in several cases.

Vocal mastery of such a gigantic role is thus a question of economy, which a young singer must first gradually develop. Indeed, each new attempt at singing the part entails a new adjustment to the vocal requirements. Above all this calls for a scaling-down towards the lyrical, which Sachs so often requires. This, really, is the Gordian Knot for a higher baritone: that he constantly has to operate in a register which *per se* is too low, and which goes against the physiological reality.

At the same time, this higher and lighter voice type serves well the melodious sound, the flowing, often highly lyrical voicing that permeates the entire role. To reach this and never to lose it must be the goal of every interpreter of Sachs. And this also means that every young singer, when studying the role, should think more of Wolfram than of Wotan, that is if he is extremely circumspect in the selection of the part.

Aside from technical mastery of the voice, this part, more than other roles, requires precise attention to and internalization of all the poetic-linguistic elements, thus total mastery of the text. In contrast to Wotan's dynamic alliteration reminiscent of ancient epics ("Stabreim-Pathos"), which is how Wagner causes him to speak, we find here the conversational tone of real human beings, which on the one hand makes the language easier to learn, on the other requires that the words be internalized completely.

It is thus recommended that the singer first gain mastery of the words from the libretto and not from the piano reduction, and that he memorize daily in a comfortable speaking voice. A natural unity of word and tone will certainly facilitate the vocal rendition, and in such a natural setting, gestures and facial expressions, and thus the entire interpretative structure, emerge almost naturally.

Rendering the cobbler poet for the stage is not particularly difficult, since Wagner's directions and remarks of the other characters in the opera make it eminently clear how Sachs is meant to be: a robust man in his late forties or early fifties, still permeated with an undiminished lust for life.

Among his companions in the guild, he never acts in the manner of a narrow-minded pedant clinging to the "rules" as represented by the town clerk Beckmesser. On the contrary, he enjoys sniffing out everything that is new, and approaches such things with tolerance. He is modest, even, no matter how superior to the others he might feel. That also makes him beloved, even popular, which causes the stubbornly tradition-bound Beckmesser to look on with such envy.

Sachs's movements, gestures, and expressions reveal natural humanity; they are often lively, even youthful and fiery, but always measured and simple, not at all self-important. As the scenes unfold, Wagner achieves a magnificent sharpening of focus upon Sachs as person and protagonist. To begin with, Sachs is more an observer, simply one of the masters, formulating his initial comment with modest reserve: "Verzeiht, vielleicht schon ginget ihr zu weit!" (Forgive me, but perhaps you have already gone too far!).

No other protagonist who appears with Sachs can maneuver himself to the fore. The unfolding action itself propels Sachs to center stage, until at last—convinced and courageous—he assumes responsibility for the fate of those dear to him. At the close of Act I, he still stands alone, opposite the others, and only gradually becomes the "*spiritus rector*" of the unfolding drama.

The organization of the scene in Sachs's house in Act II is described precisely by Wagner, not that this is followed today anymore. Sachs sings the *Fliedermonolog* while still inside the workshop: according to the stage directions, "he leans back with his arm resting on the closed lower panel of the workshop door." The work table thus remains invisible from the outside so that his head and torso lit by the shoemaker's globe[1] result in an atmospheric tableau, doubtless also in recognition of most Sachs performers' scant knowledge of the shoemaker's craft. But Wagner's instruction also corresponds with the intimacy of the monologue and the dialogue with Evchen, even though the singer's vocal production is of course hindered somewhat as a result. But what happens when, by comparsion, contemporary productions often lack house walls whose usefulness in aiding the acoustics is blatantly neglected?

Thus, so as not to hinder the power of Sachs's voice, which—God knows—he needs, upon hearing the words "Dort an der Tür" (There, by the door) David usually opens the lower door panel and moves both table and stool far enough out, so that, when Sachs sits on the stool, he has the acoustically beneficial door and house wall in back of him. When David then sings: "Was war nur der Lene?" (What was up with Lene?) Sachs disappears into the workshop for a brief moment, but then comes back to

---

1. *Schusterkugel*—a water-filled sphere which in earlier times was used as a lens to magnify and focus light.

the table still "rather short-tempered" (*kurz angebunden*): "Was stehst noch ... Gut' Nacht!" (What, still standing there? ... Good night!) and attends to his work. But he lets go of it almost immediately and loses himself in contemplation while the clarinet renders Stolzing's love motif tenderly and the strings whirr with delicate *dolcissimo* under the horn thirds, so that the listener imagines that they smell the scent of the lilac (*Flieder*), which the composer had confused seasonally with the elder (*Holunder*).

And with this *Fliedermonolog* begins the internal drama, revealing Sachs's spiritual journey, telling of his fate while preparing the development of his relationship to Walther von Stolzing, and in particular to Eva. Sachs reflects on the events in the church, especially Stolzing's trial song which he cannot get out of his mind—all this in a soft, *cantabile* tone. Even the intermittent quasi-recitative "spoken" sections should sound beautiful and should not interrupt the lyrical flow. The short eighth- and sixteenth-rests serve clear word-formation or highlighted meaning, as was Wagner's habit (and followed by Hugo Wolf so fussily in his Lieder).

The Wagner performer is always well advised not merely to know his own part in detail. Thus, even before the curtain rises on Act III, a Sachs should listen quietly to the wonderful orchestral prelude in order to achieve the appropriate basic mood from which his singing must derive in this and the following scenes.

There is a lot going on in Sachs's mind as he sits in his armchair and pours over a folio while the bright morning sun shines through the window. Most likely he slept little following the disturbances of the previous night. He is experiencing the fate of every aging man, the realization that he will have to do without his dear Eva (*lieb Evchen*). The old reports he reads in the city and world chronicles (*Stadt- und Weltchronik*) both reassure and cheer him. Buried in his thoughts about the "useless foolish anger" (*unnütz tolle [. . .] Wut*) with which people throughout the ages have chased the delusion (*Wahn*) of happiness, he hardly notices that his apprentice David has entered.

For the performance of such thoroughly intimate scenes, Sachs would have been wise not to overextend his vocal chords during Act II, and especially not to get carried away during the cobbler's song by singing with a constant *fortissimo*. A prerequisite for this is that the mental concentration of the singer does not let up at any time, not even during the various "rests." Too much outward gesturing is harmful, and hand movements especially should be kept to a minimum. The eyes and the face do the speaking, and all liveliness of sentiment should be reflected by a facial expression which never lapses into indifference. Should the singer succeed in conveying such human experience, the listener will share in the experience—a rule, incidentally, to which there is no exception in the entire repertoire.

It bespeaks a certain dramaturgical and possibly also musical clumsiness that Wagner crams the finale with two enormous monologues for Sachs, approached with approriate respect by all Sachs interpreters. In light of these, it will have been beneficial if the singer availed himself of the opportunity to lie down during the intermission before Act III, and, even more so, if he has already negotiated the gentle transition to the more tender tones following the outbursts of passionate jealousy and enthusiastic endorsement in his workshop, so that now, content, he can face the demands of the fairground scene (*Festwiese*). Should he, in addition, manage to avoid the appearance of delivering an oration to the assembled *Volk* and be seen, instead, giving expression to his innermost conviction, then may he be afforded the jubilant final applause.

—Translated by Nicholas Vazsonyi

4

The Dangers of Satisfaction: On Songs, Rehearsals, and Repetition in *Die Meistersinger*[1]

Lydia Goehr

Topsy Turvy is a recent British film about the operetta composers Gilbert and Sullivan, a marvelous portrayal of nineteenth-century English musical theater. In one scene we are shown a rehearsal for the singers, an early stage in the production of the *Mikado* when they are still learning their parts. We are shown a scene rehearsed several times. In a sense the rehearsals do not go right: the singers fail to capture the "Japanese manner." But by the time of the first performance they more or less succeed. What is interesting about the scene is that no exaggeration is given to the audience to help it see the difference between when things go right and wrong. Though comments are made and adjustments to body demonstrated—by real Japanese women!—the audience is asked just to look and listen to the repeated act. Given anything less than the most musically and dramatically trained ears, and perhaps not even with these, listeners are unable to state the difference between the song's better and worse performances, yet they grasp it. They know when the singers get it right and respond appropriately to their success. As Wittgenstein once wrote: "Someone who understands music will listen differently (with a different facial expression, e.g.), play differently, hum differently, talk differently about the piece than someone who does not understand."[2]

---

1. A version of this essay is published in *Die Musik als Medium von Beziehungsbefindlichkeiten: Mozarts und Wagners Musiktheater im aktuellen Deutungsgeschehen*, ed. Otto Kolleritsch, Studien zur Wertungsforschung, 40 (Vienna, Graz: Universal Edition, 2002).

2. Ludwig Wittgenstein, *Culture and Value*, 80. All quotations from Wittgenstein are taken from *The Collected Works of Ludwig Wittgenstein* (Oxford: Blackwell, 1998). For the original German, see Ludwig Wittgenstein, *Vermischte Bemerkungen, Eine Auswahl aus dem Nachlass*, ed. H. von Wright (Frankfurt/Main: Suhrkamp, 1994), 136.

How a director manages to convey this moment of difference deliberately in a film is a fascinating question, but it is not mine. I am interested in the claim that the differences listeners hear in musical rehearsals, the incremental improvements that differentiate one rehearsal from another, make *den Unterschied ums Ganze* (all the difference in the world) because grasping those little differences moves listeners, as it moves performers, from a state of not understanding to understanding. Yet in this move there is something paradoxical, because, though we come to grasp a difference between rehearsals, the very idea of a rehearsal-sequence involves our hearing the same thing over and over again. So grasping the difference also has to be accompanied by our seeing the sameness. But why, when faced with sameness, do we not just see the same thing over and over; how do we come to see the difference? Wittgenstein once captured the "topsy-turvy" play of sameness and difference when he remarked that: "We speak of understanding a sentence in the sense in which it can be replaced by another which says the same; but also in the sense in which it cannot be replaced by any other. (Any more than one musical theme can be replaced by another.)"[3]

In another case, Wittgenstein asked us to consider "[t]he peculiar feeling that the recurrence of a [musical] refrain gives us." He continued:

> I should like to make a gesture. But the gesture isn't really at all characteristic precisely of the recurrence of a refrain. Perhaps I might find that a *phrase* characterizes the situation better; but it too would fail to explain why the refrain strikes one as a joke, why its recurrence elicits a laugh or grin from me. If I could dance to the music, that would be my best way of expressing just *how* the refrain moves me. Certainly there couldn't be any better expression than that.—
>
> I might, for example, put the words "To repeat", before the refrain. And that would certainly be apt; but it does not explain why the refrain makes a strongly comic impression on me. For I don't always laugh when a "To repeat" is appropriate.[4]

What was Wittgenstein's point? That sometimes dancing, speaking, gesturing, or repeating a phrase will feel like (and be) the right way to respond, but never will it serve either as an explanation or as a perfect substitute for the experience.

---

3. Ludwig Wittgenstein, *Philosophical Investigations*, Part I, #531, 143–44. German: Ludwig Wittgenstein, *Philosophische Untersuchungen I* (Frankfurt/Main: Suhrkamp, 1971), #531.

4. Ludwig Wittgenstein, *Remarks on the Philosophy of Psychology*, Part 1, #90, 19. Ludwig Wittgenstein, *Bemerkungen über die Philosophie der Psychologie I* (Frankfurt/Main: Fischer, 1984), #90.

My essay is not actually about Wittgenstein but about musical understanding. It is about how listeners come to understand the difference in sameness and the sameness in difference, an understanding that makes *den Unterschied ums Ganze*. It is also about the difference between *cold* and *constructive* repetition, between repetitive acts where we end up in the place where we began because we keep doing the same thing over and over again in the same way, and repetitive acts in which development takes place, where even in doing the same thing over and over again, in each instance we do something different and thereby show a change in our understanding.

Moreover, I focus my concern with repetition entirely on Wagner's *Die Meistersinger* because it presents the dialectic between cold and constructive repetition in an exemplary fashion. "Ein schönes Lied," sings Walther von Stolzing to the melodic leitmotif of the Prize Song, "—ein Meisterlied / wie fass' ich da den Unterschied?" This opera also shows that there is more at stake in the argument about repetition than just a philosophical problem. With many philosophers, one can learn much about following rules coldly and constructively and how it is possible, as Hans Sachs sings, that a piece of music can sound so old and yet be so new (*Es klang so alt und war doch so neu*). However, to see what else is at stake, I will focus on one particular philosopher preoccupied with repetition, namely Adorno, because for him, repetition works for or against our musical understanding and for or against our social freedom, and that awareness sustained his life-long critique of Wagner. He also provided an historically motivated rationale for why, in the general formulation of the problem of repetition, a preference is shown for difference over sameness.

In one of the few positive recommendations he ever made, Adorno suggested a progressive use for a piece of technology—the radio.[5] Against his general complaint that radio was turning participants into passive listeners by authoritatively subjecting them to broadcast programs that were "all exactly the same,"[6] he saw how it might do something different. Radio could be used to give listeners the opportunity to participate in musical rehearsals. Rather than presenting them with a finished product, the completed and perfected performance, which they could only contemplate with the thought that "this is just how it is," radio could let listeners hear the sequence of correct and mistaken moves, the learning process, the process of labor, construction, and artifice, through which the work assumes a final shape.

Adorno was interested in structural listening, in promoting a view in which listeners would follow along with a work's "innere Bewegung spontan

---

5. Theodor W. Adorno, "New Music, Interpretation, Audience," in *Sound Figures,* trans. R. Livingstone (Stanford, Calif.: Stanford UP, 1999), 37–88.

6. Max Horkheimer and Theodor W. Adorno, *Dialektik der Aufklärung: Philosophische Fragmente* (Frankfurt/Main: Fischer, 1997), 129.

mitkomponiert."[7] Hearing a work, as it were, in the process of composition had two benefits: first, it would enable listeners to understand why a given work was different from any other—the uniqueness of its construction. Second, it would help shatter the illusion of the work's naturalness and inevitability, i.e., the ahistorical reaction that this is just how music is and should be, the mistaken idea that a work of genius is a product of nature and not of history and labor. Shattering this illusion would have two benefits of its own. On the side of production, it would open up listeners to an understanding or acceptance of what Adorno called works of New Music; on the side of reception, it would show listeners something different, thus perhaps encouraging them to set aside their "customary crutches of listening," the sort of listening in which listeners already know, or think they know, what to expect, where they already know, or think they know, what gives them pleasure. Listeners, Adorno explained with obvious Freudian undertones, are being driven by the infantile compulsion to repeat, to hear anything that presents itself as new in exactly the same way as the old.

Adorno was not saying simply that listeners should come to appreciate "the new" as different from "the old." He was arguing less for "the new" than for "difference in itself." Thus, in coming to hear the new as different, listeners might come to hear the old as different too. Different from what? Different "in itself." Listening to Beethoven's symphonies, for example, listeners might learn to hear each as a particular and not as the same as any other or, as he said, as falling under the general rubric of tonality or of those works "we all know and love." For it was precisely under the veneer of sameness that radio programming was offering one favorite hit of classical music as interchangeable with any other. Adorno's point was that engaging listeners constructively in the rehearsal sequence might challenge their most habituated forms of easy listening.

Challenging listening habits was for Adorno a form of philosophical critique articulated from the utopian perspective of difference. It was designed to encourage listeners to see through the superficial comforts and pleasures given by what they thought they desired most, namely the comfort of adaptation to that which had all the (false) appearance of the familiar. "The minimal differences from the ever-the-same," he once wrote, define "the difference concerning the totality." In these differences, in divergence itself, is our hope concentrated.[8]

---

7. Theodor W. Adorno, "Arnold Schoenberg," in his *Prismen: Gesammelte Schriften* 10 (Frankfurt/Main: Suhrkamp, 1977), 153.
8. Theodor W. Adorno, "Culture and Administration," in *The Culture Industry: Selected Essays on Mass Culture*, ed. J. M. Bernstein (London: Routledge, 1991), 113; Theodor W. Adorno, "Kultur und Verwaltung" (1960), in *Soziologische Schriften I,* ed. Rolf Tiedemann (Frankfurt/Main: Suhrkamp, 1972), 146.

In the autumn of 1937 and spring of 1938, on his way out of Germany, Adorno wrote his *Versuch über Wagner*. The timeliness of his text was demonstrated in his urgency to describe the tendencies—not just the features, characteristics, or qualities, but the historical or social tendencies (*Tendenzen*)—in Wagner's works that would show why their Nazi appropriation had been able so comfortably to assume the appearance of obviousness. He interpreted the works through tendencies he linked not just to a Fascist aesthetic, but also increasingly, and especially during and after his exile in America, to the *Kulturindustrie*. For Adorno, these tendencies showed a totalizing expression of Enlightenment culture and society in which the demand for sameness, adaptation, and cold repetition were eliminating every feature of individuality, freedom, and difference. Their description would show the fundamental deception upon which Nazi society thrived, namely, that that which was being explicitly promised—individuality, freedom, and difference—was just what was being most denied. In place of real pleasures afforded by individuality, freedom, and difference, the false satisfaction of easy pleasures was being offered under the illusion that what was merely apparent was real. On the one side, Adorno thought the false promises played perfectly into the infantile satisfaction with the superficial offerings of the Golden Calf; on the other, he thought listeners would become bored and that their boredom would prompt a desire for something different.

That Adorno himself wrote repeatedly about repetition, and especially in his *Versuch über Wagner,* should not surprise us. Yet we should not ignore it, because his use of a repetitive strategy was not intended to encourage repetition as such, but, where it was needed most, to break its powerful spell. The use of process, the deliberate focus on form, is comparable to the form of the psychoanalytic process in which we engage repetitively in repetitive patterns to make them known, explicit, or conscious, in order eventually to disengage ourselves from their grip.

When Adorno turned his critical ear to Wagner, and to *Die Meistersinger* in particular, he thus tried to break this opera's "Zauberspruch," its "boundless authority" over the audience. (Wittgenstein himself spoke of the "magic of bewitchment.") For not only was it, according to the propaganda, the Nazis' "greatest hit"; it was also the opera that promised the most, only then to deny it. To shatter its spell through philosophical form was Adorno's way of challenging its aesthetic power, its "Wahn," its establishment of order, harmony, inevitability, and completeness. To what end this philosophical challenge? To show the chaos, disorder, violence that was being masked beneath its disciplined surface.

How could this mask be shown for what it was? By exposing the contradictions between the opera's musical techniques and its claims for "newness," "freshness," "revitalization," and "difference" promised explicitly by the argument of its libretto. Adorno's description of its leitmotifs, gestures, and rhythms were interpreted not as techniques of constructive repetition but as failures of such: false promises or cold repetitions that effectively left the audience at the end of the opera in a place no different from where it began. Adorno criticized the libretto's argument too, as based on conservative rationalizations or appeals to nature, tradition, and order claiming to embrace the new, only to have the outcome of keeping the established order in place. The notion of subjectivity the opera promoted was not that of a freethinking subject—or even a genuine, pure, or noble one, to use the hazardous terminology of the libretto—but a static and conformist one brought into the fold, brought seemingly happily and convincingly into identification with a social structure that forbad genuine development. Throughout his book, Adorno was concerned with the impact of Wagner's operas on his audiences, with the false promises that played perfectly into the conformist demands of Nazism's aestheticized politics. Was it any wonder that in 1937 Adorno took as his task to stress the failures of *Die Meistersinger* to oppose the power of its most obvious success?

When in 1963, at the *Berliner Festspielwochen,* Adorno returned again to Wagner, he suggested a corollary to his conception of philosophical critique regarding the question how one should interpret Wagner in performance. His point for the interpretation of performance was just what it was for philosophical critique: to recognize Wagner's works to be in the grip of history, to see how much and through which terms these works had become subject to a "Wagner Orthodoxy"; to recognize that performances will always engage historically with these works that are in the grip of history, and as such will achieve a certain truthfulness only insofar as they succeed in injuring the orthodoxy. Only "experimental solutions," Adorno concluded, will perform this task today, because they are least likely to gloss over "das Falsche, Brüchige, Antinomische" implicit in the works themselves. Indeed, they will try to force *das Falsche* into the open: to let it be seen.[9]

But how does such a thing come to be seen, and does the work itself provide any clue? If it does, then our coming to see such a thing through performance or interpretation turns out to be inextricably connected to our judgment of the work's success or failure to provide that clue. Wagner's *Die Meistersinger,* I shall now argue, demonstrates that connection in an exemplary fashion, in the form of a question it tries both to raise and answer.

I therefore turn now to the opera itself to say something about its repetitive strategies with a special eye focused on this critical question of its success or failure. The most difficult question I pose is whether Walther

---

9. Theodor W. Adorno, "Wagners Aktualität," in *Ob nach Auschwitz noch sich leben lasse: Ein philosophisches Lesebuch,* ed. R. Tiedemann (Frankfurt/Main: Suhrkamp, 1997), 383.

von Stolzing's final *Preislied*, a song that has all the appearance of compositional success, in any sense symbolizes a failure of the opera. Obviously, to answer this question, we need to know what sorts of conditions determine success and failure, but this latter question is one of the deeper questions of the opera itself.

I am not recommending some kind of logical procedure with which we could conclude that if the *Preislied*'s success marks a failure of the opera, then inversely its failure marks the opera's success. Rather, I suggest that the *Preislied* stands symbolically or allegorically to the opera through *a step of reflection*, which is to say, insofar as it leaves the answer to the opera's question of success and failure understood. It would be too easy if the conditions of success and failure of the winning song simply extended to the conditions of the opera's judgment. But one of the lessons of the opera is to throw a wrench into that very equation.

If I said the opera itself should not leave the audience merely satisfied but also thinking, I would seemingly be announcing one of the platitudes of a concerned aesthetic theorist who wants thought and not just feeling to result from aesthetic experience. However, again, I would also be asking for something *Die Meistersinger* asks for itself. For this opera ends not with the *Preislied*, but with a disturbing monologue sung by Hans Sachs on its meaning and consequence. The opera does not end with what seems to be its natural or inevitable ending—with the song sung, the prize won, with its meaning assumed and shown, with the feeling that "of course it was going to end this way," with everything "gut gemacht." Instead it ends with a monologue in which Sachs explains the significance of the *Preislied* not just for its composer—why Walther must now join the Mastersingers and not simply run off with Eva—but also for the entire future of the mastersingers' tradition, and thus also for the future of art, of which the *Volk* has just served as final judge.[10] What becomes obvious in this monologue is that there is nothing obvious about the significance of the *Preislied*, and that it is the shattering of this obviousness that is intended to shift our response to the song from being one of blind satisfaction to one of critical reflection on the future of art.

I shall do no more than mention the tortured disturbance created by Sachs's appeal to the future purity of German art and his fear of foreigners. Instead I shall concentrate on the just as troubling disturbance created when he responds so seriously to Walther's interruption of the easy or "gut gemachte" satisfaction given by the *Preislied*, when Walther, refuses the

---

10. As Sachs demands early on: "lass das Volk auch Richter sein," to which Master Kothner asks: "Gebt ihr dem Volk die Regeln hin?" For some of the background on Wagner's decision not to end the opera at the end of the Prize Song, and of Cosima's involvement in that decision, see chapter 2 of my *The Quest for Voice: On Music, Politics, and the Limits of Philosophy* (Oxford: Clarendon Press, 1998).

position of master or even any association with the masters (for the German "ohne Meister" retains the ambiguity)—"[Ich] will ohne Meister selig sein." For, in his response, Sachs explains for the last time why he has shifted the burden of judgment away from the experts and given it to the *Volk,* to the one group, notably, that until the end is not made privy to his long lesson on art. Early on in the opera, Sachs asks the other masters whether they should not move the judgment of song "herab aus hoher Meisterwolk'" and turn it "zu dem Volk," "ob das ihm zur Lust geschah!" Yet on what terms is the *Volk* supposed to make its final judgment? Just on the basis of pleasure? Apparently, but given the final monologue, also with at least some understanding that the judgment will be used to guide that of the masters who represent the *Volk* by preserving its song. However, if at least part of Sachs's point is to transform the *Volk* into a moderately responsible and not merely a naively responding body, then perhaps Wagner should have ended his opera with a chorus engaged more thoughtfully in reflection, and not, as he did, with a chorus singing in praise of their and everyone else's success. But would such an alternative ending to the opera have elicited the appropriate applause?

One might think that Wagner's aim, in choosing the ending he did, was self-serving because he wanted applause for his opera. Certainly he did and said so, but why? Perhaps because, given his precarious reputation at the time, he was begging to be judged no longer by his harsh critics but by the *Volk* with whom he believed he might have better luck. As Walther sings in desperation: "Ha! diese Meister! / Dieser reimgesetze / Leimen und Kleister!— / Mir schwillt die Galle, / das Herz mir stockt, / denk' ich der Falle, / darein ich gelockt. / Fort, in die Freiheit! Dahin gehör' ich—" As is well known, much of *Die Meistersinger*'s libretto is about the harm conservative critics—specifically, Eduard Hanslick in the figure of Beckmesser—can do to composers who try to do something new. Much of Wagner's anti-Semitism is articulated in the form of a displeasure with the unwelcoming (as he experienced it) operatic establishment of *bürgerliche* managers and critics in Dresden and Saxony, who, as Master Pogner complains, place importance "nur auf Schacher und Geld." Composing an opera that would speak directly to the *Volk,* that would glorify its role in judgment, might have been his way of transforming his own perceived failure with the critical establishment into a success with the general public.

But the transition from critics to the public was not as self-serving as this explanation sounds. Wagner was also interested in the notion of a democratic theater—as Bayreuth was conceived. In this light, his argument was not so much against expertise but for a particular political conception of art in which the audience would participate in an artistic experience that would work alongside certain political transformations of community: art for the people, and, at best, a sophisticated art for an educated people, achieved through the *Schein* of sensuous form. The fact that Wagner's democratic theater was later conceived increasingly as an aestheticized microcosm of a totalitarian state—the *Gesamtkunstwerk* as aesthetic state—only demonstrated the dangerous ideological spell to which this idealistic and politicized view of art could succumb. But again my point is less with that thorny problem than with Wagner's desire that his audience not be, as his chorus of *Volk* seem to be, content merely with a happy, upbeat feeling of success and satisfaction, but that it also leave the theater with some sort of socially transformative thought.

One might suggest now that if part of *Die Meistersinger*'s argument is to show that it would be immature for a composer to remain content with the belief that his genius depends entirely on the inspiration of nature or the birds, so the argument by the end suggests that this is true of the *Volk* too. The fact that the people are in a rural setting, and in a festive Johannistag mood, certainly underscores the appearance of naturalness. However, though it might obscure, it does not belie Sachs's warning that the *Volk*'s judgment of the *Preislied* is an important one, and demands its and, by extension, our understanding. From which it follows that if the audience of Wagner's opera identifies with the *Preislied*'s audience, an identification Adorno found most disturbing, then the *Volk* with whom they should identify should ideally be one that has grasped the dangers of immaturity—the dangers, that is to say, of an audience spellbound in the atmosphere of rightness within which the *Preislied* is clearly sung. It might be a necessary step when the audience, within and without the opera, is offered a profoundly wrong version before they hear the right one. But it is also a troubling step insofar as Beckmesser's disastrous humiliation is used to inspire the contrary feeling when we hear Walther sing, that "ah yes, this is how it should be."

Let me introduce now some of the different but familiar strategies of repetition used in the opera: first obviously in the repetitive verse form of the *Meisterlied* itself, and then in how Walther's *Preislied* musically and textually repeats and develops his prior songs—the "Trial Song" and the "selige Morgentraum-Deutweise"—how it is conceived as their natural child, as the perfect combination of rules and inspiration. And in contrast to the developmental and organic relation obtaining between Walther's songs, the audience hears the cold and failed attempts to sing a *Meisterlied* of which, in a certain sense, there seems in this opera just to be only one ideal type. The range of failed and successful attempts to sing The Song is demonstrated through the repetitive structure of the art-lesson taught by Sachs primarily to Walther, but which the audience is also taken through, as in Socrates' *Meno*, as a repetitive form of pedagogical mimesis. It is a long and sometimes deliberately laborious lesson in which the audience sees, through the apprentice David's song, the limitations of talent and craft which, though in accordance with the rules of good mastersinging, nonetheless produces songs that feel, metaphorically, no better than "einem Paar recht guter Schuhe" (the cold repetition of rules by the merely talented). And then, through Beckmesser, the audience sees less the limitations than the curse of old age when it comes to be associated not with wisdom but with pedantry and corruption (repetition through theft). And then, finally, against the limitations of craft and the curse of pedantry, it sees the trials and tribulations of genius, albeit attacked but made persistent by the promise of love from Eva and the paternal encouragement of the wise Sachs. Through Walther, the audience sees the move from the immaturity of not understanding to the maturity of understanding the relation of genius to rule-following (or at least a move in that direction), because Walther, like so many of Wagner's leading tenors, never seems to get the point entirely—or does he?

One may also say that this entire learning takes place through the production of would-be or approximations of master songs, all produced as if rehearsals of the final event, the singing of the *Preislied*. And with the rehearsals all in place, like the preparation for the final performance, when we finally reach that performance, everything goes, or at least should go, just right. At the end, we all know why the *Preislied* deserves the Prize. "Das habt ihr einmal wieder gut gemacht," sings the *Volk* to Sachs. Or at least we all think we know.

Why suddenly the doubt? Because there is a risk in this rehearsal sequence that needs to be made explicit, the risk that the way the lesson is taught makes the *Preislied* appear too certain the outcome, too natural the consequence, too correct the fit. Recall Adorno's proposal for radio rehearsals. One danger in listening to a rehearsal sequence (Adorno does not mention) is that, though we come to see how a work is put together, we also come to believe that the final performance we hear is the only way to perform it. In other words, we run the risk of confusing the final performance with the work itself and forget that other ways to perform it are possible. The danger I am pointing to lies in the forgetfulness that things can go differently, a forgetfulness Adorno articulates elsewhere as the danger of overidentification of the subject with the object and the consequent loss of critical distance. So let us imagine now that we could rewrite *Die Meistersinger*'s ending to show at least that the *Preislied* is not after all the only outcome of the opera's lesson.

First, instead of offering a monologue on the significance of the *Preislied*, Sachs might have stood up after Walther's performance and informed the audience that the final Song could have been sung differently. And then he would have sung his own version. Of course we know he had already renounced his claim to Eva and hence, for this reason, could not sing his own song. But still, had he done so, he could have shown the *Volk*, instead of just telling it, that the future of German art will never be guaranteed by the success of a single song, but by preserving a tradition in which one understands what it means to be open to, and care for, new song. It is not Walther's

Preislied that matters, but that something new is recognized and accepted as such. And yet the new, as he would have shown by singing another song, may assume different, even unpredictable, expressions. For the song Sachs would have sung, he would have won, if not the girl, then the Mastersinger's crown, which he wins anyway.

Or imagine that Walther stands up after Beckmesser's debacle and sings something that seems to be completely unrelated to any song that has been heard before, leaving the masters once again puzzled. Walther might thus have been saying: "You thought you could get me to tow the line, but I really wanted to compose 'eine neue Weise.' " This scenario prompts one to ask how much difference Wagner really allows by making Walther's *Preislied* so family resemblant, familiar, to what has gone before. Put otherwise, the question is how different an act of genius can be. Nietzsche once said it cannot be too different:

> The progress from one level of style to the next must be so slow that not only the artists, but also the listeners and spectators participate in it and know exactly what is taking place. Otherwise, a great gap suddenly forms between the artist, who creates his works on remote heights, and the public. . . . For when the artist no longer lifts this public, it sinks quickly downwards and falls, in fact the deeper and more dangerously the higher a genius had carried it; like the eagle, from whose talons the turtle, carried up into the clouds, drops to disaster.[11]

Nietzsche's words fit a view of change by incremental steps for which *Die Meistersinger* seems to argue, though with the assumption that in these incremental steps can lie all the difference in the world. Like Wagner's Hans Sachs, Nietzsche wants to keep art out of the clouds. However, suppose we said that the steps should be big and obvious, as when composers announce that they are doing something really different, do it, and seem to have good reason for doing it. As we know, however, such large gestures run the risk of being ignored simply on the grounds of their being 'too different.' We don't know what to do with them: "Wer nennt das Gesang?"; "Es ward einem bang!"; "Ja, ich verstand gar nichts davon," sing the masters in response to the Trial Song. But incremental steps run a risk too: that their difference is read as not different enough, when what is different is simply absorbed into what is already known as a continuation of the same. As the *Volk* sings at the end of the *Preislied*: "Gewiegt wie in den schönsten Traum, hör' ich es wohl, doch fass' es kaum!" And then the masters: "Es ist kühn

---

11. Friedrich Nietzsche, *Human All Too Human: A Book for Free Spirits,* trans. M. Faber (Lincoln: University of Nebraska Press, 1986), #168; *Menschliches, Allzumenschliches: Kritsiche Studienausgabe,* ed. G. Colli and M. Montinari (Munich: dtv, 1999).

und seltsam, das ist wahr, doch wohl gereimt und singebar." My point is not to decide between big and little steps as a model for creativity. It is only to show that in either case the difference that exists can always be rationalized—with a "doch"—as insignificant. My concern is with the forgetfulness of difference, not the fact of it.

Let us return to the thought that the entire opera is a rehearsal for the *Preislied*, a rehearsal that the audience witnesses in order to understand its significance when it is finally performed. This thought connects us to the question I posed earlier, whether the success of the *Preislied* can tell us anything about the success or failure of *Die Meistersinger* itself. Suppose in presenting his lesson for the rightness of the *Preislied*, Wagner wanted his audience to be left thinking that it should also accept his opera, because his opera was no less than the *Preislied* of German opera. Might not the audience say that the opera is not actually so different from the operas it already knows and loves? Composed in the tradition of grand opera, it has three acts with arias, duets, and quintets. So what is so new?

But suppose Wagner was being more subtle. Suppose the *Preislied* of German opera was not *Die Meistersinger*, but an opera composed and performed contemporaneously, and in close connection, namely, *Tristan*, one of Wagner's works, to quote from the "Wahn" monologue, "die selten vor gemeinen Dingen, und nie ohn' ein'gen Wahn gelingen." Might the audience not now better appreciate Wagner's attempt to prepare it for another kind of composition which he knew was quite different?

I am suggesting that Wagner's project in *Die Meistersinger* was guided doubly, by his desire to write a successful opera, to receive quick applause, and by the desire to prepare the audience to listen to his already composed *Tristan*. The opera thus assumed a Janus, but ingenious, face regarding the character of repetition. Recall Adorno's criticisms of its strategies of repetition to show the dangers in 1937 of its Fascist appropriation. What I think Adorno did not see then (and perhaps deliberately so) was that some of the repetitive features he picked out as dangerous, regressive tendencies were also, for Wagner, deliberately cold, pedantic, conservative, and old. Wagner was intentionally not offering the emancipatory promise that *Tristan* was purportedly offering, because this new promise could not be framed in the terms of traditional opera, which Wagner was showing through *Die Meistersinger* was already, to use Hegel's words, "a thing of the past." Perhaps, to differentiate the one opera from the other, Wagner made his Hans Sachs sing of knowing "ein traurig Stück," the story of Tristan and Isolde, and of his being clever in avoiding the fortune of King Marke through his renunciation of Eva. But is not Hans Sachs's cleverness double-edged? Since, by playing it safe himself, by sadly but a little ironically agreeing with Beckmesser that he is indeed composing only "*Gassenhauer*," he shows that he knows that someone else, like the young Walther, will have to take the risk he has not taken, to avoid a future in which nothing new happens?

Tristan's anticonventional form demonstrates something *Die Meistersinger*'s conventional form does not, namely Wagner's commitment to releasing his works from the tradition that had defined opera's conventions and terms of critical judgment. In this sense, Wagner's gestures certainly seem bigger in *Tristan* than in *Die Meistersinger*. But is the difference as simple as that? Suppose *Die Meistersinger*'s argument is that if the *Volk* responded properly to the *Preislied,* and the audience properly to the opera, then each would show an openness to hearing what was truly new, not in what it was being presented as such, in the song actually heard, but, rather, in the promise of new possibilities.

We may now interpret Sachs's final monologue as a continuation of Walther's interruption in the satisfaction everyone feels with the *Preislied* in order to leave the audience questioning that satisfaction. For, by experiencing this interruption in pleasure, the audience might then thoughtfully question its satisfaction with an opera like *Die Meistersinger,* which in one sense was deliberately composed to produce such satisfaction, but in another sense was meant to leave one dissatisfied with one's satisfaction so as to create a desire to be satisfied with something different. In this sense, the failure of *Die Meistersinger* to be emancipatory, in Adorno's terms, may also be the condition that allows us to interpret the opera as a deliberate failure, a failure that could serve, we might say, as a constructive rehearsal for something like *Tristan*'s success.[12]

However, the fact that many critics during Wagner's time expressed their clear favor for *Die Meistersinger* over *Tristan* demonstrates the tenacity of conservative judgment with which Wagner was confronted. Yet it might also demonstrate the failure of *Die Meistersinger* to be the deliberate failure he partially wanted it to be, thus leaving room for what Adorno saw to be too easy a Nazi appropriation. Throughout the opera, Sachs shows us the necessity to control aesthetic illusion: to use art to achieve peace and control in the face of that "same old" madness that appears and has to appear every so often in order, as he says in his "Wahn" monologue, "for something to happen." But where in this opera itself does "Wahn" really take place? Not the controlled "Wahn" of the *Polterabend,* but the sort of indeterminacy and irresolution that shows us that *Die Meistersinger* is, on one level, the perfect outcome of Sachs's lesson on art, the next step in German opera, but also, at another level, that a different outcome for that lesson is possible.

How destructive could this indeterminacy be and how well could it serve to break the opera's spell? Imagine an ending to the opera we have not yet considered, motivated singularly now by just that moment when Walther

---

12. I leave aside the question here whether *Tristan* itself, and perhaps even more so than *Die Meistersinger* (on my reading), succumbs to regressive patterns of satisfaction.

forcefully refuses to accept the position of mastersinger—"will ohne Meister selig sein." Indeed, imagine that he tells us that, given the lesson he has just been taught, he thinks the first song he sang, his Trial Song, is still preferable to the last: more musical, more innovative. The last was the compromise—perhaps the unwanted equation between "Parnass und Paradies"—he knew he had to make. It is not an unfamiliar judgment that the first of Walther's songs is the one that shows most emancipatory potential, the most Tristanesque chromaticism some critics even say, and that the last is the most conventional, but what does this judgment do to the present argument?

I have been arguing that only perhaps in Sachs's final monologue might the real message of difference be seen, despite, and here is a danger, every appearance in its content to the contrary. Otherwise put, I have been interpreting Sachs's response to Walther's interruption of the satisfaction with the *Preislied—die Unterbrechung in der Lust,* the breaking of the spell—to mark a genuine ambivalence in an opera that wanted desperately to be familiar, easily absorbed, in order to win the prize, but a prize the opera itself also wanted to give away to another opera that promised something different. Given this ambivalence, the opera ended up in this interpretation being about the difficulties of Sachs's renunciation, his realization of what it means for him, or the opera in which he plays his part, not to take the risks that King Marke and his opera took. In other terms, I have been reading *Die Meistersinger* as an opera about courage and fear, an opera that threatens to take back what it promised or, in Adorno's words, to betray itself through its commitment to an aesthetic of developmental repetition that ends up cold. I have also been reading this opera as a philosophical allegory that seems to make a promise it deliberately does not keep so that it could tell us that the promise was being kept elsewhere.

And yet if Sachs's final monologue demonstrates a desire on Wagner's part to interpret Walther's interruption of the satisfaction with the *Preislied* for the reasons I have just stated, then Walther's own refusal of his song might demonstrate, and now quite independently of Sachs, something even stronger, namely that Sachs's entire lesson on art that generated the final satisfaction was by Walther's very singing of the *Preislied* profoundly unraveled. Sachs's final and grand monologue might therefore state the lesson of difference, but in Walther's small but determined gesture of refusal—in just one line sung—the spell of even that lesson might have been broken.

What conclusion follows from this gap I have imposed between Sachs and Walther? And how, in tandem with this, should we interpret the fact that, following Sachs's monologue, the *Volk* seems only further confirmed in its satisfaction, enthusiastically waving their hats and scarves, and singing with joy? Did the *Volk* not after all learn its lesson, or did it once again accept the words of Sachs without question? Either of these conclusions is plausible, but in a certain sense neither matters. For what matters for the audience, if no longer for the *Volk,* is that, amidst all this joy and operatic resolution, Walther's reasons for his refusal or continued disassociation with mastersinging are purposefully left unexpressed. We are only told that he is happy being in love. Sachs may well be given the last words and the *Volk* given the opportunity to jump for joy, but the final and silent gesture of irresolution still, I think, belongs to the singer who clearly wanted to keep his secret.[13]

---

13. Special thanks to Manfred Frank, Walter Frisch, Daniel Herwitz, Berthold Hoeckner, Ernst Osterkamp, Brian Soucek, and Hans Vaget.

Part II

History in/of
Die Meistersinger

5

Stereoscopic Vision: Sight and Community in *Die Meistersinger*[1]

Lutz Koepnick

It has become a commonplace among Wagner scholars to consider Sachs's interpretation of Walther's song—"It sounded so old / and yet it was so new"[2]—as the key to both the musical style and the political program of *Die Meistersinger von Nürnberg*. According to scholars like Carl Dahlhaus and Theodor W. Adorno, Wagner's *Die Meistersinger* relies on modern compositional practices in order to conjure the impression of older musical idioms. Following Wagner's own aesthetic precisely, the music of *Die Meistersinger* disguises reflection and technique as nature and spontaneity. In order to become art and interlock the archaic and the modern, art here willfully effaces its own constructive efforts. "Nowhere, not even in *Parsifal*, is Wagner's music so artificial as in the appearance of simplicity with which it clothes itself in *Die Meistersinger*."[3] Similarly, in his hope to reconstruct feelings of national belonging via the emotive sounds of German music and the German language, Wagner in *Die Meistersinger* amalgamates various modern visions of sixteenth-century Nuremberg so as to recuperate a mythical past in which art knew no separation from the everyday. Interlacing romantic, conservative, and democratic narratives of the German Renaissance, *Die Meistersinger* conceals Wagner's historical assemblage in the spellbinding guise of unmediated presence and prophetic anticipation. Wagner's Nuremberg is a dreamt one, a chimera of the nineteenth-century imagination deeply affected by the course of German history after 1848

---

1. Research for this essay was supported by a generous grant from the American Council of Learned Societies.

2. Richard Wagner, *Die Meistersinger von Nürnberg: Opera in Three Acts* [Libretto], trans. Susan Webb (New York: The Metropolitan Opera Guild, 1992), 103. Hereafter, page references are given in parentheses.

3. Carl Dahlhaus, *Richard Wagner's Music Dramas*, trans. Mary Whittall (Cambridge: Cambridge University Press, 1979), 75.

and prior to unification in 1870/71. While Wagner is at pains to give history the appearance of historical inevitability,[4] his Nuremberg—in the words of Peter Uwe Hohendahl—"derives its meaning precisely from the confrontation between past and present, between medieval community and modern industrial society."[5]

Adorno's *In Search of Wagner* employs the concept of "phantasmagoria" in order to describe this puzzling fusion of old and new, and reveal the historical index of Wagner's modern recreation of the archaic. Phantasmagorias, in Adorno's understanding, indicate the

> occultation of production by means of the outward appearance of the product.... In the absence of any glimpse of the underlying forces or conditions of its production, this outer appearance can lay claim to the status of being. Its perfection is at the same time the perfection of the illusion that the work of art is a reality *sui generis* that constitutes itself in the realm of the absolute without having to renounce its claim to image the world.[6]

Adorno's notion of phantasmagoria has often proven to be a viable formula for the analysis of how compositional technique in Wagner's music denies technique and engineers the paradoxical illusion of self-contained being. What has been largely overlooked in the reception of Adorno's critical assessment, however, is the fact that Adorno borrowed this concept from nineteenth-century developments in visual rather than sonic representation. The term "phantasmagoria" was popularized around 1800 as the name for magic-lantern shows in which back projection diverted the viewer from the actual sources of visual delight and thereby mystified the operations that generated pleasurable images in the first place.[7] The following pages seek to correct this fundamental oversight by examining what I understand to be the phantasmagorias of vision and visibility in Wagner's *Die Meistersinger*. I will argue that *Die Meistersinger* evidences the demise of traditional concepts of sight and the visual during Wagner's own lifetime, while at the same bearing the mark of mid-nineteenth-century technologies of visual illusion and scopic entertainment. It is in Wagner's or-

---

4. Lydia Goehr, *The Quest for Voice: On Music, Politics, and the Limits of Philosophy* (Berkeley: University of California Press, 1998), 48–87.

5. Peter U. Hohendahl, "Reworking History: Wagner's German Myth of Nuremberg," in *Re-Reading Wagner*, ed. Reinhold Grimm and Jost Hermand (Madison: University of Wisconsin Press, 1993), 57.

6. Theodor W. Adorno, *In Search of Wagner*, trans. Rodney Livingstone (London: New Left Books, 1981), 85.

7. Jonathan Crary, *Techniques of the Observer: On Vision and Modernity in the Nineteenth Century* (Cambridge, Mass.: MIT Press, 1992), 132–33; Terry Castle, "Phantasmagoria: Spectral Technology and the Metaphorics of Modern Reverie," *Critical Inquiry* 15 (Autumn 1988): 26–61.

chestration of seeing, I submit, that certain aspects of the social and political agenda of *Die Meistersinger,* as well as the music drama's dream-like location in neither past nor present, become the clearest.

As Jonathan Crary has demonstrated in *Techniques of the Observer,* numerous scientific, technological, and social developments in the first half of the nineteenth century triggered a revolutionary breakdown of Albertinian perspectivalism and older notions of a disembodied, monocular, and atemporal viewing subject. Contrary to Renaissance and Enlightenment theorists of sight,[8] nineteenth-century scientists such as Gustav Fechner, Johannes Müller, and Hermann von Helmholtz emphasized the importance of internal physiological stimulation and the temporal dimension of visual perception, whereas the advent of visual technologies such as photography and the stereoscope unsettled the earlier understanding of sight according to the idealist model of the camera obscura. But modern visual culture, in Crary's view, commenced not only with a return of the body and a destabilization of former naturalistic codes of representation; it not only dislodged decorporealized paradigms of vision which prevented "the observer from seeing his or her position as part of the representation"[9] and thus called for new conventions of what could be taken for real. As importantly, nineteenth-century modernization also provided the reembodied and binocular viewing subject with new mise-en-scènes of visual pleasure and consumption. Driven by a dramatic shift from production to the provision of consumer goods, nineteenth-century capitalism elevated phantasmagorical illusions to the order of the day. Industrially produced images flooded the marketplace, invaded the arenas of everyday activity, supplanted concrete experience with spectacular diversions, and helped to uphold increasingly spurious notions of community and social coherence. In face of the collapse of former orientations, meanings, and identities, it became the privileged task of visual culture to soothe minds by replaying the old within the new, and to bond emotions by disguising material objects as self-sustaining attractions.

The present essay intends to shed some light on how the figuration of sight in Wagner's *Die Meistersinger* reflects and participates in this transformation of visual culture during the nineteenth century. In order to do so, I first examine the significance of corporeal viewing for the narrative process of *Die Meistersinger,* and then explore the ways in which particu-

---

8. For more on the conception of sight during the Renaissance and Enlightenment, see, among others, Thomas Kleinspehn, *Der flüchtige Blick: Sehen und Identität in der Kultur der Neuzeit* (Reinbek: Rowohlt, 1989); Martin Jay, *Downcast Eyes: The Denigration of Vision in Twentieth-Century French Thought* (Berkeley: University of California Press, 1993), 21–148; and Barbara Maria Stafford, *Good Looking: Essays on the Virtue of Images* (Cambridge, Mass.: MIT Press, 1996), 20–81.

9. Crary, *Techniques of the Observer,* 41.

larly the final scene of Act III takes recourse to nineteenth-century modalities of seeing in order to facilitate the modern in its production of a dreamlike semblance of the past. Understood as a phantasmagoria in its more literal sense, Wagner's staging of communal integration at the end of *Die Meistersinger*, in spite of its outward historicism, indexes fundamental changes of political visibility during the mid-nineteenth century. The scene on the open meadow might allude to medieval and early-modern types of social representation as much as to Enlightenment notions of "attestive" visuality,[10] but at the same time, by celebrating the incorporation of diverse constituencies into a unified spectacle of acclamatory publicness and cultural consumption, the concluding festival encodes peculiarly nineteenth-century developments. It is with this analysis of how *Die Meistersinger* reworks different modes of public visibility that the final section will offer a new perspective on one of the most troublesome issues of current Wagner scholarship: whether or not Heinz Tietjen's 1933 staging of Act III as a spectacular Nazi party rally à la Leni Riefenstahl fulfilled or simply missed the point of Wagner's original vision.

Eyes Wide Shut

Notwithstanding a composer's intuitive affinity to sound and hearing, eyes in Wagner's dramatic and theoretical work designate the most fundamental site of human sense perception and communication.[11] It is the eye, according to Wagner's anthropology, that allows the individual to distinguish between self and other, between what is similar and what is different; it is the modality of sight that in Wagner's larger socio-aesthetic program empowers the audiences of public art to recognize themselves in the aesthetic reflection provided on stage and thus sense their specific place within a specific human collective. Good sight in Wagner is linked to a corporeal experience of organic communality; it catalyzes unmediated reciprocity between those who are familiar, and it separates that which is foreign in nature. Bad sight, on the other hand, as we shall see later, undermines communal identity because it either impairs the recognition of oneself in the other or fails to draw appropriate boundaries between dissimilar groups.

In Wagner's 1849 treatise, *Das Kunstwerk der Zukunft* (The Art-Work of the Future), the composer's doctrine of seeing finds the following formulation:

---

10. For more on the notion of "attestive" visual politics, see chapter 3 of Yaron Ezrahi, *The Descent of Icarus: Science and the Transformation of Contemporary Democracy* (Cambridge, Mass.: Harvard University Press, 1990).

11. Marc A. Weiner provides an extended analysis of eyes in Wagner as organs guaranteeing the recognition of similarity and difference, in *Richard Wagner and the Anti-Semitic Imagination* (Lincoln: University of Nebraska Press, 1995), 35–102.

> The eye apprehends the *bodily form of man,* compares it with surrounding objects, and discriminates between it and them. The corporeal man and the spontaneous expression of physical anguish or physical wellbeing, called up by outward contact, appeal directly to the eye; while indirectly he imparts to it, by means of facial play and gesture, those emotions of the inner man which are not directly cognisable by the eye. Again, through the expression of the eye itself, which directly meets the eye of the beholder, man is able to impart to the latter not only the feelings of the heart, but even the characteristic activity of the brain; and the more distinctly can the outer man express the inner, the higher does he show his rank as an artistic being.[12]

Sight's primary activity is to scan the environment and recognize physical signs of similarity and difference. In its aesthetically most portentous function, however, the eye transcends its merely receptive task, becomes an organ of corporeal expression, and establishes unmediated proximity between human beings. Alluding to the romantic conception of a return of the gaze, Wagner celebrates scopic reciprocity as a state of absolute presence and total transparency, a state in which one's feelings and thoughts can directly reach the heart of the other without requiring the alienating logic of linguistic mediation and conventionalized speech. At its best and aesthetically most relevant, then, vision in Wagner, rather than simply bridging the gap between subject and object, rather than facilitating noncoercive relationships between nonidentical particulars, either collapses differences between like-minded souls into experiences of absolute sameness, self-recognition, and cohesion; or, conversely, it reifies the appearance of the other into a manifestation of radical, incommensurable alterity: "The Self 'knows' itself by sensing its ties with its community and by discerning its difference from those who are foreign."[13]

Wagner's philosophy of sense perception and self-knowledge has little in common with the Hegelian dialectic of self and other. Neither the figure of struggle nor one's transformation by a contingent other, but instead the rather narcissistic and instinctive beholding of oneself in the other is at the center of Wagner's theory of recognition. It therefore also comes as no surprise that whoever falls in love in Wagner's music dramas falls in love at first—or, as I have argued elsewhere, at last[14]—sight. Love always enters the lives of Wagner's heroes in the form of a shock; it transpires as a rapture of visual recognition. The loving gaze, in which Wagner's vision of

---

12. Richard Wagner, *Prose Works,* trans. William Ashton Ellis (Lincoln: University of Nebraska Press, 1995), 1:91.

13. Weiner, *Richard Wagner and the Anti-Semitic Imagination,* 45

14. Lutz Köpnick, *Nothungs Modernität: Wagners "Ring" und die Poesie der Macht im neunzehnten Jahrhundert* (Munich: Wilhelm Fink, 1994), 225–45.

unbridled transparency and reciprocity culminates, suspends the ordinary continuum of time and discovers the absolute in a sudden moment of enchantment. Walther von Stolzing and Eva Pogner, in the opening scene of *Die Meistersinger,* neatly illustrate Wagner's optics of instantenous love. Affection here sets in as a silent drama of looking, of meeting the other's gaze and communicating passion through the enraptured eye. Wagner's demanding stage directions describe Walther's and Eva's initial exchange of glances in the interior of St. Catherine's church as follows:

> Walther von Stolzing is standing at some distance away, leaning on the side of a column, his gaze fixed on Eva, who turns repeatedly around to him with mute gestures. . . . By means of a gesture, Walther puts a wistful question to Eva. . . . Eva, by look and gesture, attempts to answer; but she drops her eyes again, ashamed. . . . Walther tenderly, then more urgently. . . . Eva: timidly repulsing Walther, but then quickly gazing soulfully at him. . . . Walther: enchanted; solemnest protestations; hope. . . . Eva: smiling happily; then, ashamed, lowering her eyes. . . .Walther, in extreme suspense, fixes his gaze on Eva (13–15).

Whereas Wagner first envisions the initial encounter between Walther and Eva as one of inquisitive gestures *and* attentive glances, he quickly moves on to present their gazes as gesture in and of themselves. It is the moment when the eye commands the ability simultaneously to behold and to express affection, to see and to be seen, the moment in which true love comes into being. Understood as a corporeal window to the mind and soul, the eye in this opening scene is by no means figured as merely passive or receptive, as an organ of disembodied speculation or pure knowledge. Instead, both Eva's and Walther's eyes communicate the body as a subject and object of desire. Sight in Wagner has erotic power, and it is the titillating sentience of seeing and being seen, the reciprocal sensation of gestural vision, which causes Eva—cognizant of the customs of place—to withdraw her gaze well before any word has been spoken between the new lovers.

Similar to his aria "Fanget an!" in Act I, Walther's fervent gaze at Eva embodies an intimate mode of looking in which neither convention nor tradition seems to restrain the natural genius's emotional plenitude. Vision, for Walther, is beyond rules and norms. It transcends time and space, and it knows no limits to what can be shown or known. Yet as it transforms a public space (the church) into a highly private playground for the imagination, Walther's loving gaze—in spite of its aesthetic viability—is of little use to offer an operative blueprint for successful procedures of communal integration. It is instead in the figures of Beckmesser and Sachs that we can better understand how Wagner's *Die Meistersinger* probes different models of public vision and visibility and plays through their impact on the conditions, limits, and rule-bound forms of community. As we will see, at the core of this probing is the proposition that the visual is of critical importance for the translation of individual passion and madness into publicly communicable forms. Public festivals, in the perspective of *Die Meistersinger,* serve as simulacra of ritual sacrifice; they channel destructive energy into social order and convert Walther's unbound gaze into reliable and accessible codes of reciprocal seeing.[15]

Throughout the music drama, Beckmesser is typified by skewed forms of looking, by self-inflicted chiasmas bearing witness to the town clerk's greed, egotism, and instrumental reason. Beckmesser, as it were, wants to see too much; he hopes to enforce a spontaneous return of the gaze, yet does not even dare to meet the other's look. Beckmesser's eyes are wide shut. His look is driven by calculating interest, only to be rewarded in the end for his manipulation of sight with public obscurity. During the song competition in Act III, Beckmesser's humiliating performance for instance in no small measure stems from his failure to focus on Sachs's text. He secretly looks at the manuscript, "tries to read the paper; isn't able to" (241), and hence, in the judgment of the *Volk,* produces nothing other than nonsense. Likewise, at the end of Act II, Beckmesser fails to recognize what David notices at first sight, namely that Beckmesser delivers his song to a stand-in, to Magdalene rather than Eva. Beckmesser's blindness in this scene triggers the violent turmoil that concludes Act II. Like bad singing, bad looking in *Die Meistersinger* leads to social disintegration; it undermines social well-being and promotes destructive outbreaks of rage and madness. It is therefore only consequential that Beckmesser, at the end of *Die Meistersinger,* must vanish into oblivion, must be removed from the public stage of vision and visibility, so that the fragmented community may live again. That Beckmesser "rushes away in a rage and disappears into the crowd" (243) is the last thing we hear and see of him in Wagner's music drama. Redirecting the town community's latent violence, the spectacular festival on the open meadow sublimates the noisy blindness of the riot into a new order. Beckmesser is sacrificed, is earmarked as the one who looks differently, so as to reinforce the boundaries of that which is familiar and communal.

It has often been pointed out that the cobbler-poet Sachs, conceived by Wagner in 1851 as "the last manifestation of the art-productive spirit of the *Volksgeist,*"[16] serves as a mediator between Walther's rule-defying ro-

---

15. My understanding of Wagner's festival as a "simulacrum of ritual sacrifice" is informed by the work of Jacques Attali, for whom music's principal function is to bond people in common rituals and make them forget the general violence that resides behind the appearances of everyday life. See Jacques Attali, *Noise: The Political Economy of Music,* trans. Brian Massumi (Minneapolis: University of Minnesota Press, 1985), 21–45.

16. Wagner, "A Communication to my Friends," *Prose Works,* 1:329.

manticism and Beckmesser's manipulative, self-destructive formalism. Sachs represents a tradition of art that aspires to convert authentic inspiration into codifiable technique. Integrated into the circuits of the everyday, his preferred art "must constantly keep in touch with the natural spirit of the *Volk* or its 'free' individuals to avoid becoming overly artificial."[17] A similar point, I suggest, can be made with regard to Sachs's role in *Die Meistersinger*'s many dramas of looking. Sachs's gaze oscillates between the romantic bliss of private inspiration and the need for a public recoding of communal cohesion. In the opening of Act III, we witness Sachs as a meditative reader situated in the midst of a prosaic environment, the workshop. In contrast to Beckmesser, Sachs's eyes are focused on the text; his view is not marred by covetousness. The setting in fact is reminiscent of a genre painting, offering what Friedrich Schiller would call a "sentimental" restoration of bygone times.[18] What we see on stage is an intimate *tableau vivant* which reenacts romanticized notions of the past as affective simulation: "Sachs is sitting in a large armchair at this window, through which the morning sun shines brightly on him; he has a large folio before him on his lap, and is absorbed in reading it" (175). Contemplative reading in this scene, far from arresting Sachs in passivity, endows the cobbler-poet with complete authority over the visual field. Sachs's auratic posture coerces David, who has barely recovered from the previous night's turmoil, to assume a position of repentant submissiveness. Sachs's transfigured appearance as a romantic reader simultaneously attracts and rejects; it puts David in the role of the irreverent son whose foremost desire is to secure the paternal authority's forgiveness.

Sachs's figuration as both an absorbed and an absorbing reader sets the stage for his public celebration by the crowd in the last scene of Act III. Unlike Beckmesser, who is rejected by the assembled *Volk* as an unlikely suitor for Eva even prior to his song—"What? He? He's wooing? Doesn't seem like the right one!" (239)—Sachs enters the scene in the charismatic posture of a latter-day media star, of a figure that compels and fascinates. Sachs is hailed triumphantly by the *Volk*; he is greeted as one who offers something for everyone and thus integrates the community across existing divisions of social status, age, and gender. Interestingly enough, Wagner's stage descriptions depict Sachs's spectacular entry as part of a larger "spectacle [Schauspiele]" (235), a theater within the theater. As importantly, it is through the medium of sight, not song or speech, that Sachs initially connects to the jubilant crowd gathered in front of the festival stage: "Sachs, who, motionless, has gazed above the crowd as if absent-minded, finally

---

17. Goehr, *The Quest for Voice*, 71.
18. Friedrich Schiller, "Über naive und sentimentalische Dichtung," in *Über das Schöne und die Kunst: Schriften zur Ästhetik* (Munich: dtv, 1984), 230–308.

rests his gaze familiarly upon them, and begins with a voice affected by emotion, but quickly growing firmer. . . ." (235). One might suspect at first that Sachs's affable gaze at the crowd simply elevates Walther's and Eva's earlier drama of reciprocal visuality to a public setting; and that, therefore, Sachs's popularity relies on the fact that his eyes can meet the eyes of the *Volk* in a scene of mutual and spontaneous recognition. What is important to keep in mind, however, is that Sachs's look at the crowd emerges within a highly choreographed and codified spectacle, an annual ritual of sights and sounds that depends on identifiable sets of rules and staging principles. Sachs's amicable gaze at the *Volk*, rather than—like Walther—doing away with all rules, and rather than—like Beckmesser—manipulating given codes for personal agendas, follows the customs and routines of the festival in order to transcend them. What is staged and orchestrated must take the appearance of the natural and spontaneous, what is rule-bound and a product of technique must disguise premeditation and be tested in front of the crowd, so that communal traditions lose their stifling effects and open themselves up to continual renewal. It is to the way in which the festival scene of Act III, in its very staging of visual reciprocity and transparency, expunges every trace of effort and willfulness, and to the way in which Sachs's appearance on the open meadow reflects the vicissitudes of political publicness in the middle of the nineteenth century, that I will turn my attention in the following final sections of this essay.

Engineering the Real

Wagner's *Meistersinger* premiered on 21 June 1868 in Munich. Most of the sets were designed by Angelo II Quaglio and Christian Jank, with the notable exception of the final festival scene, devised by Heinrich Döll, the *Königliche Hoftheatermaler*. Quaglio and Döll had visited Nuremberg one year prior to the premiere in order to study the local architecture and animate their historicist imagination. Wagner's expectations for the first staging of *Die Meistersinger* were more than demanding. Privileging spatial depth and three-dimensional configurations over painted backdrops and perspectivalist foreshortenings, Wagner required the majority of sets and buildings to be "praktikabel."[19] According to Wagner's requests, the Munich premiere was meant to reembody rather than merely represent historical Nuremberg, to cast an imagined past into plastic, tangible forms. Moreover, instead of recycling props, sceneries, or costumes from existing opera productions, Wagner called for a completely new design, one which would set authoritative standards for any future realization of Wagner's music drama. Neither trouble nor cost were spared to put *Die Meistersinger* on

---

19. Detta Petzet and Michael Petzet, *Die Richard Wagner-Bühne König Ludwigs II.* (Munich: Prestel Verlag, 1970), 167.

Ludwig II's royal stage, or so it appeared to the eyes of contemporary observers; the Munich magazine *Punsch* spoke mockingly, and in startlingly unaesthetic terms, of the premiere as an "action requiring colossal working capital."[20]

Döll's 1868 design for the open meadow (see figure 5.1) was dominated by a majestic tree stretching its leafy branches from the left side of the set all the way into the right third of the upper part of the stage. Three wooden poles provided a visual counterpoint to the tree on the right edge of the design. They were decorated with flags, banners, insignias, and garlands, some of which intertwined with the branches of the tree. The mastersingers' stage occupied the left foreground, while a number of food stalls and amusement stands inhabited the slightly tilted background. Partly "practicable," partly painted, the river Pegnitz meandered through the far end of the stage, visually tying the three-dimensional set designs to the atmospheric backdrop, the painted skyline of medieval Nuremberg. In Döll's design, the natural and the man-made thus appeared in organic, prestabilized harmony. Tree and poles, garlands and branches, merged into a virtual roof under which the mastersingers' procession could safely unfold. Natural settings provided a scene for human interactions just as much as society transformed nature into a mirror of human passion. As a result, both nature and the signs of civilization took on the character of the ornamental: nature was shown as architectural and architecture copied natural forms. Döll's decorative incorporation of tree and garland thus opened up, and framed, a stage-like space within the stage on which the boundaries between exterior and interior realms, private and public, the open and the intimate, collapsed. Döll's stage delimited a space that naturalized social affairs and socialized nature, a space that remained utterly incomplete without human populations.

Contemporary reviewers of the Munich premiere praised Döll and Quaglio for their unprecedented combination of realism and illusionism. In the eyes of many reviewers, the set design offered a virtual reality,[21] a self-contained space of artifice and simulation, powerful enough to trigger in the audience overwhelming experiences of identification and corporeal immersion. Praising the street set of Act II, the *Neue Berliner Musikzeitung*, for instance, wrote: "Here, one does not see any painted houses but rather complete cardboard buildings that imitate reality, as well as streets, plazas, and perspectives that create an almost perfect illusion."[22] In the view of Wagner's critics, the set designs for the premiere succeeded in casting

---

20. Ibid., 160.

21. On Wagner and virtual reality, and on the total artwork as an anticipation of the *Startrek* holodeck, see Peter Hein, *The Metaphysics of Virtual Reality* (New York: Oxford University Press, 1993), 124–27.

22. Petzet and Petzet, *Die Richard Wagner-Bühne König Ludwigs II.*, 167.

Sight and Community in Die Meistersinger 83

Figure 5.1. Heinrich Döll's 1869 set for Act III of *Die Meistersinger*: Meadow on the banks of the Pegnitz. Herrenchiemsee, König Ludwig II-Museum. Reprinted from Detta & Michael Petzet, *Die Richard Wagner-Bühne König Ludwigs II.* (Munich: Prestel, 1970), 161, with permission from the Bayerische Verwaltung der staatlichen Schlösser, Gärten und Seen.

Nuremberg as second-degree nature. They incorporated the past into the framework of what historians of early film would later call an aesthetics of attraction and astonishment, an exhibitionist aesthetics privileging display and sensuous immediacy—the exhilarating illusion of space, effect, and movement—over narrative causality and integration.[23]

According to the *Neue Zeitschrift für Musik*, the opera's course of visceral sensations culminated with the open meadow scene of Act III: "This colorful variety of poetry, sound, and scenery, this rapid series of gripping and surprising instrumental effects, these kaleidoscopic figments of the imagination, which barely allow eye and ear to come to their senses, must also convert the most stubborn opponents."[24] True to Adorno's contention that the favorization of effect over structural coherence in Wagner's music dramas already foreshadowed the twentieth-century culture industry in embryonic form,[25] Wagner's critics commended in particular Act III of the Munich premiere as a spectacular ride through space and time, as a captivating displacement of ordinary experience much closer to the logic of a Hollywood blockbuster than Wagner could have ever imagined. The sensuous appeal of the open meadow was thereby only enhanced by the fact that Wagner's score allowed for only thirty-seven bars of music, or roughly three minutes, to convert Sachs's house of Act III, scenes 1–4, into the festival plain. Döll's festival set had to be placed right behind Quaglio's and Jank's workshop design, while a rather intricate horizontal and then vertical maneuver of the proscenium curtain—which in some sense anticipated the function of a fade in/fade out in cinematic punctuation technique—was meant to transport the viewer smoothly from one locale to the next. A site for spectacular diversions and dramatic presentations within the opera itself, the palpable set for the open meadow was designed to address the senses of the audience as a miraculous presence, as a product presenting itself as self-producing, as a phantasmagoria. It engaged the viewer's curiosity and solicited the audience's identification, not simply with what could be seen and heard on stage, but with the very apparatus that made the opera's virtual recreation of the past possible in the first place.

Die Meistersinger as a precinematic cinema-of-attractions? As Hollywood *avant la lettre*? We would do well, I believe, not to push Adorno's

---

23. Tom Gunning, "The Cinema of Attraction(s)," *Wide Angle* 8.3–4 (1986): 63–70, and Tom Gunning, "An Aesthetic of Astonishment: Early Film and the (In)Credulous Spectator," in *Viewing Positions: Ways of Seeing Film*, ed. Linda Williams (New Brunswick, N.J.: Rutgers University Press, 1995), 114–33. For a critical reassessment of Gunning's model, see David Bordwell, *On the History of Film Style* (Cambridge, Mass.: Harvard University Press, 1997), 139–49.

24. Petzet and Petzet, *Die Richard Wagner-Bühne König Ludwigs II.*, 167.

25. Andreas Huyssen, "Adorno in Reverse: From Hollywood to Richard Wagner," in his *After the Great Divide: Modernism, Mass Culture, Postmodernism* (Bloomington: Indiana University Press, 1986), 16–43.

accent on the prophetic status of Wagner's music drama too far, not least of all because the figuration of the visual in Die Meistersinger, as much as it may foreshadow the orchestration of pleasure in mainstream cinema, at the same time bears testimony to scenes of visual pleasure and illusionism in Wagner's own time. As Jonathan Crary and others have shown, the mid-nineteenth century was preoccupied not only with physiological theories of seeing but also with new technologies of visual illusion that helped convert ocular astonishments into marketable commodities. All kinds of visual gadgets and imageries inundated private leisure activities with what, according to Martin Jay, "at its worst was a new form of visual pollution, the rise of what would soon be called—the word was coined in Munich in the 1860s, possibly as a corruption of the English 'sketch'—kitsch."[26] Among the myriad of "-scopes" and "-ramas" that reorganized nineteenth-century visual culture starting around the 1820s was the stereoscope, which, thanks to its equal bearing on the development of scientific discourse and popular consumption, was one of the most outstanding. Let me briefly recount the story of the stereoscope and its significance to mid-nineteenth-century observers before indicating how the modern reorganization of visual culture influenced the conception and design of Wagner's *Meistersinger*.

Developed by Charles Wheatstone in 1838 and most comprehensively theorized by David Brewster in 1856,[27] the stereoscope (see figures 5.2 and 5.3) drew attention to the physiological basis for binocular disparity and the synthetic operations of subjective vision—the intellectuality of apprehension, as Schopenhauer called it in Kantian terms.[28] Allowing the observer to view two distinct perspectives as one, and to experience flat images with a startling illusion of spatial depth and tangibility, the stereoscope called into question the assumed congruence between the physical world and the mind's perception of it. The stereoscope's three-dimensional images were solely a product of the viewer's perception; they relied on physiological activities that on the one hand translated the apprehension of disjointed images into an illusionary impression of unity and realistic palpability, while on the other hand coalescing *successive* perceptions into

---

26. Jay, *Downcast Eyes* 122. For more on the origin of kitsch in the nineteenth century, see also Matei Calinescu, *Five Faces of Modernity: Modernism, Avant-Garde, Decadence, Kitsch, Postmodernism* (Durham: Duke University Press, 1987), 225–64.

27. Sir David Brewster, *The Stereoscope: Its History, Theory, and Construction with Its Application to the Fine Arts and Useful Arts and to Education* (London: John Murray, 1856); see also the various essays on the stereoscope by Brewster and Wheatstone in Nicholas J. Wade, ed., *Brewster and Wheatstone on Vision* (London: Academic Press, 1983).

28. Arthur Schopenhauer, "Vom Sehn," in *Kritik des Sehens,* ed. Ralf Konersmann (Leipzig: Reclam, 1997), 195–96.

Figure 5.2. Wheatsone's original stereoscope. From Hermann von Helmholtz, "Recent Progress in the Theory of Vision (1868)." Printed in *Selected Writings of Hermann von Helmholtz*, ed. Russell Kahl (Middletown, Conn.: Wesleyan University Press, 1971), 202. Reprinted by permission of Wesleyan University Press.

an apparition of temporal simultaneity and presence.[29] By rendering coherent what in fact was differential both spatially and temporally, the stereoscope elucidated the fact that nothing about the real and the natural in normal vision should ever be taken for granted. While the "reality effect" in the stereoscopic experience was hailed as striking indeed, the device at the same time helped discount epistemologies which defined the "real" without reference to the corporeal, ever-shifting positions of the observer. Whatever people saw as real, natural, unified, and secure from now on had to be understood in part as the work of rapid, subjective, and fundamentally unstable physiological operations.

So tantalizing were the phantasmagorias produced by the stereoscope that the instrument occupied a privileged place, not just in theoretical optics, but in popular scientific discourse around 1860. While stereoscopic images were mass-produced and mass-distributed for newly emerging leisure markets, Hermann von Helmholtz, in a number of well-noted public lectures in the late 1850s and 1860s, explored the principles of stereoscopic vision as proof of the fact that all knowledge was gained through empirical experience rather than inborn ideas. Prompting in the viewer a

---

29. Following Brewster's account, the impression of three-dimensional space in the stereoscopic experience "is not obtained from the mere combination or superimposition of the two dissimilar pictures. The superposition is effected by turning each eye upon the object, but the relief is given by the play of the optic axes in uniting, in rapid *succession,* similar points of the two pictures. . . . Though the pictures apparently coalesce, yet the relief is given by the subsequent play of the optic axes varying themselves *successively* upon, and unifying, the similar points in each picture that correspond to different distances from the observer." Brewster, *The Stereoscope,* 53; also quoted in Crary, *Techniques of the Observer* 120–22.

Sight and Community in Die Meistersinger

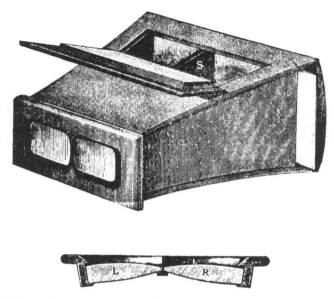

Figure 5.3. The ordinary stereoscope of Brewster. From Hermann von Helmholtz, "Recent Progress in the Theory of Vision (1868)." Printed in *Selected Writings of Hermann von Helmholtz*, ed. Russell Kahl (Middletown, Conn.: Wesleyan University Press, 1971), 203. Reprinted by permission of Wesleyan University Press.

process of false inductions, stereoscopic representations of real objects—according to Helmholtz—exemplified the rule for all illusions of sight, namely, that "we always believe that we see those objects which would, under conditions of normal vision, produce the retinal image of which we are actually conscious."[30] What makes the stereoscope special, however, is that it triggers illusionary perceptions that do not simply go away once we learn about the mechanisms which originate them in the first place. To illustrate this point, Helmholtz compared the seductive apparition of the real in the stereoscopic experience to the appearance of authenticity we accord to the performance of good stage actors. Stereoscopic seeing, like theatrical spectatorship, relies on adopted codes and conventions according to which we see as nature what is a product of art, skillfulness, and technique. Similar to the physiological laws of binocular vision, competent actors extend sensations of liveliness and immediacy even if the viewer knows perfectly well that what s/he sees is a performance. "We are all, so

---

30. Hermann von Helmholtz, "Recent Progress in the Theory of Vision (1868)," in his *Selected Writings*, ed. Russell Kahl (Middletown, Conn.: Wesleyan University Press, 1971), 217.

to speak, jugglers with the eyes,"[31] Helmholtz concluded, thereby suggesting that experience teaches us to understand how to render the theatrical and the illusory as real and to overlook the ineluctable incongruence of mind and matter.

Though scientists, public promoters, and private consumers disagreed about the extent to which the effacement of the mechanism's operation was indeed at the heart of the stereoscopic sensation, the nineteenth-century's exploration of binocularism signaled an end of Albertinian perspectivalism and point of view, a disjunction between experience and its causes, that drew attention to the synthetic, corporeal and—in Helmholtz's understanding—acrobatic aspects of subjective vision. It is, I submit, precisely this paradoxical coupling of realism and spectacle, reference and theatricality, palpable experience and illusion, that mid-nineteenth-century debates about binocular vision in turn shared with Wagner's contemporary re-vision of the German past in *Die Meistersinger*. Though I point out the similarities between the tropes that informed public debates about the stereoscope during the 1850s and 1860s and the staging and reception of Wagner's opera in 1868, my intention is not to propose any deterministic relationship between these two; nor is it my ambition to encourage Wagner scholars to document whether or not the master spent his spare time peeping through stereoscopic lenses. Rather, my point here is to show that the orchestration of sight in *Die Meistersinger* was bound up with much more comprehensive ruptures in modern visual culture, ruptures that effected the reconfiguration of spatial perception, the institutionalization of a decentered observer, and the concomitant emergence of new realist codes of seeing.

In trying to reconstruct how stereoscopic images might have been perceived by mid-nineteenth-century spectators, Jonathan Crary has argued that stereoscopic representations deranged conventional optical cues by presenting a multiplanic patchwork of intensities within a single image:

> Certain planes or surfaces, even though composed of indications of light or shade that normally designate volume, are perceived as flat; other planes that normally would be read as two-dimensional, such as a fence in the foreground, seem to occupy space aggressively. Thus stereoscopic relief or depth has no unifying logic or order. If perspective implied a homogenous and potentially metric space, the stereoscope discloses a fundamentally disunified and aggregate field of disjunct elements. Our eyes never traverse the image in a full apprehension of the three-dimensionality of the entire field, but in terms of a localized experience of separate areas.[32]

---

31. Hermann von Helmholtz, "Über das Sehen des Menschen (1855)," in *Philosophische Vorträge und Aufsätze*, ed. Herbert Hörz and Siegfried Wollgast (Berlin: Akademie-Verlag, 1971), 75.

32. Crary, *Techniques of the Observer*, 125.

Stereoscopic representations, according to Crary, prompted the viewer's eye to follow a choppy path into the depths of the image. They assembled local zones and receding planes of three-dimensionality, aggregated discontinuous fields of clarity, and thus obstructed any perception of space as homogenous or coherent.

Its spectacular integration of the natural and the social notwithstanding, Döll's stage design for the scene on the open meadow evidences some of the features typical for stereoscopic imagery and seeing. With its layered planes of action, its various areas of depth and flatness, and its pronounced modeling of the foreground, Döll's set—prior to the entry of the mastersingers—suggests the multiplanic, aggregate space of stereoscopic representation. Decentering the homogenizing principles of monocular point of view, the amorphous deep-space of Döll's set design thereby closely followed Wagner's own intentions for the opening of Act III, scene 5:

> The Pegnitz River winds through the area: at the nearest point downstage, the narrow stream can be used [praktikabel gehalten]. Boats bearing colorful flags continually ferry the arriving, festively dressed burghers of the guild, with wives and children, across to the bank of the festival meadow. To the side, right, a raised platform, with benches and chairs on it, has been set up; it is already decorated with the banners of the guilds which have arrived; in due course, the banner-bearers of the still arriving guilds will put their banners up on the singers' platform so that at last it is completely enclosed on three sides. Tents with drinks and refreshments of all kinds border the remaining sides of the main downstage space. In front of the tents, things are going along already merrily: burghers, with wives, children and journeymen are sitting and reclining there. The apprentices of the Mastersingers, festively dressed, richly and charmingly adorned with flowers and ribbons, exercise in merry fashion the office of heralds and marshalls, with thin staves which are also decorated with flowers and ribbons. They receive those disembarking at the riverbank, organize the procession of the guilds and lead these to the singers' platform, in front of which, after the banner-bearers have planted the flags, the guild burghers and journeymen amuse themselves at will among the tents. At this moment, after the scene changes, the shoemakers will be received as planned at the riverbank and led downstage (227–29).

Erratically jumping between different areas of action, Wagner's vivid stage descriptions envisioned a non-linear dispersal of various activities across different zones and planes of the stage. According to Wagner's ethnographic imagination, the *Volk* of Nuremberg was meant to enter scene 5 as an unstructured and discontinuous body, as engaged in a non-regulated multiplicity of enterprises, some of them ceremonial and festive, others simply amusement-centered and jocular. Döll's stage design translated Wagner's "thick description"[33] of (imaginary) local customs into a stunning architectural configuration, whose violation of proper perspectival relations seemed to undo the borders between the illusionary and the real, between past and present. The set's disparate planes and perspectives invited the viewer's eye to follow a choppy path into the stage's multifarious depth. Far from coalescing all its elements into one homogenous field of vision, Döll's stage prior to the beginning of the festival presented a conglomerate of separate and more or less disjunct areas of spatial coherence, a stereoscopic space par excellence. In doing so, the design—like stereoscopic sight—encoded the "real" as an aggregate of individual scenes and manifold surfaces, of sculptured depth and horizontal flatness. Yet, as we will see in the final section of this essay, after the arrival of the mastersingers on the open meadow, *Die Meistersinger* aspires to nothing less than to make this decentered space cohere again, to suture the discrete into a unified whole, and thereby to recast the planar organization of stereoscopic space according to the codes of monocular vision and geometric perspective.

Good Looking?

Corrupt, self-absorbed forms of looking at the end of Act II result in the disintegration of social harmony. Prioritizing private desire over the claims of community, Beckmesser is struck with symbolic blindness and thus unleashes what must remain hidden behind civilization's irenic facade: murderous antagonism.[34] The final scene on the open meadow, by way of contrast, serves the reconstruction of social cohesion and communal identity, the concealment of what can break society apart. It provides a spectacular framework in which, among others, acts of reciprocal visuality restore peace and order and at the same time remove from sight that which no longer is defined to belong (Beckmesser). Once the crowds have entered the stage and gathered in an amphitheatrical setting around the mastersingers' platform, once the crowds have recognized themselves enthusiastically in Walther's artistic performance on stage, little is left of the scene's initial impression of decentered multiplicity and discontinuity. Stereoscopic depth and heterogeneity give way to a horizontal *tableau* of social reconciliation, a highly choreographed spectacle of sights and sounds condemning—to borrow a phrase by Peter Wollen—"the viewer to a world in which we can see everything but understand nothing."[35]

---

33. I borrow this term from anthropologist Clifford Geertz, *The Interpretation of Cultures* (New York: Basic Books, 1973), 3–32.

34. For a persuasive reading of *Die Meistersinger* in terms of Sigmund Freud's *Civilization and Its Discontent*, see Paul Robinson, *Opera and Ideas: From Mozart to Strauss* (Ithaca: Cornell University Press, 1985), 210–61.

35. Peter Wollen, Introduction, in *Visual Display: Culture Beyond Appearances*, ed. Lynne Cooke and Peter Wollen (Seattle: Bay Press, 1995), 9.

Arthur Groos has recently demonstrated in great detail the extent to which Wagner's fair on the open meadow, far from recreating sixteenth-century processions, indexes the *mise en scènes* of nineteenth-century festival culture and its attempt to establish a "secular liturgy for celebrating the *Volk*."[36] Surely, Wagner's *Volk* in *Die Meistersinger* does not yet constitute a modern mass; instead, it is figured as a self-conscious collective with a common will to action. However, what Wagner's *Volk* in the final scene of Act III shares with the clientele of patriotic festivals around 1850 is both a vision of the nation as a sacred space and an emphatic middle-class orientation. Similar to historical celebrations during the mid-nineteenth century, the festival in *Die Meistersinger* is predominanetly organized and consumed by bourgeois constituencies, by artisans, their families, apprentices, and journeymen. Wagner's festival meadow supplies the middle class with a site to celebrate itself, while any signs of monarchic leadership—in stark contrast, for instance, to Albert Lortzing's conservative reconstruction of Nuremberg in *Hans Sachs* (1840)—are conspicuously absent. Freely blending historical fact and historicist fiction, nostalgia, and utopia, Wagner's festival, in particular by staging the aristocrat Walther's assimilation to popular taste, thus seems to consecrate the fact that an "aristocratic order has been replaced by a bourgeois artistic one."[37]

Given my foregoing discussion of the phantasmagorical role of the visual in *Die Meistersinger*, Groos's remarks on the fusion of liberal and nationalistic elements, of bourgeois self-consciousness and historicist spectacle, of political religion and public art, during the final scene of Act III warrants further discussion. Let us first recall, however, that Wagner's central proposition in *Die Meistersinger* is that social cohesion depends on the community's ability to deter any rigid separation between art and politics, between mastersong and the everyday. Neither the mastersingers' pedantic formalism nor Walther's genius for self-expressivity initially meets this demand. Cast into the role of the astute mediator between tradition and innovation, Sachs's point is neither to glorify nor to dismiss rule-bound behavior, but rather to expose aesthetic codes and practices to popular trials so as to probe their continued pertinence. The ritualistic festival on the open meadow serves precisely this purpose. If the *Volk* here assembles around its singers, then only to authenticate whether or not public art still expresses the people's natural spirit, whether or not the masters' songs are

---

36. Arthur Groos, "Constructing Nuremberg: Typological and Proleptic Communities in *Die Meistersinger*," *19th-Century Music* 16.1 (Summer 1992): 27. For more on nineteenth-century political festival culture, see George L. Mosse, *The Nationalization of the Masses: Political Symbolism and Mass Movements in Germany from the Napoleonic Wars through the Third Reich* (Ithaca: Cornell University Press, 1975).

37. Groos, "Constructing Nuremberg," 30.

still in touch with the popular and thus own the ability of bonding minds and emotions. Contrary to a common contention, Sachs therefore is not a liberal democrat tallying yeas and nays but a grass-roots populist; his primary function is to ensure that cultural expressions continue to provide something for everyone and thereby elevate the particular to the organic whole of the community.

Because the aesthetic in *Die Meistersinger* is conceived as necessarily political, it is in terms of political models of visual representation that we must examine exactly how the festival of Act III translates individual tastes and practices into representative and shared expressions of belonging.[38] Wagner's populist stance at the end of *Die Meistersinger* in fact draws on two different traditions of representativeness and public will-formation. On the one hand, as a highly theatrical self-celebration of the bourgeoisie, the reconciliatory spectacle on the open meadow clearly recycles medieval and early modern understandings of representation in which public displays were meant to make something invisible visible and thus endow given authorities with "auratic" legitimation. Occupying a stage within the stage, the song contest identifies representative figures so as to indicate social status and reinforce existing social stratifications. Political and social representation here is wedded, not to public debate or critical reasoning, but to "personal attributes such as insignia (badges and arms), dress (clothing and coiffure), demeanor (form of greeting and pose) and rhetoric (form of address and formal discourse in general)."[39] Similar to feudal and absolutist models of representation, social cohesion in Wagner's Nuremberg depends on both the stage-managing of public appearance and the presence of people before whom power and status can be displayed.

On the other hand, Wagner's scene on the open meadow also alludes to Rousseau's idea of the festival as a nontheatrical site of total participation,

---

38. For a different reading of national community-building in *Die Meistersinger*, see Hans Rudolf Vaget, "The 'Metapolitics' of *Die Meistersinger*: Wagner's Nuremberg as Imagined Community," in *Searching for Common Ground: Diskurse zur deutschen Identität 1750–1871*, ed. Nicholas Vazsonyi (Cologne: Böhlau Verlag, 2000), 269–82. While I share Vaget's interest in the "metapolitical" aspects of Wagner's nationalism in *Meistersinger*, I find his application of Benedict Anderson's overused terminology unsatisfactory. As he tries to tell apart the aesthetic, the political, and the metapolitical aspects of Wagner's nationalism, Vaget ends up collapsing the theoretical and the analytical dimensions of Anderson's concept of imagined community. As a result, Vaget takes the appearance of belonging for granted and neglects the extent to which ideas of community in Wagner operate as ideology effacing their own constructedness.

39. Jürgen Habermas, *The Structural Transformation of the Public Sphere: An Inquiry into a Category of Bourgeois Society*, trans. Thomas Burger (Cambridge, Mass.: MIT Press, 1989), 8.

pure presence, and unhampered transparency.[40] For Rousseau, outdoor festivals such as the wine harvest in his own *La nouvelle Héloise* permitted invigorating experiences of social communion in which the General Will, as theoretically developed in *The Social Contract,* would come to the fore. On Wagner's open meadow, Rousseau's vision of reciprocity and plebescitarian immediacy plays a central role in reestablishing broken social bonds. "So lovely and dear," the *Volk* comments on Walther's prize song, "how distantly it hovers, / yet it is as if we're experiencing it with him!" (249). Walther's song not only reaches the heart of the spectator directly, but in driving art beyond mere representation it effaces the division of performer and viewer and unlocks a space of unmitigated presence and total participation. Wagner's open meadow, in Jacques Derrida's words, "is the place where the spectator, presenting himself as spectacle, will no longer be either seer (voyant) or voyeur, will efface within himself the difference between the actor and the spectator, the represented and the representer, the object seen and the seeing object."[41] It therefore should come as no surprise that neither discussion nor vote is necessary to confirm Walther's triumph over Beckmesser. What in fact allows Walther to win the contest is nothing other than his ability to stimulate a direct communion of the souls. Endowing the body politic with the sensation of having but one interest and one will, Walther's victory requires no formal casting of votes precisely because his presentation overcomes the very need for settling public disputes by means of technical procedures. Walther revitalizes the community's power to express its will directly, not through registering ballots and a statistical apparatus, but through acclamation. Rather than simply *representing* communal identity, the festival is meant to *embody* what holds Nuremberg's people together in a substantive, vital manner, through—as Carl Schmitt would put it in 1923 in a different context—"something taken for granted, an obvious and unchallenged presence."[42]

The fusion of theatrical and festal, representative and acclamatory, celebratory and attestive, feudal and bourgeois forms of public visibility in *Die Meistersinger* might at first be seen as simply yet another instance of Wagner's personal oscillation between the historical and the historicist. It speaks, so much is clear, against any iconoclastic effort (such as Wieland Wagner's of 1963) of rendering the open meadow a carnivalistic site of

---

40. See Jay, *Downcast Eyes,* 90–94.
41. Jacques Derrida, *Of Grammatology,* trans. Gayatri Chakravorty Spivak (Baltimore: Johns Hopkins University Press, 1976), 306.
42. Carl Schmitt, *The Crisis of Parliamentary Democracy,* trans. Ellen Kennedy (Cambridge, Mass.: MIT Press, 1986), 16–17. For more on Schmitt's shifting critique of representation and publicness, see in particular John P. McCormick, *Carl Schmitt's Critique of Liberalism: Against Politics as Technology* (Cambridge: Cambridge University Press, 1997), 157–205.

mockery, parodic role reversal, and unbound libido, a kind of Shakespearean outbreak of popular anarchy and raw merrymaking. For, whether understood as a neo-feudal theater of power or as a Rousseauean festival of total participation, the song contest of Act III clearly does not constitute a Bakhtinian festivity; it is far from interrupting the continuum of history, space, and power so as to celebrate the "*joyful relativity* of all structure and order, of all authority and all (hierarchical) position."[43] What is at stake on Wagner's open meadow is not a carnivalistic displacement of authority but instead the regrounding and naturalization of social order, the domestication of destructive madness in stylized spectacles of transparency and mutual recognition.

Rather than charting a transfigured or, as it were, misunderstood sixteenth century, the principal ambiguity of political visibility and publicness in Wagner's *Die Meistersinger* bears testimony to the vicissitudes of publicity between the mid-nineteenth-century decline of classical bourgeois culture and the late-nineteenth-century arrival of postbourgeois mass culture. Jürgen Habermas, in his seminal account of the transformation of the bourgeois public sphere, discusses mid-nineteenth-century developments in terms of a refeudalization of the public sphere. Inasmuch as the realm of cultural expressions became subsumed under the law of the market, Habermas's no doubt idealized culture-debating public of the eighteenth century was transformed into a culture-consuming public. Nonverbal communication took the place of reading and debate, discussion itself turned into a fetish, and prefabricated arguments and acclamatory settlements displaced the possibility of rational justification and decision-making. In this shifting climate of publicness, political institutions had to address their citizens increasingly like consumers. The political and in particular the idea of the nation were converted into items of middle-class consumption, while public relations experts engineered forms of consent which had little in common with the unanimity resulting from time-consuming processes of critical discussion and deliberate persuasion:

> Publicity once meant the exposure of political domination before the public use of reason; publicity now adds up the reactions of an uncommitted friendly disposition. In the measure that is shaped by public relations, the public sphere of civil society again takes on feudal features. The 'suppliers' display a showy pomp before costumers ready to follow. Publicity imitates the kind of aura proper to the personal prestige and supernatural authority once bestowed by the kind of publicity involved in representation.[44]

---

43. Mikhail Bakhtin, *Problems of Dostoevsky's Poetics,* trans. Caryl Emerson (Minneapolis: University of Minnesota Press, 1984), 124.

44. Habermas, *The Structural Transformation of the Public Sphere,* 195.

Sachs's role on the stage of the open meadow is that of a modern publicity maker who is intimately familiar with the engineering of friendly dispositions. He embraces the refeudalizing scenes of bourgeois publicness in order to substitute formal debate with cultural consumption. Sachs in fact succeeds not only in marketing the aura of representative figures as consumer goods, but—with the help of Walther's talents—in allowing the crowd to consume its own appearance, its semblance of organic communality, as the most thrilling of all sensations. What under the later aegis of industrial mass culture would be administered by the culture industry, is supplied here in the guise of the popular festival. The festival elevates the middle-class members of the crowd to the level of commodities. It creates a framework in which political leadership can present itself as an object of pure sensory amusement. *Die Meistersinger* thus shrouds the refeudalization of bourgeois culture in Wagner's own times into a phantasmagoria of total participation and transparency. Rousseau's nontheatrical festival in Wagner takes the form of the theatrical itself; in Wagner's own words, it becomes a "spectacle of the people's jubilation" [Schauspiele des Volksjubels] (235). Yet as it supplants the negotiation of different opinions with an erasure of difference through argument-free acclamation, the spectacle's ultimate function is to produce a lonely crowd. Both in Wagner and in the context of nineteenth-century capitalist modernization, the spectacle engineers a crowd unable to recognize symbolic materials and cultural differences as potential sources of emancipation. "What binds the spectators together is no more than an irreversible relation at the very center which maintains their isolation. The spectacle reunites the separate, but reunites it *as separate.*"[45]

Yet if the final scene of *Die Meistersinger,* rather than resurrecting the German past, indexes the decline of the classical bourgeois public sphere and, simultaneously, previews the refeudalization of political visibility in the age of commericialized culture, did Heinz Tietjen's infamous staging of the festival as a Nazi mass rally à la Riefenstahl, with its eight hundred performers on stage and its overwhelming integration of singing and moving chorus,[46] get it right after all? Does Wagner's phantasmagoria of belonging foreshadow or even authorize Hitler's spectacular equation of Nuremberg and Bayreuth? It is only if we deny the constitutive tensions and historical ambivalences of political visibility in *Die Meistersinger* that we can answer these questions in the affirmative. The figuration of vision and visibility in Wagner's music drama, as I have argued in this essay, indicated fundamental transformations of nineteenth-century visual culture. *Die Meistersinger* at once evidenced the advent of new codes of realist representation and the dethronement of monocular, disembodied per-

---

45. Guy Debord, *Society of the Spectacle* (Detroit: Black and Red, 1983), 29.
46. Dietrich Mack, *Der Bayreuther Inszenierungsstil* (Munich: Prestel-Verlag, 1976), 27.

spectivalism. The scene on the open meadow, I have suggested, tried to resurrect the past—monocularism—through the stereoscopic gaze of the present, while at the same time presenting exterior realms as interior spaces and positing reciprocal relationships between nature and society. The image of the crowd on the Bayreuth stage and the Nuremberg rally-ground during the Nazi period, by way of contrast, reflected very different principles and historical circumstances. Both Riefenstahl and Tietjen considered the masses as deanimated material for an abstract, self-contained geometry of power. As importantly, however, the ornamentalization of the masses in Nazi Nuremberg and Nazi Bayreuth owed in no small part to yet another decisive turn of modern visual culture, namely the breakthrough of cinema and its power to engineer auratic residues through mechanical mass-reproduction. The implied viewer of both Nuremberg's and Bayreuth's mass rallies was not the event's actual participant or witness, but the cinematic spectator; the modern design and choreography of the crowd adhered to intrinsically cinematic principles.

In his famous critique of the fascist stage-managing of politics, Walter Benjamin theorized as follows what in the final analysis separates the phantasmagorias of seeing in Wagner's festival scene from the orchestration of public vision and visibility in Hitler's Nuremberg and Bayreuth:

> Since the innovations of camera and recording equipment make it possible for the orator to become audible and visible to an unlimited number of persons, the presentation of the man of politics before camera and recording equipment becomes paramount. Parliaments, as much as theaters, are deserted. Radio and film not only affect the function of the professional actor but likewise the function of those who also exhibit themselves before this mechanical equipment, those who govern. Though their task may be different, the change affects equally the actor and the ruler. The trend is toward establishing controllable and transferable skills under certain social conditions. This results in a new selection, a selection before the equipment from which the star and the dictator emerge victorious.[47]

Benjamin thought of the relation of fascism to bourgeois society as analogous to the relation between film and nineteenth-century theater.[48] This

---

47. Walter Benjamin, "The Work of Art in the Age of Mechanical Reproduction," in *Illuminations: Essays and Reflections*, ed. Hannah Arendt, trans. Harry Zohn (New York: Schocken Books, 1969), 247.

48. Andrew Hewitt, *Fascist Modernism: Aesthetics, Politics, and the Avant-Garde* (Stanford, Calif.: Stanford University Press, 1993) 168–69. For more on Benjamin's critique of the fascist spectacle, see Lutz Koepnick, *Walter Benjamin and the Aesthetics of Power* (Lincoln: University of Nebraska Press, 1999).

Sight and Community in Die Meistersinger 97

analogy proves instructive to point out critical differences between Wagner's and the Nazis' views of the crowd. What remained ambivalent and tension-ridden in Wagner, an unabashedly eclectic reworking of different source materials and historical references,[49] in the Third Reich's appropriation of *Die Meistersinger* became a phantasmagoria of unrestricted accessibility and self-contained presence. Sachs and Walther may foreshadow media stars of the twentieth century; their popularity on the open meadow may anticipate the illusive recreation of aura and authenticity through the film industry's star cult. But what we cannot find in the political actor Sachs is a camera-oriented dictator whose will is meant to triumph not simply over the masses but also over the modalities of postauratic representation. The Nazi spectacle systematically exploited the means of industrial mass culture so as to manufacture a post-bourgeois community of the *Volk*. The politics of vision and visibility in *Die Meistersinger*, by contrast, remain inseparable from Wagner's however uneasy association with nineteenth-century bourgeois culture[50] and what we must understand as his theatrical view of politics.[51]

---

49. Hohendahl, "Reworking History," 58.

50. Egon Voss, "Wagners 'Meistersinger' als Oper des deutschen Bürgertums," in Richard Wagner, *Die Meistersinger von Nürnberg: Texte, Materialien, Kommentare* (Reinbek: Rowohlt, 1981), 9–31.

51. For more on Wagner's understanding of politics as theater, see Köpnick, *Nothungs Modernität*, 17–42.

6

"The Most German of all German Operas"[1]: *Die Meistersinger* through the Lens of the Third Reich

DAVID B. DENNIS

> *The music of the Nazis is not the Prelude to* Die Meistersinger, *but rather the Horst-Wessel-Lied; they deserve credit for nothing else, and no more can or should be given to them.*
>
> —Ernst Bloch[2]

In college classrooms across the United States, a common feature of many courses covering modern German history is a screening of Leni Riefenstahl's propaganda film promoting the 1934 Nazi Party rally at Nürnberg. Usually *Triumph des Willens* (Triumph of the Will), which includes no narration, is presented with commentary by instructors or explanatory notes. These explications often include assertions that the music accompanying Riefenstahl's opening imagery comes from Richard Wagner's *Die Meistersinger von Nürnberg*: "For 68 seconds the screen remains dark. From this cinematic 'void' there gradually emerges the solemn, swelling sound of the overture from Wagner's *Mastersingers of Nuremberg*," reads one guide to the movie. "Herbert Windt, a classical composer, created the Wagnerian-style orchestral scores which provide a background to the film,"

---

1. "Richard Wagner und das Kunstempfinden unserer Zeit: Rundfunkrede von Reichsminister Dr. Goebbels," *Völkischer Beobachter,* 8 August 1933.

2. Ernst Bloch, "Über Wurzeln des Nazismus" (1939), in *Politische Messungen, Pestzeit, Vormärz,* vol. 11, *Gesamtausgabe* (Frankfurt am Main: Suhrkamp, 1970), 320.

Die Meistersinger *through the Lens of the Third Reich* 99

this summary continues. "The Wagnerian motif was apparently suggested by Riefenstahl but was a natural and appropriate choice."[3]

Such claims are generally taken for granted: students, general readers, and even scholars have little difficulty accepting associations between Wagner's nationalistic music drama and National Socialist self-promotion in film. However, the main premise of this contention is simply not true: while *Triumph des Willens* later refers to *Die Meistersinger*,[4] the film does not open with music from Wagner's opera. As a forbidding Nazi eagle appears on the screen, swastika in its talons, and the camera pans to title and credits styled as if carved in stone, the music climaxes in a potent, martial theme—apparently of Windt's own design.

Riefenstahl did decide on nonoriginal music to accompany the famous sequence showing sublime cloud banks surrounding Hitler's plane. Woven into contrapuntal texture and performed by full orchestra, the identity of this theme remains obscure for several bars, but it gradually reveals itself as the haunting and ultimately cursed tune of *Die Fahne hoch!*—better known as the *Horst-Wessel-Lied*. It is with full statement of this party *Kampflied* that Hitler's plane breaks through the clouds to a spectacular aerial view of the towers, ramparts, and pitched roofs of Dürer's city in its prewar glory. No matter how appropriate melodies from Wagner's tribute to *Alt-Nürnberg* might have been for this cinematic moment, Riefenstahl did not employ them. Confirming the gist of the above observation by philosopher Ernst Bloch, the premier Nazi propaganda film—which has strongly influenced perceptions of Hitler and his movement, especially in American universities—opens and closes with rousing versions of the *Horst-Wessel-Lied*.

Debunking this particular myth about the function of Wagner's most popular opera in Nazi propaganda should not be taken as an effort to disassociate *Die Meistersinger* from National Socialist culture. The case, however, serves as a warning against accepting assumptions about the reception of musical works without careful consideration of relevant sources. Contrary to Bloch's admonition, scholars have frequently insisted that Hitler's personal interest in and Goebbels' manipulation of *Die Meistersinger* "turned the entire opera into a Nazi anthem."[5] As the present chapter will demonstrate, evidence in the record of *Die Meistersinger*'s reception by Nazis does support such claims; but some inferences about the opera's meaning within National Socialist discourse do not hold up under closer scrutiny.

---

3. Linda Deutschmann, *Triumph of the Will: The Image of the Third Reich* (Wakefield, N.H.: Longwood Academic, 1991), 28–30.

4. The third scene—from 0:12:42 to 0:14:27 on the Connoisseur Video Collection cut of the film (The Film Preserver, Ltd., 1992)—consists of a series of shots of Nürnberg at daybreak, backed by the *Wach auf* melody from the prelude to Act III.

5. Frederic Spotts, *Bayreuth: A History of the Wagner Festival* (New Haven, Conn.: Yale University Press, 1994), 165.

Central to Wagner scholarship in recent years has been an intense debate over the extent to which the composer's well-documented hatred for Jews colored his dramas and music. Interpretations of *Die Meistersinger* as one of the "most blatantly anti-Semitic"[6] of Wagner's creative works focus on the character of the *Merker*, Sixtus Beckmesser. Anti-Jewish symbolism is "woven into the ideological fabric" of *Die Meistersinger* as its characterization of Beckmesser "incorporates unmistakable anti-Semitic stereotypes."[7] The broader implication of such assessments of Beckmesser, his singing,[8] and the treatment he receives is that Wagner communicated via *Die Meistersinger* coded instructions that Germans first physically abuse (for comic relief, as in the "Riot Scene" of Act II), and ultimately eliminate Jews from their community (since, in the original version, Beckmesser flees the stage in disgrace).

Most essential to arguments about the anti-Semitic significance of Beckmesser is the assertion that whereas persons considering the opera today may not recognize the character's implicit Jewishness, pre-1945 audiences immediately grasped its references to "a common stock of anti-Semitic stereotypes."[9] Since the end of the Second World War, "such ideological implications in Wagner's writings and music dramas have been increasingly denied or repressed, as the cultural vocabulary of the world in which he is read and performed has changed." As a result, "an obvious dimension of the Wagnerian artwork" became "an issue of open debate" after the defeat of Nazism.[10] Shifting expectations have "led to a widespread disavowal of precisely the racist and exclusionary dimension of his essays and music dramas that would have been so obvious to a nineteenth-century audience."[11]

---

6. Marc A. Weiner, *Richard Wagner and the Anti-Semitic Imagination* (Lincoln: University of Nebraska Press, 1995), 84.

7. Barry Millington, "Nuremberg Trial: Is There Anti-Semitism in *Die Meistersinger?*" *Cambridge Opera Journal* 3.3 (1991): 247–60, here 247. Millington explains further: "The characterization of Beckmesser draws directly on a common fund of nineteenth-century anti-Semitic stereotypes, specifically on the description of Jews in Wagner's pamphlet, *Das Judentum in der Musik* (1850). [. . .] From the start, he is represented as the outsider, the Other, and is made painfully and cruelly aware of his Otherness in the course of the opera. [. . .] Beckmesser is shallow and one-dimensional: he has no redeeming features. Wagner's hatred for everything he represents is so total that for once he loses his sure dramatic touch" (Ibid., 249).

8. Beyond his physical and dramatic representation, Millington and others perceive in the very music of Beckmesser's part "a parody of the Jewish cantorial style" (Ibid., 249–57).

9. Ibid., 255.

10. Weiner, *Anti-Semitic Imagination*, 2.

11. Ibid., 13.

Unfortunately for this argument, however, no one has yet supported it with direct reference to records proving that this dimension of *Die Meistersinger* was part of the "cultural vocabulary" of nineteenth-century Germans, or—more to the point—was articulated by the anti-Semitic radical right that ultimately dominated German politics and targeted Jews for extermination. Setting aside, for a moment, the separate matter of Wagner's intentions: did German audiences address the Beckmesser character as obviously anti-Jewish in the years leading up to the Holocaust? "The question demands a study of its own," admits a supporter of this view.[12] But thus far, none has appeared.[13]

Assessing the interpretation of Wagner's operas as anti-Semitic, one reviewer declared that "it will never be possible to calculate the precise degree of Wagner's complicity in the crimes of twentieth-century fascism."[14] This may be true, because we probably cannot verify whether Germans who perpetrated genocide were motivated by experiences of Wagner's operas—via wartime productions at Bayreuth, for instance. But by directing our attention to records of their cultural politics, we can evaluate the extent to which the volkish right and the Nazi Party employed his works as high-cultural propaganda instruments for spurring a generation of "willing executioners." In the end, I suggest, the crucial question is not whether Hitler and his immediate followers perceived Wagner's opera as anti-Jewish, but whether the music and text of *Die Meistersinger* were effectively implemented to indoctrinate Germans with anti-Semitic ideology. Is there proof that the opera itself was explicitly used to motivate actions against Jews, or, more broadly, to create a cultural atmosphere that encouraged people to do so?

To determine if specific characters of *Die Meistersinger* inhabited the "anti-Semitic imagination" of Germans in and around the Nazi movement, I have studied a wide array of sources. These include all the material collected in secondary assessments of Wagner's place in German political culture, especially that of the right wing, including Hartmut Zelinsky's *Richard Wagner: ein deutsches Thema* (1976) and Berndt Wessling's *Bayreuth im dritten Reich* (1983). I have also examined every article on *Die Meistersinger* that appeared in the *Bayreuther Blätter* from 1878 through 1938 (its last edition); in the *Zeitschrift für Musik* from 1933 to 1943; in *Die Musik* from 1933 to 1943; and in the *Zeitschrift für Musikwissenschaft* from 1918 through 1935.[15] Outside music scholarship, I have checked journals such as the *National-*

---

12. Millington, "Nuremberg Trial," 260.

13. Millington does "no more than suggest a few pointers for future research" (Ibid.).

14. Thomas Grey, "Bodies of Evidence," *Cambridge Opera Journal* 8.2 (1996): 185–97, here 196.

15. These sources include articles with telling titles like "Richard Wagner als Künder der Arischen Welt," "Richard Wagners Regenerationslehre und ihre Bedeutung für die Gegenwart," "Richard Wagner in unserer Zeit," and "Richard Wagner—nationalsozialistisch gesehen."

sozialistische Monatshefte (1935–41), *Volk im Werden* (1933–35), *Volk und Rasse* (1929–38), the *Zeitschrift für deutsche Bildung* (1925), and the *Zeitschrift für deutsche Geistesgeschichte* (1935–38). Besides serials, I have assessed publications devoted to linking Wagner with anti-Semitic, volkish, and then Nazi culture, including Paulus Cassel, *Der Judengott und Richard Wagner* (1881); Houston Stewart Chamberlain, *Richard Wagner* (1896); Karl Grunsky, *Richard Wagner und die Juden* (n.d.); Curt von Westernhagen, *Richard Wagners Kampf gegen seelische Fremdherrschaft* (1935); Peter Raabe, "Wagners *Meistersinger* und unsere Zeit" (1935); Karl Ganzer, *Richard Wagner und das Judentum* (1938); Richard Stock, *Richard Wagner und die Stadt der Meistersinger* (1938); and Johannes Bertram, *Der Seher von Bayreuth* (1943). Moreover, I have surveyed a wide range of literature considered central to German racist culture as a whole: Houston Stewart Chamberlain's *Die Grundlagen des neunzehnten Jahrhunderts* (1899) and his correspondence with the intensely anti-Semitic Cosima Wagner;[16] the works of Richard Benz;[17] the racist theories of Ludwig Ferdinand Clauss[18] and Hans F. K. Günther;[19] Richard Eichenauer's *Musik und Rasse* (1937); the collected articles and speeches of Joseph Goebbels;[20] Alfred Rosenberg's *Der Mythus des 20.*

---

16. Paul Pretzsch, ed., *Cosima Wagner und Houston Stewart Chamberlain im Briefwechsel 1888–1908* (Leipzig: Philipp Reclam Verlag, 1934).

17. Richard Benz, *Blätter für deutsche Art und Kunst* (Jena: Eugen Diederichs, 1915); Richard Benz, *Die deutsche Romantik: Geschichte einer geistigen Bewegung* (Leipzig: Philipp Reclam, 1937); Richard Benz and Arthur von Schneider, *Die Kunst der deutschen Romantik* (München: R. Piper, 1939); Richard Benz, *Die Welt der Dichter und die Musik*, 2nd ed. (Düsseldorf: Diederich, 1949); Richard Benz, *Geist und Reich: Um die Bestimmung des Deutschen*, 3rd ed. (Jena: E. Diederichs, 1933); Richard Benz, *Märchen-Dichtung der Romantiker: Mit einer Vorgeschichte* (Gotha: F. A. Perthes, 1908).

18. Ludwig Ferdinand Clauss, *Die nordische Seele: Artung, Prägung, Ausdruck* (Halle: 1923); Ludwig Ferdinand Clauss, *Rasse und Seele: Eine Einführung in die Gegenwart* (München: J. F. Lehmann, 1926); Ludwig Ferdinand Clauss, *Die nordische Seele: Eine Einführung in die Rassenseelenkunde* (München: J. F. Lehmann, 1934); Ludwig Ferdinand Clauss, *Rasse und Seele: Eine Einführung in den Sinn der leiblichen Gestalt*, 3rd ed. (München: Lehmann, 1934).

19. Hans F. K. Günther, *Rassenkunde des deutschen Volkes*, 2nd ed. (München: J. F. Lehmann, 1923); Hans F. K. Günther, *Rasse und Stil: Gedanken über ihre Beziehungen im Leben und in der Geistesgeschichte der europäischen Völker, insbesondere des deutschen Volkes* (Munich: J. F. Lehmann, 1926); Hans F. K. Günther and G. C. Wheeler, *The Racial Elements of European History*, trans. G. C. Wheeler (New York: E. P. Dutton and Co., 1928).

20. Joseph Goebbels, *Goebbels-Reden,* ed. Helmut Heiber (Düsseldorf: Droste Verlag, 1971); Joseph Goebbels, *Signale der neuen Zeit: 25 ausgewählte Reden* (Munich: Zentralverlag der NSDAP, 1934); Joseph Goebbels, *Der Angriff: Aufsätze aus der Kampfzeit,* ed. Hans Schwarz van Berk, 5th ed. (Munich: Zentralverlag der NSDAP, 1936); Joseph Goebbels, *Das eherne Herz: Reden und Aufsätze aus den Jahren 1941/42* (Munich: F. Eher, 1943).

Jahrhunderts (1930) and his collected essays.[21] Finally, I have inspected every major article on Wagner in general (numbering almost three hundred) and on *Die Meistersinger* in particular (over thirty) that appeared in both of the major Nazi newspapers, the *Völkischer Beobachter* (1920–45) and *Der Angriff* (1927–33).

This investigation has uncovered no evidence that Nazi cultural politicians, or their volkish forbears and associates, referred in public discourse to the character of Sixtus Beckmesser as Jewish, or to his fate in *Die Meistersinger* as foreshadowing National Socialist policies against Jews. Observing that the extreme German right did not openly discuss Beckmesser's features as Jewish is striking when one considers that its spokesmen otherwise had no reservations about launching anti-Semitic diatribes within their treatments of Wagner. Brutish attacks on Jews do appear throughout Nazi writings about this composer and his works, including *Die Meistersinger*. For instance, in its section about this opera, Curt von Westernhagen's 1935 book, *Richard Wagners Kampf gegen seelische Fremdherrschaft*, directly addressed the composer's hatred for Jews. When in 1869 Wagner reprinted the notorious essay, *Das Judentum in der Musik*—where, according to Westernhagen, he first started to "track down, or rather, ferret out the race problem"—the composer jeopardized the success of *Die Meistersinger*, which had premiered only a year earlier: "As [Wagner] put it, 7000 Jews declared war on him, but 70,000 or 700,000 Jews would be more like it—because all Jewry recognized right away the danger it faced if the race question were seriously raised." The "blood question," Westernhagen insisted, was an "undertone" in Wagner's thinking that gradually became louder and more distinct until it "sounded as the notion of regeneration, of racial rebirth."[22]

Consistent in National Socialist reception of *Die Meistersinger* was the assumption that a Jewish-led conspiracy had tried to block performance of the work and, where that failed, undermine its popularity through sharp criticism—until the Nazi "seizure of power" that is. Richard Stock stated this theory bluntly in *Richard Wagner und die Stadt der Meistersinger*, a publication inspired by performance of the opera at the 1935 Nazi Party rally in Nürnberg. Stock harped on the fact that Wagner had wished to premiere the opera in Nürnberg, believing that the home of Hans Sachs

---

21. Alfred Rosenberg, *Kampf um die Macht: Aufsätze von 1921–1932*, ed. Thilo von Trotha (Munich: F. Eher nachf., 1937); Alfred Rosenberg, *Gestaltung der Idee: Reden und Aufsätze von 1933–1935*, ed. Thilo von Trotha (Munich: F. Eher nachf., 1943); Alfred Rosenberg, *Das politische Tagebuch Alfred Rosenbergs aus den Jahren 1934–35 und 1939–40*, ed. Hans-Günther Seraphim (Göttingen: Musterschmidt, 1956); Alfred Rosenberg, *Letzte Aufzeichnungen: Nürnberg 1945–46* (Uelzen: Jomsburg Verlag, 1996).

22. Curt von Westernhagen, *Richard Wagners Kampf gegen seelische Fremdherrschaft* (Munich: J. F. Lehmann, 1935), 25. All translations are the author's.

and Albrecht Dürer was a "sanctuary of Germanness," and that this city of medieval handworkers and world-renowned German tradesmen was a "mighty bulwark against Jewish sponging and wheeling-dealing." But in Wagner's time, the responsible officials were "infected and weakened by the anti-German spirit of Jews" who had become more and more powerful since the revolutions of 1848. So the "honorable wish of the master—hated as an enemy of the Jews—was denied."[23]

Spouting a view common among Nazi Wagnerians, Stock insisted that the plot operated beyond the city of Nürnberg, throughout German lands, from Wagner's lifetime until Hitler finally "made good on this terrible injustice to the great German genius." *Die Meistersinger* had come into being "in a state of spiritual, or cultural-political banishment" imposed by Jews and other "enemies of German unity and traditional German culture." Leading the cabal, Jewish critics and literati—who were "popping out of the ground like poisonous mushrooms" during Wagner's era—attacked his most "deeply German" opera in the "bitterest and dirtiest ways," driven by the "undying hatred that this rootless race holds against volkish originality and creativity." In their view, the "Great Antisemite"—as this composer "bravely" revealed himself to be, by ruthlessly "tearing the mask from the face of this parasite on the cultural life of the *Volk*"—had to be "exterminated."[24]

Besides treatment of *Die Meistersinger* at the hands of critics, Nazi supporters claimed that the "Pan-Jewish (*Alljudas*) battle" against Wagner also took the form of insinuations that the composer was not of pure "nordic" stock. "From time to time," the *Völkischer Beobachter* complained, "there arises some humbug suggesting that the greatest of all German geniuses, Richard Wagner, had some Jewish blood in his veins."[25] These claims were based on rumors that Wagner's mother had been the lover of Ludwig Geyer (whom she married after her first husband, Carl Friedrich Wagner, died) at the time of the composer's conception. The *Völkischer Beobachter* strove to "overcome this filth and break through these lies once and for all" with a two-pronged argument: first by demonstrating that

---

23. Richard Wilhelm Stock, *Richard Wagner und die Stadt der Meistersinger: Den Grossen von Bayreuth Richard und Cosima Wagner zum Gedächtnis in ihrem 125. und 100. Geburtsjahr* (Nuremberg: Verlag Karl Ulrich & Co., 1938), 7. To prove his assertions about the critical attack on Wagner, Stock provided extensive extracts from the so-called *Schmähartikeln* that Jews and their supposed coconspirators launched against *Die Meistersinger*. In none of these examples did there appear any criticism of the opera as containing anti-Semitic imagery, although Stock insisted that the authors hated Wagner primarily for his anti-Jewish views (Ibid., 138 ff.).

24. Stock, *Wagner und die Stadt*, 7, 71, 138.

25. J. St-g, "Der alte Schwindel von Richard Wagners Blutbeimischung," *Völkischer Beobachter*, 12 December 1929.

relations between Ludwig Geyer and Wagner's mother were "innocent until they married"; second, by insisting that, in any case, Geyer was not Jewish.[26] But ultimate proof that Richard Wagner was a "German of Nordic stamp" resided in his music, particularly that of *Die Meistersinger*. According to the *Völkischer Beobachter*, there was only one correct answer to these accusations and it was best stated by Wagner's son, Siegfried: "All one has to do is listen to the first three beats of the *Meistersinger* Prelude to know that my father was not of Jewish descent."[27]

Clearly, Nazis and their supporters had no qualms about fomenting anti-Semitism via articles and statements about *Die Meistersinger*. But nowhere in these writings appeared insinuations about the Jewishness of Beckmesser. As we will see below, the focus in most Nazi reception of *Die Meistersinger* was on the character of Hans Sachs, but the few references made to the *Merker* treated him as an irritating but nonetheless respectable member of Nürnberg society—indeed a figure of undeniable aesthetic authority derived from long-standing traditions within the singers guild, and therefore a formidable opponent to Walther and his youthful, free-wheeling ways. In his 1935 essay, "Wagners *Meistersinger* in unserer Zeit," Peter Raabe, then president of the Reichsmusikkammer, insisted that Beckmesser was "conceived as a high-ranking civil servant."[28] Elsewhere, the incorrigibly volkish *Bayreuther Blätter* discussed the *Merker* as the leader of an influential group within the guild which included other mastersingers such as Kothner and Zorn, together comprising a conservative "party."[29] These Hitlerites, therefore, did not openly discuss Beckmesser as an Outsider, but rather as a highly influential Insider whose main sin was that of artistic pedantry.

With regard to Beckmesser's singing, Nazi interpreters tended to explain his "difficulties" on the basis of increasing anger and confusion as his plans go awry. Describing the second act, a 1943 summary of the operas by Johannes Bertram—notorious for his nazified Wagnerism[30]—averred that "as the hammer-blows of the shoemaker acting as *Merker* begin to sound in the summer night, Beckmesser sings ever louder and more breathlessly, trying to drown out the hammering; ultimately he completely loses his senses,

---

26. Ibid.
27. Miss., "Alljudas Kampf gegen Richard Wagner," *Völkischer Beobachter*, 29 December 1927.
28. Peter Raabe, "Wagners *Meistersinger* in unserer Zeit," in *Die Musik im dritten Reich: Kulturpolitische Reden und Aufsätze* (Regensburg: G. Bosse, 1935), 68–72, here 69.
29. Gustav Roell, "Neue Beiträge zu alten Problemen: 3. Die Prügelszene in den *Meistersingern von Nürnberg*: Eine Würdigung des Dramatikers Richard Wagner," *Bayreuther Blätter* 56 (1933): 141–43, here 142.
30. Mork, *Richard Wagner als politischer Schriftsteller*, 221–22.

and all control over himself and his song."[31] No suggestion was made here, or in other Nazi-era explications, that Beckmesser's performances are representative of an inherent, "racially determined" incapacity to sing. The Riot Scene, moreover, was addressed as the point when "everything crazy, one-sided, cranky, and overdone is once again put into healthy order—driven with inexorable irony and, when necessary, kicks and punches."[32] Violent imposition of *Ordnung*, yes: but not explicitly a strike against Jewishness. Rather, the "battle" was being waged against the supposed "objectification and desecration of music."[33]

Even if such phrases might be interpreted as coded references to aesthetic tendencies perceived by Nazis as Jewish, the question arises as to whether there would have been reason in Hitler's Germany to use code for readings of *Die Meistersinger* as an anti-Semitic artwork anytime after January 31, 1933—let alone in 1943, as the Shoah raged. If they so perceived him, what restrained proto-Nazis, Nazis, and their fellow travelers from publicly identifying the opera's antagonist as a Jew? Obsessed with conspiracy theory, Wagner's immediate circle might have worried about Jewish responses to blatantly anti-Semitic stereotypes in his works. Wagnerians on the anti-Semitic right continued to complain that Jewish-led interests were out to harm Bayreuth throughout the Weimar era. But if Nazi cultural leaders considered Beckmesser a cipher for the "Jewish problem," why did they not popularize this view once their party ruled artistic and political life in Germany, when it would have so clearly served the propaganda aims of the Third Reich? Since National Socialist cultural politicians and their supporting "experts" sought every opportunity to link other aspects of Wagner's life and work with anti-Semitic ideology, could their failure to do so in the case of *Die Meistersinger* have been a simple omission? That they did so neither before nor after 1933 suggests that whatever their personal views about the opera might have been, Nazi leaders did not regard Beckmesser as a useful symbol for representing Jewry, its supposed treachery against the German *Volk,* and the need for its elimination.

Nonetheless, though Beckmesser was not featured in National Socialist culture, *Die Meistersinger* was. From the early stages of the movement, performances of the opera received special attention in the main Nazi newspapers. In August 1923, the *Völkischer Beobachter* complained that too many foreign visitors were taking advantage of low exchange rates for German currency and, by their attendance, marring productions of *Die*

---

31. Johannes Bertram, *Der Seher von Bayreuth: Deutung des Lebens und Werkes Richard Wagners* (Berlin: Buchmeister Verlag, 1943), 317.

32. Ibid., 317.

33. Wilhelm Zentner, "Richard Wagner und die Volksbildung: Ansprache gehalten bei der 26. Hauptversammlung des Bayerischen Volksbildungsverband," *Zeitschrift für Musik* 100.7 (1933): 699–701, here 700.

Meistersinger at the Munich Festival. The paper even proposed that foreigners be forbidden entrance to the Munich theater during the festival. "No one, except perhaps hopelessly stupid Marxists, will deny that this is a matter of national interest" since "of all our rich possessions, practically nothing is left to us but our holy German art."[34] As their resources expanded, however, Nazis were able to arrange concerts by and for their own kind, and music from *Die Meistersinger* was prominent in the programs. A favorite high-cultural propaganda initiative of the Nazis during their *Kampfzeit* was a "Richard Wagner Morning Festival": sunrise performances highlighting *Am stillen Herd* and Walther's *Preislied*.[35] Moreover, the very first concert of the *NS Symphonieorchester* (also known as the *Orchester des Führers*) in January 1932 included the prelude to *Die Meistersinger* along with works of Carl Maria von Weber and Anton Bruckner.[36]

Once in power, Nazis treated themselves to a *Meistersinger* binge. Their so-called seizure of power coincided, significantly, with the fiftieth anniversary of Wagner's death, and Hitler marked both events by attending a "Richard Wagner Celebration" in the Leipzig Gewandhaus just two weeks after assuming the office of Reich Chancellor. The program included the *Meistersinger* prelude, which the Mayor of Leipzig described in his commemorative address as a work that "represents this son of Leipzig in the finest light of his Germanness—a Germanness that is once again striving to become self-aware, and conscious of its strength."[37] Only a month later occurred the most notorious example of *Meistersinger* nazification. On 21 March 1933, ceremonies arranged for the Day of Potsdam culminated in a performance of *Die Meistersinger* at Berlin's Staatsoper. Having attended the torchlight parade along Unter den Linden, Hitler and the rest of his government arrived for the third act of the opera.[38] The *Völkischer Beobachter* reviewer, Hugo Rasch, covered the evening rhapsodically. In his eyes, this was a scene of "German worthiness," unforgettable for one like him, who "never lost his feeling for the German *Gemeinschaft*, even during the last few decades of confusion." German women "dressed taste-

---

34. St-g, "Wagners Blutbeimischung." This problem later took care of itself, to a degree: treating the Munich production of *Die Meistersinger* in 1932, the same reviewer remarked that fewer Americans were in the audience because of the bad economic conditions in the United States (J. St-g, "Beginn der Wagner- und Mozart-Festspiele in München: Auftakt: *Die Meistersinger von Nürnberg*," *Völkischer Beobachter*, 21 July 1932).

35. Advertisement, "Richard Wagner Morgenfeier," *Völkischer Beobachter*, 25 February 1932.

36. "Das nationalsozialistische Reichs-Symphonie-Orchester," *Völkischer Beobachter*, 19 March 1932.

37. "Richard-Wagner-Gedächtnisfeier in Anwesenheit des Reichskanzlers," *Völkischer Beobachter*, 14 February 1933.

38. "Der Festablauf am 21. März," *Völkischer Beobachter*, 21 March 1933.

fully—not decorated with jewels or erotic makeup"; men wore tuxedos or "dress brown uniforms." The spirit of a "great community of fate, always present in even the least meeting of our storm troopers, lived just as much here," despite social differences among the audience members. Gratitude rose from formerly heavy hearts toward their "savior," who followed the opera "with that unique light in his eyes and his penetrating comprehension of the performance." Whoever noticed how, during the third act, "the *Volk* of Nürnberg instinctively turned toward the Führer, sitting in the royal seats," and then how "the eternally beautiful *Wach auf, es nahet gen den Tag* emerged from the choir to touch each and every heart," sensed that the "moment of Germany's transformation" had arrived. A worthier conclusion to the symbolic festivities of the day was "inconceivable" to this enthusiast.[39]

Curt von Westernhagen was similarly overwhelmed by the Day of Potsdam experience, writing that this synthesis of politics and culture was symbolic of the "German essence which, at its best, combines will to action with deep reflection." It was likewise indicative of Wagner's contemporaneity, requiring that

> we consider what the master had to say to the German *Volk* about issues that shake us to the core: about the notion of a German Revolution and the rebirth of myth; about the eternal significance of classical Greece and the universal artwork; about folk festivals and the genius as spokesman for the *Volk*; about religious revival out of the spirit of German myth and German mysticism; and about the heroic wise men of German history.[40]

"Thus was the birthday of the Third Reich solemnly observed, in the spirit of Potsdam and Bayreuth's Wagnerian tones," editorialized the newly "synchronized" *Zeitschrift für Musik*.[41] But the Day of Potsdam ritual was not the last time that *Die Meistersinger* would sound at the "altar of the nation" in the fateful year of 1933. With August came the first Bayreuth Festival in the Third Reich, and it likewise opened with a production of *Die Meistersinger* "in the presence of the Reich Chancellor." Curbing a tradition initiated at the first postwar Bayreuth production in 1924, Hitler insisted that the audience not rise at the end of the opera to sing national or party anthems. On his command, each person who entered the Festspielhaus received a card reading, "The Führer requests that guests refrain from sing-

---

39. Hugo Rasch, "Die Festvorstellung in der Staatsoper," *Völkischer Beobachter*, 23 March 1933. See also Westernhagen, *Wagners Kampf*, 96.
40. Westernhagen, *Wagners Kampf*, 7.
41. Paul Bülow, "Adolf Hitler und der Bayreuther Geistesbezirk," *Zeitschrift für Musik* 100.7 (1933): 677–80, here 677.

ing the *Deutschland-* or *Horst-Wessel-Lieder,* or making any similar demonstrations at the end of the performance. There is no more splendid expression of the German spirit than the immortal work of the master himself."[42] This directive earned Hitler respect among Nazi Wagnerians as a true aficionado: "When I sat," wrote Paul Bülow, "in that memorable opening performance of *Die Meistersinger,* right in front of the seats for government officials, and saw the serious face of the Führer transfixed by the powerful third act, I knew that he had come not only as a our leading politician, but as a plain and simple listener, ready—just like the rest of us—to give himself wholly over to the eternal magic of the music."[43]

But by exploiting Wagner's opera it was not just privileged Bayreuth audiences that the new regime wanted to impress. That evening the performance was broadcast throughout Germany, and Joseph Goebbels took advantage of the occasion to make an extended radio address. Printed in full by both Alfred Rosenberg's *Völkischer Beobachter*[44] and his own newspaper, *Der Angriff,*[45] the propaganda czar's speech verified the prominence of *Die Meistersinger* in Nazi culture. "There is certainly no work in all the music literature of the German *Volk* that so closely relates to our times and our spiritual condition," Goebbels opened. "How often in recent years," he asked rhetorically, has the *Wach auf* chorus been heard by "faithful Germans" as a tangible symbol of the "reawakening of the German *Volk* out of the deep political and spiritual narcosis that it entered in November of 1918?" Towering over all Wagner's other music dramas as "the most German of all," *Die Meistersinger* is the "incarnation of our *Volkstum,*" representing "everything that marks and fills the German soul."

Goebbels continued by extolling the pro-Wagner spirit of the new regime: "Richard Wagner's heirs can today rest assured that the master and his work are safe and secure" in the care of a regime whose head personally visited "sites of Wagnerian creativity during the very first year of the German Revolution, paying humble homage to the greatest musical genius of all time." He concluded this *Meistersinger* radio address with an extended reference to the opera's finale as a manifesto of National Socialist cultural policy. "May the German people never lose this spirit of respect for the great men of the nation!" Only then would the new Reich "do justice" to the demand that Richard Wagner made via Hans Sachs in the close of "the most

---

42. H. H. Stuckenschmidt, "Bayreuther *Meistersinger*: Die Eröffnung der Festspiele," *BZ am Mittag,* 22 July 1933.

43. Paul Bülow, "Der Führer und das Haus Wahnfried," *Zeitschrift für Musik* (April 1939) 362–65, here 362.

44. "Richard Wagner und das Kunstempfinden unserer Zeit: Rundfunkrede von Reichsminister Dr. Goebbels," *Völkischer Beobachter,* 8 August 1933.

45. "Reichsminister Dr. Goebbels huldigt Richard Wagner," *Der Angriff,* 7 August 1933.

German of all German operas": "Therefore I say to you: honor your German masters! Then you will conjure up good spirits; even should the Holy Roman Empire dissolve in mist, for us there would yet remain holy German art!"

Though lengthy (included here are only his direct references to the opera), this transmission was not Goebbels' last word on *Die Meistersinger,* even during the first year of the government. On 15 November 1933, he presided over the opening of the *Reichskulturkammer,* the institution he designed to dominate cultural life in the Third Reich, and this event also included propagandistic use of *Die Meistersinger.* Immediately after Goebbels' inaugural speech, the *Völkischer Beobachter* reported, amid "stormy applause for the Reichsminister," sounded the *Wach auf!* chorus: "A hopeful awakening! Music for—as Dr. Goebbels so perfectly put it—marching into the shining future of German culture."[46] On top of this glut of *Meistersinger* performances associated with the new state in 1933, linkage between the opera and National Socialism was formalized two years later, when Hitler ordered that the opera be staged during each *Reichsparteitag* in Nürnberg. Nazi Wagnerians were ecstatic. By deeming this the "official" opera of the N.S.D.A.P. rallies, Richard Stock gushed, the "political genius, Adolf Hitler, has established in the city of *Die Meistersinger* an eternal monument to the artistic genius, Richard Wagner."[47]

Through 1935, National Socialist statements about Wagner's Nürnberg opera mainly addressed its significance for the existing German nation. However, with the first stages of Hitler's march toward war, *Großdeutsch* aspects of Nazism gradually became more apparent in the discourse of *Meistersinger* reception. Within months of the *Anschluß,* the *Völkischer Beobachter* reviewed a production of the opera at the Salzburg Festival—Nazi luminaries, including Goebbels, in attendance—and therein hinted at a pan-Germanic reading of *Die Meistersinger*'s nationalistic implications. The *Völkischer Beobachter* interpreted performance of *Die Meistersinger* for the festival's opening as "a symbol, a program, and a promise in one": a symbol because "once sounded, these cheerful notes will henceforth influence how the Salzburger Festival will proceed"; a program because this was "a sublime expression" of what a "German music festival" must do, namely, provide a "communal experience" designed to "eliminate prejudices based on wealth, class, and education"; finally, a promise because "whoever just heard this 'honor your German masters!'" will "never forget" the promises made by this regime vis-à-vis pan-German cultural traditions.[48] Thus were confirmed fears from abroad about the future

---

46. "Die Reichs-Kultur-Kammer eröffnet: Der Führer bei der Feier in der Berliner Philharmonie," *Völkischer Beobachter,* 16 November 1933.

47. Stock, *Richard Wagner und die Stadt,* 7, 28.

48. Dr. Antropp, "Festlicher Auftakt in Salzburg: *Die Meistersinger* unter Furtwängler in Anwesenheit von Dr. Goebbels," *Völkischer Beobachter,* 25 July 1938.

Germanification of the "international" music festival in Mozart's birthplace.[49]

Two years later, in November 1940, *Völkischer Beobachter* coverage of a *Meistersinger* performance in Strasbourg—the heart of newly reclaimed Alsace-Lorraine—proposed a revanchist reading of the opera. "The first *Meistersinger* production in liberated Alsace moved the heart as powerfully as the experience of a storm." In the present political atmosphere, the opera seemed to represent "recent events," especially when the singer playing Hans Sachs delivered the "powerful warning" contained in his closing address "with stirring emotional effect, while turning directly toward the Alsacian audience." This was a moment that "allowed everyone to relive in their deepest hearts what has taken place in the last few months, and a reminder that they have every right to celebrate in this hour." The concluding chorus seemed an expression of "unbounded joy in response to these developments"; Alsacian listeners took part in this finale "as if they were themselves the *Volk* of the *Festwiese*, giving thanks for all these feelings of happiness to a German master who has become a symbol of the richest and most worthy aspects of German existence."[50]

Even after Germans began to experience the whirlwind reaped by such expansionist attitudes, *Die Meistersinger* remained at the center of wartime cultural life. Partly as a propaganda measure, and partly as a way of channeling funds into Hitler's beloved Bayreuth, the government "rewarded" armaments workers and wounded soldiers with trips to Wagner's Festspielhaus for entertainment and edification. To reduce costs, the 1943 festival—"enhanced" with participation of choruses from the Hitler Jugend, the Bund Deutscher Mädel, and the SS Standarte Wiking—was limited to a single Wagner opera: *Die Meistersinger*. "Thirty thousand front soldiers and armaments workers experienced sixteen performances of the *Meistersinger von Nürnberg* as guests of the Führer at the Fourth Wartime Festival in Bayreuth," wrote an enthusiastic Richard Stock. "To these brave front-fighters and their faithful comrades from the forges of German arms," he explained, no other work could have been more symbolic of the "profound goals" being furthered by their "heroic actions" than this "hymn to the honor of German masters." Hitler's invitations to the wartime festivals repaid a "debt of thanks that we owe to the best of the nation for risking their lives to protect the eternal treasure of German culture."[51] The

---

49. Pierre-Jean Jouve, "In Memoriam Salzbourg," *La Nouvelle Revue Française* 51.299 (1938): 177–86; J.-C. Boutroux, "Souvenirs de Salzbourg," *Le monde musical* 49.5 (1938): 118–19.

50. Erwin Bauer, "Die Meistersinger von Nürnberg," *Völkischer Beobachter,* 18 November 1940.

51. Richard Wilhelm Stock, *Richard Wagner und seine Meistersinger: Eine Erinnerungsgabe zu den Bayreuther Kriegsfestspielen 1943* (Nürnberg: Verlag Karl Ulrich, 1943), 157.

Nationalsozialistische Monatshefte also extolled this terrible scene, complete with bandaged soldiers marching up Bayreuth's famous Green Hill, as a triumph of Nazi culture. "Even amid the hardest of military exertions," Erwin Völsung bragged in this Nazi journal, the German people "astonishes the rest of the world" by "pausing" to honor a genius who provided an "inexhaustible source of strength for overcoming the pain and suffering of our battle with fate." Greeted with great enthusiasm, *Die Meistersinger* seemed to Völsung a "particularly appropriate choice for fulfilling the special wartime mission of this festival."[52] Equally fervent about the motivational value of the *Kriegsfestspiel*, Robert Ley, head of the German Labor Front (DAF) and its *Kraft durch Freude* (Strength through Joy) movement, proclaimed at a press conference that it "conspicuously demonstrates holy faith in our Fatherland and uncompromising will to defend the life of our *Volk*." Even in the fourth year of war, Ley continued, relying on the "indestructibility of its highest qualities and the protection of the German sword," the "most worthy representatives" of the German *Volk* had once again gathered at "one of the holiest of sites consecrated to German art" in order to pledge themselves to the "eternal values of its artistic genius," as called for by Hans Sachs: "Honor your German masters, then you will conjure up good spirits!"[53]

Whatever divisions may have existed within the leadership of National Socialist cultural politics, the principals were consistent in their efforts to associate the words, music, storyline, and imagery of *Die Meistersinger* with what they perceived as the progressive tenets of the National Socialist world view. Besides Goebbels, his fierce competitor, Alfred Rosenberg, made regular references to the opera in his theoretical works and his journalism. In his best-known publication, *Der Mythus des 20. Jahrhunderts,* Rosenberg made an extended reference to Wagnerian characters, including Hans Sachs, as models for the "Nordic soul." The "essential message of all Western art," Rosenberg held, is manifested in Richard Wagner's: that the "nordic soul is not contemplative, that it does not lose itself in individual psychology, but willfully determines cosmic-soulful laws." This "ideal of inner beauty" is realized in Wotan, in King Mark, and in Hans Sachs. The "power of heroic will" (*des Heroisch-Willenhaften*) is the "secret medium which links together all of our thinkers, researchers, and artists: this is the substance of the greatest works of the Western world, from Graf Rüdiger to the *Eroica,* to *Faust,* to Hans Sachs; it is the force that forms everything."[54]

---

52. Erwin Völsung, "Bayreuther Kriegsfestspiele 1943: *Die Meistersinger von Nürnberg,*" Nationalsozialistische Monatshefte 14.157 (1943): 405–7, here 405.

53. Cited in ibid., 405.

54. Alfred Rosenberg, *Der Mythus des 20. Jahrhunderts: Eine Wertung der seelisch-geistigen Gestaltenkämpfe unserer Zeit* (Munich: Hoheneichen-Verlag, 1940), 433. Rosenberg was apparently referring to Ernst Rüdiger, Graf von

Coming from the self-proclaimed philosopher of the movement, these pseudo-intellectual concepts were often reproduced by Rosenberg's sycophantic underlings writing about *Die Meistersinger* for the *Völkischer Beobachter* and elsewhere.[55]

Peter Raabe, who assumed the *Reichsmusikkammer* presidency after Richard Strauss vacated the position, likewise chimed in with an article on the significance of *Die Meistersinger* "in our times." Subsequently published in his collection, *Die Musik im dritten Reich,* this might be taken as one of the clearer efforts to establish an "official" line for Nazi reception of the opera. In Raabe's view, *Die Meistersinger* was not merely the "most German artwork of our operatic stage," but beyond this, the Nazi movement had "absorbed" this music drama as a "very special expression of itself," as an "affirmation of its principles, wishes, and demands." Each member of the party "finds himself and his plans confirmed" in *Die Meistersinger*. For them, it symbolizes the dawning of a new age: "the spirit of youth marching forward over decaying formalism; victory of progressives over those stuck in sterile old ways." In this struggle, Wagner's *Meistersinger* constituted a "battle cry" that emboldened those "taking the field against stagnation and prejudice." At the same time, however, it was a Hymn of Reverence for achievements realized long before. In Raabe's view, the modern era "lacks reverence" to a shocking degree: "greenhorns" who haven't yet achieved a thing "deny the value of previous German accomplishments," even though these earned for the country a worldwide reputation as the "land of thinkers and poets." People must be "forced to comply with the dictum, 'Do not scorn the masters.'"[56]

Though much of their reception took the form of references to *Die Meistersinger* as a general indicator of broad concepts they intended to impose on Germany, Nazi *Kulturpolitiker* stressed some particular themes as most resonant with their ideology. Volkish ideologues were deeply attracted to the image of Nürnberg they perceived in Wagner's work. Although Leni Riefenstahl did not use music from *Die Meistersinger* to accompany her opening shots of the city, they were inextricably associated in

---

Starhemberg, 1638–1701, an Austrian field marshal who served against the Ottomans in Hungary and was made military commander of Vienna in 1680. He defended Vienna with a small garrison against a large Ottoman army in the summer of 1683 (*The Columbia Encyclopedia,* [New York: Columbia University Press, 1995]).

55. For example, Bertram, *Seher von Bayreuth,* 327; Bülow, "Adolf Hitler und der Bayreuther Geistesbezirk"; and "Das grosse Hassen: Marxistische Hetze zum Wagner-Jahr," *Völkischer Beobachter,* 1 February 1933. Note also that while Rosenberg treated Sachs as a model "nordic" type, he made no mention of Beckmesser.

56. Raabe, "Wagners *Meistersinger,*" 71–72.

National Socialist reception. Thoughts of *Die Meistersinger* generally triggered two related but separate concepts of Nürnberg. Foremost were notions of the *Altstadt* as a symbol of unified German culture reaching back to the Reformation. Encompassing the creative spirit of Dürer, Sachs, and Wagner alike, the medieval outline of the city served in the National Socialist imagination as a bastion of "stable German art."[57] Particularly the image of the *Festwiese,* as Wagner represented it in the opera's final scene, provided Nazi propagandists with a symbol of timeless cultural stability extending from the Middle Ages. "As we can see in the history of medieval Nürnberg," wrote Richard Stock, "the Hallerwiese was long a symbol of German unity and amity." In the fifteenth century, it was an important meeting place for German princes and clans; thereafter, the Hallerwiese was commonly referred to as the "Allerwiese" (the meadow for all), which "best proves its volkishness." But it was in *Die Meistersinger,* that "Richard Wagner afforded this site its eternal significance."[58]

As Kurt Hoffmann, a self-described "apprentice musician," avowed in pages of the *Bayreuther Blätter* (using the third-person voice), Nazi Wagnerians made pilgrimages to the "City of *Die Meistersinger*" to wander its streets with sounds and images from Wagner's opera resonating in their thoughts. "In the heart of the wanderer, the nighttime city—with silhouettes of its buildings and towers gleaming in moonlight, with its secret nooks and crannies, fairy-tale wells, and dark gates—became a veritable reincarnation of the music by Wagner he had experienced the previous day." In the otherwise quiet little alley of Hans Sachs, this volkish fantasy continued, "did there not suddenly appear right in front of his quaint old shoe shop—in a fantastic, visionary way—a riotous bustle of people swearing, screaming, and punching at each other: an uproarious *Johannisnacht* tumult that seemed almost real?" The next morning, he received an even more powerful vision. Beneath the pitched roofs and towers "raged the '*Überall Wahn*' of the bustling citizenry," but up above, as if emerging from the rays of the sun, he perceived an image of the mastersingers parading with their ancient guild flags "in honor of the most genuine representatives of the creative German *Volk*." Hans Sachs also came forth, and at that very moment the "magnificent *Meistersinger* theme resounded in the spirit of the enchanted dreamer, as if played by a thousand-member orchestra—while a powerful choir entered with its unforgettable injunction: Honor your German masters! Then you will conjure up good spirits!" Thoughts intertwining Reformation-era Nürnberg and *Die Meistersinger* coordinated perfectly with the antimodernist strain of the National Socialist outlook. Even amid the "desert of degenerate postwar culture," *Die Meistersinger*

---

57. Emma von Sichard, "Feste deutscher Kunst," *Völkischer Beobachter,* 22 May 1930.

58. Stock, *Richard Wagner und die Stadt,* 163.

triggered in this "seeker" thoughts of "the most enriching German essence," contemplation of which spared him from spiritual ruin until the "strengthened Germanness" of the new era finally "broke through to liberate his thoughts and actions."[59]

But it was not the *Altstadt* alone that fascinated and inspired fanatics, for the "City of *Die Meistersinger*" was no longer just an "important old" but "once again a new epicenter of our German cultural will."[60] Hitler and his followers had ostensibly saved the city from "Jewish-democratic spirit," first by "forever" linking Nürnberg and Wagner's opera with the annual Nazi *Parteitage,* and then via even more troubling measures. Richard Stock found it a satisfying coincidence that Wagner, the great "anti-Semite" so "viciously attacked by Jews and their collaborators," was so honored *in Nürnberg*, the "very city from which Julius Streicher launched his war against worldwide Jewry," and where, during the *Reichsparteitag* of 1935, "our Führer proclaimed the Laws for the Protection of German Blood—the Nürnberg Laws."[61] It was on the basis of this wide range of associations, drawing together Wagner, Hitler, Streicher, and the Nürnberg Laws, that *Die Meistersinger* was ultimately linked to the darkest aspects of Nazi policy.

Nevertheless, the main political connotations that National Socialist reception drew from the opera had to do with social relations within the volkish *Gemeinschaft,* not treatment of those whom Nazis considered outsiders. Fundamental to Nazi interpretations of *Die Meistersinger* was the active role played in it by the German *Volk,* particularly in the last scene. As a contemporary critic put it, it was the "extraordinary volkishness" perceived in the work that made it the "official opera of the jubilee year 1933"[62] and—as others have subsequently said—into the operatic "anthem" of the Third Reich as a whole. But while exalting Wagner's representation of the *Volksgeist,* Nazis had to be careful not to slip into democratic terms of reception. Concentrating on volkish and National Socialist implementation of Wagner, it is easy to forget that parallel traditions associating him with democratic and socialist politics did exist within European culture.[63] Until 1933, at any rate, Nazi Wagnerians had to compete with interpretations of *Die Meistersinger* forwarded by German republicans and leftists who, as a contemporary observed, proclaimed *Die Meistersinger* a "democratic pageant." In the opinion of National Socialism's opposition,

---

59. Kurt Hoffmann, "Meistersinger-Erlebnis: Ein Bayreuther Stimmungsbild," *Bayreuther Blätter* 60 (1937): 151–52.
60. Stock, *Richard Wagner und die Stadt,* 9.
61. Ibid., 9.
62. Stuckenschmidt, "Bayreuther *Meistersinger."*
63. David Large and William Weber, eds., *Wagnerism in European Culture and Politics* (Ithaca, N.Y.: Cornell University Press, 1984).

"nowhere in all theatrical art is the sovereignty of the German people so beautifully affirmed as in this ringing celebration of democracy." From perspectives to the left of the N.S.D.A.P., even if Wagner's political acumen "became undone during his middle age," the "black-red-and-gold principles of 1848, for which he had sacrificed so much, remain triumphant in the ingenious *Meistersinger*."[64]

To offset these competing claims, *Reichsmusikkammer* President Raabe sharply distinguished Nazi opinions of the *Volk* represented in Wagner's opera from the *demos* construed by the Left. "The *Festwiese* scene is particularly misunderstood," he held, since it is often perceived as an endorsement for the (in his opinion) "unfortunate notion that at such festive events, persons of every class, every professional rank, and every level of education should interact with each other in brotherly fashion," just as when strangers mingle during *Karneval*. "In jest," Raabe continued, such things are occasionally possible and somewhat entertaining; but they will always have something "forced and unnatural about them." When they see the "joyous cavorting" in the *Festwiese* scene of the *Meistersinger*, some think that Wagner offered a "model for general fraternization of this sort." But this view is unfounded: did Wagner not quite clearly mandate that the scene represents "no more and no less than a festival celebrated by burghers?" One should not overlook, Raabe insisted, that "Wagner depicts neither farmers, nor soldiers, neither the mayor, nor councilmen mixing with the *Volk*." Throughout *Die Meistersinger,* Wagner "sang a rapturous 'hallelujah' to the burgher—or rather, to the *modest* lower middle class (as separate from Philistines)." Therefore, the composer "would have had a fit if he learned that today the word 'burgher' is often treated with the disrespect that the Socialists heap on the word 'bourgeois,' thereby ingratiating themselves with the proletariat they coddle so much." In the end, Wagner was no egalitarian; he "championed the honor of German burghers and considered that class strong enough to stand up for itself."[65]

However defined, Wagner's representation of the *Volk* was fundamental to Nazi reception of *Die Meistersinger,* but uppermost in their considerations of the opera was Hans Sachs's relationship with it—as a leader who emerged from the people to herald a German future grounded in a stable past. "It is the *Volksgeist* itself," insisted Johannes Bertram, that reveals itself in the "monumental *Gestalt* of Hans Sachs." Opposing the "sterile artistic tradition" personified in Beckmesser—whose "inflexible rules atrophy the pulse of the soul"—the cobbler "places himself immediately on

---

64. Bernhard Diebold, "Der Fall Wagner: Eine Revision," in *Richard Wagner: Ein deutsches Thema: Eine Dokumentation zur Wirkungsgeschichte Richard Wagners 1876–1976,* ed. Hartmut Zelinsky (Frankfurt am Main: Zweitausendeins, 1976), 190–92.

65. Raabe, "Wagners *Meistersinger,*" 69–71.

the side of Eva, that of naive *Volk* spirit." In the voice of her "virginal soul" he senses "the will of the *Volk*," and therefore demands: "Let the *Volk* judge; it will surely agree with the child."[66] Benno von Arent, Reich Theatrical Designer who staged performances at the Deutsche Oper in Berlin,[67] underscored the "popular" origins of Sachs in explications of his designs. "Today we no longer consider it an incidental fact, and certainly not a deficiency, that this poet Hans Sachs was a shoemaker." "To the contrary," wrote Arent, "we admire him and his poetry all the more" because of his craftsman status. For this reason Arent placed tools "clearly in the foreground" of the workroom in his productions, as signs of Sachs's "dual mastery," conveying the sentiment: "Honor the work; respect the worker!"[68] But Nazi perceptions of Sachs did not identify him merely as a man of the people, but as a man of the people fated to lead it. "From the very start of the opera," opined Johannes Bertram, Hans Sachs is the "leading force at the center of the proceedings—or better, *over* the proceedings," which he "steers skillfully" by virtue of his "deep comprehension of seemingly superficial events." Indeed, the shoemaker acts as the "transcendent director of the whole drama."[69] Parallels between Nazi assessments of Sachs and the *Führer-Prinzip* that underlay both ideology and bureaucracy of the Third Reich should not be overstated, but are undeniable. The volkish genius embodied in Sachs "is comparable to the focus of a lens," reads the *Official Bayreuth Festival Guide* for 1927. At that point, or in that person:

a thousand individual rays are gathered and then radiated back into life— with unimaginable strength. There is no other way to grasp the achievements of Bismarck, or the works of Wagner. The genius can reveal himself to the world as both proud and modest: "I am not the small 'I' of this single person with my incidental name; I am the *Volk*. I am the will, energy, unity, belief, love, hope, present, and future of my people." This individual is no dictator, but one willed [*Gewollter*]; no despot, but a force of nature. He is both the messiah [*Berufene*] and the elected one [*Auserwählte*].[70]

Anticipating the longed-for genius-leader, Hans Sachs's words preoccupied Nazi interpreters. Mediating, it seemed, between Richard Wagner and Adolf Hitler, Sachs's warnings and directives were studied for every modicum of contemporary relevance. Placing themselves in the shoes of Walther

---

66. Bertram, *Seher von Bayreuth*, 312.
67. Spotts, *Bayreuth: A History of the Wagner Festival*, 185–86.
68. Cited in Stock, *Richard Wagner und die Stadt*, 26.
69. Bertram, *Seher von Bayreuth*, 312.
70. Walter Lange, "Richard Wagner Verkünder deutschen Niederganges und Aufstieges," in *Offizieller Bayreuther Festspielführer*, ed. Karl Grunsky (Bayreuth: Verlag der Hofbuchhandlung Georg Niehrenheim, 1927).

von Stolzing, eager to learn from "the master," Nazi cultural-politicians derived from Sachs's teachings material that was vital to a volkish onslaught against modernist tendencies in German art. "Hans Sachs instructs the young master" and by association, the nation as a whole, that "while the spirit of his song must be derived from the heart of the Volk, its form must grow out of the experience of long-standing mastery." It is to communicate this tenet that *Die Meistersinger* ends with Hans Sachs's admonition, repeated by all who are present, "with raised hands acknowledging Sachs as the leading spirit of the Volk, the avowed representative of German art: 'Honor your German masters! Then you will conjure up good spirits; even should the Holy Roman Empire dissolve in mist, for us there would yet remain holy German art!'"

Sachs's *Schlußwörter* were fundamental to National Socialist interpretations of *Die Meistersinger*: repeated in virtually every analysis of the opera, and many other contexts besides, they became a mantra of Nazi cultural politicians. Primary use of the slogan was directed, naturally, against cultural modernism: "Besides Wagner's charge: 'Children, build anew!' [*Kinder, schafft Neues!*] let us not forget his reminder: 'Honor your German masters.' We are mindful of the still unredeemed artistic revolutionaries of the past."[71] But Nazi propagandists also identified and highlighted broader implications in the finale: "When, in his closing speech, Hans Sachs exalts German style and German art, calling for battle against the enemy both within and without, against Latin [*welschen*] smoke and Latin mirrors, it goes straight to the heart of every German."[72]

This example brings us full circle: it is undeniable that, as here, a significant strain of Nazi *Meistersinger* interpretations invoked the finale of Wagner's opera as a summons to "battle." However, even very close attention to reception records does not clarify precisely at whom they perceived Sachs to have taken aim: "modernists," "enemies within and without," "Latins," "Philistines," or Jews? Explicitly targeted are the former; only implicitly—and never directly mentioned—are the latter. The main thrust of National Socialist politicization of *Die Meistersinger* was not to motivate action against enemies, but to inspire praise for traditional cultural heroes, however defined. For confirmation let us turn to Hitler himself. In February 1933, on the fiftieth anniversary of Wagner's death and just days after assuming the position of Reich Chancellor, Hitler promised to erect a monument to "the master" in Leipzig, the city of Wagner's birth. Conforming to notions about German nationalist "sacred sites,"[73] plans called

---

71. Westernhagen, *Wagners Kampf*, 26.

72. Max von Millenkovich-Morold, "Richard Wagner in unserer Zeit," *Zeitschrift für Musik* (May 1938): 469–73; here 470.

73. George L. Mosse, *The Nationalization of the Masses: Political Symbolism and Mass Movements in Germany from the Napoleonic Wars through the Third Reich* (New York: H. Fertig, 1975), 47–72.

for a memorial amid a grove of oaks. The altar (*Gedenkblock*) would be fashioned of a piece of marble ten square meters around and five meters high, with relief carvings communicating the "fundamental motifs" ascribed to Wagnerian creativity: "Myth, Fate, Love, and Redemption." On 6 March 1934, Hitler dedicated the foundation stone for this never completed monument:

> Today's German generation [. . .] draws from the eternal forces of our Volk because it strives to emulate its best spirits. Thus has it found its way to this city already in the second year of national revival, in order—through me as Chancellor of the Reich—to place the deepest thanks of the nation at the feet of [Leipzig's] great son. As a testament of solemn promises to live up to the wish and will of the master, to continue maintaining his everlasting works in ever-lively beauty, and to draw coming generations of our Volk into the miracle world of this mighty tone poet, I lay the cornerstone of this national monument to Richard Wagner.[74]

Given that Hitler was transparently invoking, even imitating Hans Sachs on this occasion for saluting his deepest personal hero, it should come as no surprise that on the keystone he dedicated that day—explicitly for the Wagner monument, but implicitly for National Socialist culture as a whole—were carved the words: *Ehrt eure deutschen Meister!*

Whether or not Hitler also conceived Auschwitz as a tribute to his master is a question that remains open. Debate on this issue rages, since opinions range from angry certainty that Wagner begot Hitler to staunch disbelief in Wagner's moral responsibility for the crimes of his fans. This inquiry does not judge whether German anti-Semites might have wielded features of *Die Meistersinger*—particularly the character of Sixtus Beckmesser—as ideological weapons against the Jewish people; it only attempts to determine if there is proof that they did so. The public record of volkish and Nazi cultural politics indicates that this opera was primarily utilized as an icon of cultural conservatism, rather than as propaganda for fomenting racist hatred. Focusing on Hans Sachs, Nazis highlighted principles of discipline and tradition, largely overlooking the character who could combine these strictures with free expression to produce "art of the future": Walther von Stolzing. It was partly by de-emphasizing Walther—or rather, his symbolic role in the aesthetics of the future—that Nazis minimized Wagner's modernist tendencies and reputation, and consequently undermined formulation of a "progressive" National Socialist culture to which they paid little more than lip service.

---

74. "Der Führer legt den Grundstein zum Nationaldenkmal Richard Wagners," *Völkischer Beobachter*, 7 March 1934.

http://worldwidewagner.richard.de: An Interview with the Composer Concerning History, Nation, and *Die Meistersinger*

Peter Höyng

To Helen McNabb

You might have been as surprised as I when it turned out that I would be interviewing Richard Wagner. You might also imagine my excitement, sense of anticipation, even anxiety. Would I come across like a Sixtus Beckmesser, the pedantic fool mixing up his lines in an attempt to woo not Eva this time but the author and composer himself? Or would I seem as critical, even sarcastic, as Friedrich Nietzsche in his polemic *Der Fall Wagner*? Only when I recalled how this most unlikely circumstance came about did I grow calmer, a story I would like to share with you.

Given my other scholarly commitments, I was somewhat hesitant to accept an invitation to contribute to a book about *Die Meistersinger von Nürnberg*, or to be more precise, to write a chapter about "Hans Sachs and the (Re)Construction of German History in *Die Meistersinger*." However, with all the electronic tools available nowadays which can ease the scholar's task, I decided to agree. I began my research by browsing the internet, searching through various data banks and also signing up for a listserv on "Richard Wagner." At this listserv—the salon of the twenty-first century, a virtual salon, of course, where people from distant places share their interest on a chosen subject—I posted a somewhat generally worded request for some hints or help in regard to my project, the nexus of German history and the opera. The next day I found a rather angry response signed "Wagner." I was baffled at first; then thought someone was trying to be cute; then it occurred to me that Wagner is, after all, a common German name; finally I became somewhat apprehensive at the thought that someone in the Wagner family—it is a rather large clan, after all—might have responded. Though the reply was a little harsh, pompous, and arrogant, I answered politely, thanking the person for her/his ideas on the German nation as a history of salvation, a nation still in search of an identity. As if I did not know that?

While pondering the next phase of my research, another e-mail arrived, this time signed "Richard Wagner." I could not help feeling that this verged on the tasteless: it was neither original nor particularly funny. At the same time, however, it was mysterious, alluring, and intriguing to receive an e-mail with that name. I was already caught in the web without being fully aware. As a child I had a healthy fear of webs and the creatures than spin them, but now, as an adult who perhaps should have known better, instead of running away, I stayed and played with its virtual incarnation for real.

Soon after that e-mail, an exchange developed centering initially, as you might imagine, around the respondent's identity. Not only did he insist that he was none other than Richard Wagner himself, but eerily the messages sounded just like him, too. Being acquainted with Wagner's letters, his autobiography *My Life,* and his numerous essays including *German Art and German Politics,* and *On German Art,* I could not help sensing that the answers were in his spirit. Though I remained more than just skeptical, he reminded me that around the time of his *Parsifal* he had became not only a vegetarian but also a believer in reincarnation. Relenting slightly, I asked him who he is these days. He hesitantly identified himself as a computer specialist working for one of the very large data banks. In other words, he was not only using the world wide web but was very much a part of creating it. This was a little more than I could take. I started feeling a little like Nathaniel from E. T. A. Hoffmann's tale *Der Sandmann.* Nathaniel is not only haunted by his own belief in an evil spirit, named Coppola, but fails to notice that the object of his love, Olimpia, is a puppet and not a real woman. But, for Nathaniel, Olimpia is real! Was I just as blind, just as naive, transfixed by R. W.?

As you can imagine, he—I am not allowed to reveal his real new identity—is completely frustrated with his current life since it lacks all the extravagance, high drama, eroticism, and, above all, artistic expression of his former life as R. W. In a curious twist, he has become more like an Alberich, sunk deep in the myriads of information banks, the new form of idolatry. At heart, though, he lusts for salvation, and finds his only moments of relief when dreaming of his former life. In his dreams, he confessed, he lives the life of Amfortas and so, half jokingly, he called me his Parsifal since I seemed to have sympathy for him. But I thought of myself least of all as Parsifal, since I had nothing but trivial questions for him, or so it felt, and my sympathy was more a surprised fascination than true compassion. Actually, the more evident and more likely it became that it was the reincarnated Richard Wagner—a virtual R. W. in other words—the more and more inhibited, the less daring and provocative I became. I had become self-conscious, which he, in turn, did not like. He seemed to enjoy his coming out and encouraged me to be as frank as possible.

Thus, I half jokingly asked him one day whether he would be willing to grant an interview for a forthcoming book devoted to his opera *Die Meistersinger von Nürnberg*. He agreed, though he set three conditions. First, he would not meet with me in person; second, I was not to address his current life; and third, to restrict the discussion to *Die Meistersinger* and German history. He would consider this interview as a kind of test for his coming out.

Still filled with misgivings, and somewhat concerned that I was making a fool of myself, I decided to turn to my friend and editor, Nicholas Vazsonyi. To be quite honest, I was dumbfounded when he agreed to the concept of the "interview" as well as to Wagner's terms after I finally dared to tell him the whole story. We concluded that even if it were not really R. W., it might be interesting to consider what Wagner himself might say, given the ongoing and essentially unresolvable debates. At the very least, then, this suggests an intriguing mind game, pushing the bounds of the possible, legitimated on the grounds that this would remain true to Wagner's own legacy. Aware of Wagner's complex personality, and of how self-consciously and successfully he manipulated his image, we went into this thing with our eyes open—or were our "eyes wide shut?" You will have to decide. Since Wagner's music dramas strive for nothing but virtual reality, the fact that this interview would be nothing but real virtuality adheres to his own aesthetic of creating a truth that is false. What efforts and apparatus, musically and theatrically speaking, did Wagner set into motion in order to present on stage a world that, using Schiller's term, is nothing but "schöner Schein" only for the sake of truth?! An idealistic truth that reality never reveals?! I mean, who has ever encountered Wotan, Donner, Froh, and Loge, or Fricka, Freia, and Erda other than on stage? And, as a final thought of legitimizing this most unlikely interview, is the character of Walther von Stolzing not a paradigm for licensing artistic freedom? Is he not the one who overrides all the existing and confining rules in order to express himself in a way that is inherently more truthful? As you can see, my doubts never left me, but the day of the interview finally arrived, and here it is: slightly edited. I can only hope that you find it informative and that you will know what to make of his answers.

Is it okay if I call you Mr. Wagner?

Sure.

Mr. Wagner, this interview is about your opera Die Meistersinger von Nürnberg *and its relationship to German nationhood, history, and identity. It will be for readers in English.*

As you know, I was always very fond of England, and in particular of America. I actually had plans to dedicate *Parsifal* to the American people.[1]

[How ironic then, to know him these days as a computer clerk in the U.S. Unfortunately, he stipulated not to talk about his current life. I interpret that as an escapism that seems in more than one way so characteristic of him.]

You are presumably also aware that your music dramas, including Die Meistersinger, *are an integral part of the operatic repertoire in England and the U.S. This is all the more striking to me when considering that* Die Meistersinger *in particular addresses German history, art, and politics, and therefore would seem of rather limited interest outside Germany.*

You should not be surprised by my success. Though I was concerned throughout my life with politics in Germany and German politics, it would be absolutely wrong to conclude that my music dramas express nothing but German concerns, and that goes for *Die Meistersinger* as well. One can, for example, easily enjoy *Die Meistersinger* as a witty opera. In my first draft from 1845, I actually called it a "comic opera," and even later, when I worked on it again in earnest, I still considered it a "grand comic" opera,[2] simply because I use humorous elements when Sixtus Beckmesser and Walther von Stolzing become rivals and want to win respect and love from Eva, Pogner's daughter.

Sure, one can smile every once in a while, but overall it is a quite serious opera.

Yes and no. I vividly recall my first reading of the completed libretto. After I had finished the dramatic text in Paris, I believe it was in 1862, I met Countess Pourtalès. As I wrote in my autobiography, she "permitted me to visit her. In spite of being in mourning after her profound loss, she did not wish to leave her great sympathy for me unexpressed; when I told her what I was working on, she asked about my libretto: she countered my regret that she would certainly not find the lively and humorous character of my *Meistersinger* to her taste at this time with a friendly request that I read it to her, for which purpose she invited me to spend the evening with her. She was the first person to whom I had the opportunity to read my completed

---

1. "On February 1, 1880, Wagner informed the family circle that he proposed to move to Minnesota, build a house and drama school there, and dedicate *Parsifal* to the Americans," Martin Gregor-Dellin, *Richard Wagner: His Life, His Work, His Century,* trans. J. Maxwell Brownjohn (New York: Harcourt, 1983), 482.

2. Ulrich Müller and Peter Wapnewski, *Wagner Handbook,* trans. John Deathridge (Cambridge, Mass.: Harvard University Press, 1992), 73.

text, and it made such a significant impression on both of us that we often could not help bursting out into hearty laughter."[3]

This is a nice anecdote from your unusually eventful life, Mr. Wagner, but you would not deny that seeing nothing but a comedy in Die Meistersinger *would be a very superficial understanding and would actually miss one of the main points. After all the work ends with the chorus singing:*

Ehrt eure deutschen Meister,
dann bannt ihr gute Geister!
Und gebt ihr ihrem Wirken Gunst,
zerging' in Dunst
das Heil'ge Röm'sche Reich,
uns bliebe gleich
die heil'ge deutsche Kunst! (III, 5)

This is hardly humorous. It is a bold statement in which art serves as the basis of German cultural identity.

Indeed it is, and I never was really very happy with this ending anyway. I considered more than once abandoning it altogether.[4] Anyway, you started wondering why *Die Meistersinger* is of interest to an audience outside Germany. If you do not appreciate my anecdotal answer, then let me . . .

. . . I did not say that I am not appreciative of your story . . .

. . . point out that any decent person will realize that *Die Meistersinger* is also about the conflict of old versus new art as represented in the rivalry between Sixtus Beckmesser and Walther von Stolzing. It is a drama about narrow-minded book knowledge and the creative use of an art form, in short, it is a conflict between mediocrity and genius. This aspect, together with the humor, explains why *Die Meistersinger* can be enjoyed by any person who is interested in the arts and considers himself to have a mind open to the way in which the arts enable us to see the world anew.

Thank you, Mr. Wagner. It seems to me that you are in tune with one of your great admirers and conductors today, Daniel Barenboim, who also stressed in a recent conversation with the scholar Edward Said that Die Meistersinger *is first and foremost about "the relation between mediocrity*

---

3. Richard Wagner, *My Life*, trans. Andrew Gray, ed. Mary Whittall (Cambridge: Cambridge University Press, 1983), 675.
4. Cf. John Warrack, *Richard Wagner: "Die Meistersinger von Nürnberg."* Cambridge Opera Handbooks (Cambridge: Cambridge University Press, 1994), 31.

and genius, between artist and dilettante, between the new and the old in the person of Stolzing."[5]

Actually, Mr. Barenboim is in tune with me, not the other way around!

Fair enough. Let me then rephrase my question based on your wonderful remarks. Beside the universal themes of love and generational conflict and beside the higher level issue of art in society, there is a major strain dealing with the specifics of Germany and German identity. And that is the issue I would like to have our readers understand somewhat better. After all, understanding Die Meistersinger *today requires addressing three layers of German history. The first is relatively "modern." Your opera premiered in Munich in 1868, just two years after the formation of the Northern German State under Prussian aegis and only three years before the German Empire was created in the wake of the Franco-Prussian war. The second layer is your specific reference to the city of Nuremberg during early modern times, i.e., shortly after Luther's Reformation in 1517. Nuremberg was then still a prosperous and economically important city in Europe. Finally, when dealing with* Die Meistersinger, *one can hardly overlook a third historical layer, German history of the twentieth century, and specifically the first half.*

Don't be so overly careful. There is no need to tiptoe around the Nazi's appropriation of my works. I am aware of my disgusting "brother Hitler," to quote one of my more sophisticated admirers.[6] I was quite sure that you would bring up this tricky topic.

Thank you, I am glad we can agree so easily that this rather difficult and unpleasant issue needs to be addressed. After all, it is impossible not to associate the most shameful and disastrous episode of German history with Nuremberg. Not only did the Nazis stage their biggest party rallies there[7] *but, in addition, the shameful racial laws against Jews from 1935 are also referred to according to their geographic origin. It was all the more significant that the same city became synonymous with Germany's defeat in the trials after the Second World War. Therefore, one must face this issue in the*

---

5. "Daniel Barenboim and Edward Said: A Conversation," *Raritan* 18.1 (1998): 1–31, here 19.
6. Cf. Thomas Mann, "Bruder Hitler (1939)," in his *Essays*, vol. 4, *Achtung Europa! 1933–1938*, ed. Hermann Kurzke and Stephan Stachorski (Frankfurt/M: Fischer, 1997), 305–12. Also in Thomas Mann, *Gesammelte Werke* (Frankfurt/M: Fischer, 1960), 12:845–52.
7. Cf. Joachim Köhler, *Wagners Hitler: Der Prophet und sein Vollstrecker* (Munich: Siedler, 1999), 352.

context of Die Meistersinger. *But perhaps we should start with the first layer, the 19th century, the period of the opera's creation. How did you pick the material for* Die Meistersinger, *and why?*

You have to understand that I always read a lot of literature, and that I was drawn in particular to the authors of German Romanticism: Novalis, Heinrich Wackenroder, E. T. A. Hoffmann, Clemens Brentano, and Achim von Arnim. They nurtured my own romantic inclinations with their notions of the unmitigated genius, their sense for the quaint, and their fascination for mystery and fairy tale. I was always captivated by their mysterious and dreamlike stories. They believed in the higher power of poetic truth. Above all, they helped rediscover the values of the Middle Ages, a period that had been all but forgotten.

Especially during the Age of Reason or the period of Enlightenment the Middle Ages were either ignored or seen as a time to ridicule.

That's right. The authors I just mentioned saw medieval times not as outdated or inferior compared to modern times. Instead they discovered that in those distant times concepts like *Treue* (loyalty), simplicity, and the sacredness of wonders had a real meaning. Above all, they thought of those times as being more poetic—in which people had a stronger sense of and affinity for the arts. Just think of the wonderful collection of songs, *Des Knaben Wunderhorn,* by Brentano and von Arnim, published in 1806, the year when Napoleon occupied Prussia. These texts, together with the Wars of Liberation against Napoleon in 1813, triggered a symbiosis that became so crucial for the German mindset during the entire nineteenth century. The Wars of Liberation, where ordinary Germans joined the fight for freedom, also marks the birth of a new German identity. They desired a united land as well as the rights promised to them by the princes and the kings. But, as you probably know, these promises were broken after 1815, and so it was left to us artists, authors, and other intellectuals to keep this German spirit awake.

I assume you refer here, for example, to the brothers Grimm?

Quite right. But keep in mind, they were the two most prominent figures only because of their collection of fairy tales. Don't forget there were many more intellectuals like them hoping to keep the German spirit alive. The brothers Grimm also established *Germanistik,* the study of German language and literature dating back to the early Middle Ages. And within this context the five volumes of *Geschichte der poetischen Nationalliteratur der Deutschen* (History of Poetic National Literature of the Germans) by yet another professor, Georg Gottfried Gervinus, became most influential.

His history of German literature wasn't a dry academic book with a lot of facts in it but was for all those people like me who were concerned about the German nation.[8] All this taught us to cherish the treasures of older German literature especially in times of political oppression or instability. As you and your readers are fully aware, most of my themes, motifs, and ideas derive from medieval texts: *Lohengrin, Tannhäuser, Der Ring des Nibelungen, Tristan und Isolde,* and *Parsifal.*

But Die Meistersinger *is not set in the Middle Ages. How come you chose the early modern period?*

Here again, Gervinus was quite influential because, like me, he valued true German folk arts.

Indeed. I recall that he "rejected the exclusive aristocratic literature of the so-called high medieval times . . . and welcomed the breakthrough to the folk literature of the sixteenth century."[9] I suspect this refers to authors like Hans Sachs and the mastersingers.

Exactly.

However, you also departed quite strongly from Gervinus's approach when using aristocratic literature such as Tristan *by Gottfried von Straßburg and* Parzival *by Wolfram von Eschenbach.*

I never was a slave to anyone or any single idea. I thought you knew this.

Of course. Anyway, what prompted you to look into Hans Sachs and the mastersingers?

Didn't I already address this in *My Life*?

Let me see.

Why not quote me again instead of forcing me to retell everything that is already documented?

Well, sure. I wish you were a bit more patient. I only thought that . . .

Just read it and don't be so timid. By the way, I am not the only one who despises this bookish self-righteousness.

---

8. Jost Hermand, *Geschichte der Germanistik* (Reinbek: Rowohlt, 1994), 44.
9. Ibid., 44.

Sure, you are right. Okay. You wrote: "My first idea was to undertake a thorough study of Grimm's polemic on the masters' way of singing, Über den altdeutschen Meistergesang *(About the Old German Mastersong) (1811); then I had to get hold of old Wagenseil's* Chronicle of Nuremberg . . ."[10]

See, there you have it. Now it all comes back to me. Wagenseil was a professor in Altdorf, close to Nuremberg. In his chronicle he added an essay titled "Von der Meister-Singer holdseligen Kunst" (Concerning the Mastersingers' Delightful Art). This title was already familiar to me since, as a boy, I had read E. T. A. Hoffmann's wonderful short stories "Der Kampf der Sänger" and "Meister Martin, der Küfner, und seine Gesellen" from his collection, *Die Serapionsbrüder* (1819/1821).[11] In "Der Kampf der Sänger," you find, for example, the whole idea of the mastersingers gathering at the Wartburg that became so important for *Tannhäuser.*

Forgive me for being bookish again, but please let me quote for our readers the beginning of "Der Kampf der Sänger": "At the season when spring and winter part company, on the night of the equinox, a man sat in his lonely chamber with Johann Christoph Wagenseil's book, Von der Meistersinger holdseliger Kunst, *open before him."*[12]

That's right. That's just like me with all my books from the Imperial library in Vienna, when . . .

Indeed. As you stated in your autobiography: "I sat down eagerly in my hotel and appropriated excerpts from the Chronicle, which I soon used in my libretto in a manner that astonished those who knew nothing on the subject."[13]

I really don't like to be interrupted!

Excuse me. But you just insisted that I use your own published texts when appropriate!

I did? Keep going, please.

Anyway, I think there are two important aspects to that quote.

---

10. Wagner, *My Life*, 668.
11. Gregor-Dellin, *Richard Wagner*, 37–38.
12. E. T. A. Hoffmann, *Poetische Werke* (Berlin: Walter de Gruyter, 1957), 6:19.
13. Wagner, *My Life*, 668.

What do you mean?

First, that your friends were unaware of Hans Sachs and of the mastersinger tradition, in particular.

Without my opera this wonderful tradition of truly popular, I mean non-commercial, art from and for the people would still be forgotten or unknown.

Even if you criticize me again for my Beckmesserness, I would like to remind you that Albert Lortzing wrote his opera Hans Sachs *based on a play by Johann Ludwig Deinhardstein before you had started on* Die Meistersinger, *and Wackenroder . . .*

For heaven's sake. You are really an egghead. The point is: How often is Lortzing's opera performed today? You see, there is a reason why no one cares about Lortzing, and why I completely forgot about him. Please get it into your head that, without my work, no one would be aware of the wonderful tradition of the mastersingers.

You're probably right on that one.

What do you mean "probably"? I am completely right!

Okay. Second, you mentioned that you "appropriated" your material, your historical sources. I would like to stay on this topic for while, i.e., how you dealt with your material and stories.

Only, if you don't continue to be so academic about it.

I'll try my best, Mr. Wagner. As far as I can tell, you neither studied the life of Hans Sachs nor read any of his dozens of plays or his thousands of Meistergesänge, *or his many poems and proverbs, or . . .*

Keep in mind, not all of them were published at that time, just one worthwhile anthology existed, if I remember correctly. But you probably know that better than I do.

What do you mean "probably"? Just kidding: you mean the anthology by Büsching, published between 1816 and 1824?

Whatever. What are you getting at, anyway? I was an artist, not a nerdy historian.

That's my point. On the one hand, you try to create in your opera a Nuremberg that is supposed to look like the sixteenth century, and at the same time you take a lot of liberty with historical truth. For example, you ignore the long-standing political conflict between the city and the rulers of the surrounding territory, the so-called Markgrafen. *Indeed the only aristocrat, Walther von Stolzing, seems all too easily accepted by the oligarchy, i.e., the city council represented by Pogner and Sixtus Beckmesser. Contrary to expectation, the noble outsider is greeted by the bourgeois elite of Nuremberg, a fairy-tale scenario more than a reflection of political or economic reality in Nuremberg. You also ignore class conflicts among the diverse social groups within Nuremberg. Nor is there any mention of Hans Sachs as the author of rather obscene or racy carnival plays. No mention either of Nuremberg's great tradition of sculpture and painting, above all of Sachs's contemporary Albrecht Dürer.*

Actually, Eva mentions Dürer in the first scene of act one when she compares Walther to King David.

So who's becoming pedantic now?! Aside from that minor reference, there is no mention of his art and the role of the fine arts in the city of Nuremberg. Furthermore, you portray Nuremberg at a time when its economic decline . . .

Enough! I told you I was an artist, and it was never my intention to write a historical opera about Nuremberg, nor was it my intention to become a slave to history or what you call historical truth. Just think of Friedrich Schiller. As you know, he wrote *Don Carlos, Wallenstein, Maria Stuart,* and *Wilhelm Tell,* all of them based on historical events. By the way, except for *Wallenstein,* all of these plays were used for operas! This shows you what a great German playwright he was. Anyway, even though Schiller studied and taught history, he was never submissive to mere historical facts. Of course not. He appropriated history in order to create dramatic catharsis, not for amusement and effect, but in order to present a general human conflict and in order to present a higher historical truth.[14] I was no different. The key is that for the sake of some great idea you have to disregard something that historians are after and which they call truth. I think this rather idealistic view is one of the things that makes German artists, musicians, philosophers, or writers of the last two and a half centuries so important and great. As I wrote so poignantly in one of my essays, as a German one tries to strive for "the thing one does for its own sake, for the very joy

---

14. Cf. Richard Wagner, "German Art and German Policy," in *Richard Wagner's Prose Works,* vol. 4, *Art and Politics,* trans. William Ashton Ellis (London: Paul, Trench, Trübner, 1895), 35–148, here 88–93.

of doing it [...]." On the other hand, utilitarianism "is the principle whereby a thing is done for the sake of some personal end, ulterior to the thing itself."[15] The latter I consider untypical of the German mentality.

In other words, it doesn't bother you that your Nuremberg in Die Meistersinger *is a highly constructed image of the past?*

If that term pleases you, then by all means use it. But you should not forget that by your own definition each historical representation is constructed. Not only was Grimm's essay on the *Meistersinger* or Wackenroder's image of Nuremberg quite inventive, or—to use your jargon—constructed, but my Nuremberg in *Die Meistersinger* is as much an emplotment as is the notion of historical truthfulness. The historicist's idea of showing how things truly were—as my contemporary, the highly regarded historian Leopold von Ranke claimed he was doing—and thus becoming submissive to historical factualism, is as much a false notion as assuming that I wanted to be a historian in my opera. As I said earlier, I felt close to Gervinus, who claimed he was *making* history not writing it.[16] I was first and foremost an artist who used historical material as such. Any great artist will do so. Otherwise you end up merely a realist, as someone who tries to imitate reality. Instead, all serious artists interpret the nature of things and do not become imitators of what they perceive as reality.[17]

You are, of course, drawing on a long-standing debate, going all the way back to Aristotle's Poetics, *where the distinction between literature and history is drawn and where poetic truth emerges as something higher than historical writing. If your primary goal was not to write a historical opera, one has to ask what your intentions were in composing* Die Meistersinger?

One of my intentions was to show that *Die Meistersinger* serves "as the prime of classic Humanism." Hans Sachs, in particular, resembles "the old-German mode of poetry."[18] In materialistic times like ours and those of political uncertainty, I wanted to show how art can have a truly formative effect on people.

I assume you want to say on the German people.

When I composed this opera, I had Germany and the German people in mind, no doubt about it. But one can universalize this theme nevertheless.

---

15. Ibid., 107.
16. Hermand, *Germanistik*, 45.
17. Cf. Wagner, "German Art," 82.
18. Ibid., 107.

I expressed my idealism very clearly when I wrote: "Art is the only cultivatrix of the Folk."[19]

Granted. But let's be a bit more specific about what you call political uncertainties. Do you refer here to the differences between your first draft of Die Meistersinger *and the revisions you made in Vienna and then in Paris in 1861 and 1862?*

No, not necessarily. But I am glad you mention this draft because it also proves my point about being an artist and not a historian. As you know, I always worked on my music dramas over a long period of time, and many of my works underwent frequent revisions, which I consider a normal process for any serious artist.

I have the feeling you are being too vague, too general.

What do you mean?

Why, for example, did you change the role of Hans Sachs? In the 1845 draft, he is still quite young and he, not Walther, wins the bride. In addition, the draft shows more of a revolutionary tone, less a national one.[20]

Yes, I guess, I was younger, a bit more revolutionary. It was all too easy for me to identify with Hans Sachs. Keep in mind that in 1845 the hope still existed that there might be parliamentary representation for all of Germany, meaning that the thirty-something states would have lost their sovereignty. As you might recall, the King of Prussia, Friedrich Wilhelm IV, refused to become emperor in 1849 when, although the representatives of the Frankfurt parliament asked him to become the head of a united Germany, the princes of the other German states did not. The princes did not understand the true German spirit.[21]

If you bring up the events of 1849 and this first attempt for a representational system of a united Germany, I would like to ask you about your role during the Dresden uprising. At that time, you were thirty-six, with a position as the court's music director. Not exactly a position from which to participate in revolutionary activities.

---

19. Ibid., 67.
20. Cf. Peter Uwe Hohendahl, "Reworking History: Wagner's German Myth of Nuremberg," in *Re-Reading Wagner,* ed. Reinhold Grimm and Jost Hermand (Madison: University of Wisconsin Press, 1993), 39–60, here 45–47.
21. Richard Wagner, "What is German?" in *Richard Wagner's Prose Works,* vol. 4, *Art and Politics,* trans. William Ashton Ellis (London: Paul, Trench, Trübner, 1895), 149–69, here 164.

An Interview with the Composer 133

Well put. But keep in mind, first I was nothing more than an observer at the revolt in Dresden, in May 1849.[22] Only when the fight against Prussian troops gained momentum did I decide "to surrender myself to the stream of events,"[23] and support the revolutionary forces, among them Bakhunin. However, after the bloody defeat of the revolutionaries not only in Dresden, but in all of Germany and elsewhere in Europe, I was forced to reconsider my position somewhat.

You had to go into exile for supporting the revolutionary side, i.e., fighting for a democratic, representational, and anti-aristocratic system.

Yes, a warrant for my arrest had been issued in Dresden on suspicion of participation in the revolt, and thus I could no longer count on safe asylum in any of the German federal states. My good friend Franz Liszt's recommendation was in favor of Paris, where I eventually ended up. It's all in my autobiography.[24]

A successful revolution would have meant the first unified and democratic state in Germany. Instead, it took until 1918, when the German Empire of 1871 was dismantled and the first republic, the Weimar Republic, was constituted. Did you change your position on Die Meistersinger *for political or personal reasons?*

Both. Anyway, after the defeat of 1849, and after I read the sources for *Die Meistersinger*—the ones we mentioned earlier—I modified my position on German nationhood. Now I saw that, for the German spirit, art represented the best foundation for future political change. So I retained my revolutionary position not only in art. After 1849, I was still convinced that the German aristocracy, the princes, had to change their attitude towards the German people. They had to open their heart to the German spirit. Now you can see why Walther von Stolzing is portrayed so favorably: his class needed a model of a truly new German spirit. That's why I made such a bold statement when writing: "If the German Princes are not faithful guardians of the German spirit . . . then their days are numbered."[25] Thus, the collapse of the German Reich in 1918 after the catastrophic war came as no surprise to me. It just proved my point.

By the way, did you notice how deeply involved we are in political and historical questions? The artistic freedom that you claimed over historical truth seems so linked to political ends.

---

22. Wagner, *My Life*, 390–95.
23. Ibid., 402.
24. Ibid., 415.
25. Wagner, "German Art," 42.

What do you mean by "seems"? It is. I always hoped that my art, and in particular my music drama, would rejuvenate the German spirit. In that sense, as I said earlier, I was always like Schiller who thought that art can educate the people.

But when Schiller promotes his idealistic notion of aesthetics, he is neither preoccupied with the German people nor German identity. Actually, listening to your answers, it's not Schiller but rather Heinrich Heine who comes to mind. He was also in exile in Paris. In fact, there was a whole German community of exiles there. Of course, Heine died in exile while you left Paris. Heine poems also have that political trajectory, especially Deutschland: Ein Wintermärchen *(Germany: A Winter's Tale), where he laments Germany's backwardness and political conservatism.*

Back then, when Heine had "become the father of literature," as I wrote, I had my problems with him simply because he mocked "every kind of earnest literature."[26] In contrast to him, I wanted to reawaken the holy nature of art. In particular, my concept of music drama sought to stimulate all human senses while simultaneously speaking to the mind.

Let me second this with one of your strong statements where art and politics are so intertwined. You wrote that in this fusion "lies the spiritual seed and kernel of all national-poetic and national-ethical culture, that no other art-branch can ever truly flourish, or ever aid in cultivating the Folk, until the Theater's all-powerful assistance has been completely recognized and guaranteed."[27]

Isn't this wonderful? I have no regrets writing this statement. It also explains to you that, compared to this position, Heine's irony and wittiness were in my eyes nothing but cynical and offered no way out of the misery.

Do I understand you correctly, though, that you would reevaluate your position on Heine today?

Yes, after all, it also grieved him very much that Germany lacked freedom. But first and foremost he had political freedom in mind, and I was concerned with my artistic freedom. Retrospectively, I can see that we were unified in our opposition to Prussia's brute force, and to the narrow-mindedness that was and is unfortunately so abundant—especially in Germany—but not only there.

---

26. Ibid., 68.
27. Ibid., 69.

Does your conciliatory attitude towards Heine have anything to do with your former admiration for him when you were first in Paris between 1840 and 1842?

I am glad you mention this. Yes indeed, I always admired Heine's truly literary talent and his strong romantic inclinations. As you and I know, I am indebted to him since my opera *Der fliegende Holländer* is based on his idea.[28] However, even there his tone is too witty and I wanted to make a truly passionate and romantic libretto out of his short text.

I am glad that you remember your early admiration for him. Your rejection of him in later years is linked to your anti-Jewish feelings and your outspoken anti-Semitism. Is that right?

Let me state quite clearly, that I am not trying to shy away from my former resentment against some Jews.

Well, you couldn't even if you tried.

Please don't interrupt me again; especially not on this important point. As I wrote earlier, I clearly thought that "the Jew set right this bungling of the German's, by taking German intellectual labor into his own hands." I thought that we had to stop this "travesty of the German spirit" before the nation really took "this simulacrum for its mirrored image" and that "we have to inquire how to save it from such a shameful doom."[29] Back then I really thought that "the German Princes supplied the misunderstandings, the Jews exploited" them financially.[30] As you see, I am still aware of my published essays which show my all too passionate political engagement. I do wish I could annul these writings but I know that I cannot erase my published statements. That is my real personal tragedy. I am aware that I am cursed because of them, excluded from salvation like Tannhäuser or Kundry . . .

. . . or the Flying Dutchman . . .

. . . However . . . however, I want to make absolutely clear that my music dramas themselves have nothing in common with my written assertions. You will not find anything against Jews in my works. Jews were and still

---

28. Cf. Heinrich Heine, *Aus den Memoiren des Herren Schabelewopski* (1822–1826), in his *Werke*, vol. 2, ed. Helmut Holtzhauer (Berlin: Aufbau, 1974), 281–339.
29. Wagner, "What is German?" 159.
30. Ibid., 158.

are some of my very best interpreters as you know very well. You mentioned earlier Daniel Barenboim. He and James Levine—some of the best conductors of my music dramas today—are vocal in their unrestricted devotion. Do you assume that they are stupid or naive?

Of course not! Nor is it my intention to embarrass you personally. But at the same time, your defense seems weak when I think, for example, of the ending of Die Meistersinger. *To advocate the notion of a "genuine" German art is one thing, but it is quite different to be racially exclusive, especially in light of twentieth-century German history. I am thinking of the final chorus of* Die Meistersinger:

> Habt Acht! Uns dräuen üble Streich'!
> Zerfällt erst deutsches Volk und Reich,
> in falscher welscher Majestät
> kein Fürst bald mehr sein Volk versteht;
> und welschen Dunst mit welschem Tand
> sie pflanzen uns in deutsches Land;
> Was deutsch und echt, wüßt' keiner mehr,
> lebt's nicht in deutscher Meister Ehr'." (III, 5)

You said "in light of twentieth-century German history." I think it is unfair to use this passage that I wrote in the 1860s and then connect it to Hitler's barbaric racial politics between 1933 and 1945. That I was against Jews at times is something that I unfortunately cannot deny. But you have to put my essays into the historical context for which you have so strongly argued. Take for example my essay *Judaism in Music* from 1850. I published it anonymously because I did not want to be known for being against Jews. After all I was a revolutionary in exile and it could have hurt my fragile position. This essay was simply motivated by my jealousy and hatred of Meyerbeer's success. At that time I still had to fight hard to have my genius fully recognized.

Why then did you decide to republish the essay in 1869 this time with your name, an essay so full of hideous arguments?

I see you are trying to corner me like so many others. But let me tell you, I think it was a mistake, and I should have listened to Cosima who feared that my polemic against Jews and my belief in a Jewish conspiracy would hurt my reputation. That's why I didn't include it in the 1871 edition of my collected works.[31] After all, not only were some of my dear friends like Herrmann Levi, Karl Tausig, or Joseph Rubinstein Jewish but, even more

---

31. Cf. Jacob Katz, *The Darker Side of Genius: Richard Wagner's Anti-Semitism* (Hanover, N.H.: University Press of New England, 1986), 71.

importantly, so many in my audience were Jewish. In fact "Jews were included in the foremost ranks" of my "followers in the battle" over my "direction of art,"[32] for which I was and still am very thankful.

That's what some of your defenders always do, mention your Jewish friends. That always seems to me like a very cheap maneuver and an attempt to hide your deep resentment against Jews.

It might look cheap to you, but it is true that my anti-Jewish sentiments, which, by the way, were quite common in Germany, did not stop me from appreciating . . .

. . . those who helped your career.

I think you go too far here and don't understand the times I lived in. I thought you are an honest scholar who tries to look objectively at all sides within the historical context.

How is it that you are suddenly so concerned with the historical context?

Because some people try to drag my art through the mud because of the deep seated fears against a Jewish conspiracy that I once had. Do people actually know, for example, that I managed to prevent my name from being used for the anti-Semitic movement that started around 1879?

Yes, I am aware of it. At home you were anti-Semitic for ideological reasons,[33] and beyond Wahnfried *you distanced yourself from the growing movement for opportunistic reasons. You had and still have strong support from Jews as you mentioned just a while ago. Is this how you try to deal with the radicalized and extremist anti-Semitism of Nazi politics?*

Well, keep in mind that in *Wahnfried* I also had dear Jewish friends! But I don't want to use this reminder to escape your criticism. I am painfully aware that I cannot expect any full acquittal in light of this barbaric Hitler, simply because of the anti-Jewish statements I unfortunately published.[34] At the same time it is nonsense to assume that I promoted his kind of despotic politics with my art. It is too simplistic to reinterpret everything I said or wrote because of the way Hitler and his Nazis adopted and misused my art.

---

32. Cf. ibid., 68.
33. Cf. ibid., 114.
34. Cf. ibid., 132.

You might call it unfortunate that of all people Hitler turned out to be one of the most devout followers of your art. But I don't find it merely coincidental that he called Die Meistersinger *"our true German Folk Opera," and used Nuremberg of all places for his party rallies and his racial laws in 1935. Nor is it a coincidence that he gave the order that same year for the* Festwiese *in the final scene to be recognized as the location for his party rallies. Talk about the virtual becoming real: the Nazi reality imitated not only art but imitated your fabricated historical image.*[35]

The fact that this scoundrel Hitler thought he understood my art shows you one thing and one thing only: he didn't understand how to distinguish between art and politics. He was a lunatic, and it is scandalous to blame me for this crazy man's policies. Let me be very clear: his dictatorial German state is not at all what I had in mind when working on *Die Meistersinger* or when I spoke of German greatness.

But the fact remains that your music dramas, together with your statements, made it all too easy for the art to be misused.

I admit that in light of the political tragedy in and of Germany during the first half of the twentieth century, my writings can all too easily be mistaken. However, judge me by my deeds, and above all by my musical works that have survived all of this political mess and misinterpretation. The popularity of my music is in and of itself a triumph of the arts, just as Walther's artistic freedom overcomes the masteringers' narrow-mindedness.

I understand that you would like to step out of Hitler's shadow by drawing a distinction between your political writings and your music dramas. However, you are the one who outspokenly interlocked them, not I. Look at the quote I mentioned earlier about "creating a national culture and cultivating the Folk by creating a new totality of music drama." If this is not clear advocacy for the fusion of art and politics then what is? In fact, this is the quintessential definition of what historian Friedrich Meinecke termed "Kulturnation," a nation united by culture and not by political constitution.[36]

Well, that was very much the mood in Germany in the nineteenth century. I was by no means the only one who thought along these lines. But once again let me be very clear. My writings are one thing and my artistic work another. Of course I wouldn't say today what I wrote back then. I want to

---

35. Cf. Köhler, *Wagners Hitler*, 352–54, 381.
36. Friedrich Meinecke, *Weltbürgertum und Nationalstaat*. In his *Werke*, vol. 5, ed. Hans Herzfeld (Munich: Oldenburg, 1962), 23.

be judged by my music and nothing else. And let me point out to you: I am and will be judged by my music only. Look at what someone like the wonderful and Jewish conductor Daniel Barenboim has to say about my works! You quoted him earlier.

Okay. If you only want to be judged by your works then let's return to Die Meistersinger. *There again you find this fusion of art and politics.*

Yes, indeed. But you quoted the last lines of the chorus at the beginning:

> Ehrt eure deutschen Meister,
> dann bannt ihr gute Geister!
> Und gebt ihr ihrem Wirken Gunst,
> zerging' in Dunst
> das Heil'ge Röm'sche Reich,
> uns bliebe gleich
> die heil'ge deutsche Kunst! (III, 5)

Now, however much you want to criticize me, it should at least be clear that these lines are unbelievably prophetic, especially in light of the events of the twentieth century. Let me explain: The Third Reich is long gone but my music survived and is still a testimony to the greatest German spirit.

Point taken, Mr. Wagner. However, I would also argue that your music dramas have many layers of meaning including racial politics, however latent.[37] Let me quote a highly respected colleague, Edward Said. In regard to the final act of Die Meistersinger, *he writes that:*

> there is a transformation, first of all, from the domestic world, the cobblers, the streets of Nuremberg . . . to this vast official gathering-place where the Meistersingers and the townsfolk all get together and it is a rally of some sort. In addition, Sachs is proclaimed as the great figure for the city . . . what he's really saying is that once one acknowledges the presence of something new and gifted like Stolzing, there is nevertheless the need to follow, and the collective is, in a sense, most important. Finally, there's the idea of the outside as threatening: there's a kind of xenophobic quality to it, *in* the opera . . . which is troubling.[38]

As I told you before, there was a strong movement in German society that thought German art could lead the way to the creation of a national identity. There was nothing wrong with this idea of "Kulturnation." It was

---

37. Cf. *Richard Wagner and the Anti-Semitic Imagination*, 13, 359.
38. "Daniel Barenboim and Edward Said," 21.

quite normal in the second half of the nineteenth century to refer to one's national identity and to seek out its strength. The French did it, the British did it, and eventually so did the Germans.

But the British and French identified themselves through their constitution and political strength, not through their culture. Besides, there is a difference between national identity and strength on the one hand, and imperialist or chauvinistic politics on the other.

If you insist on distinguishing between "Kulturnation" and "Staatsnation" then you should also be fair and mention how chauvinistic the British and French were!

I just implied that. However, that doesn't excuse your exclusion of an ethnic group whom you wanted to prevent from enjoying the same rights as other Germans. After all, the Jews didn't receive the same full civil rights until 1871. In this context Cosima's remark is striking, to say the least. She wrote in her diary that when visiting Nuremberg in 1877, you were in a Meistersinger *mood except when you were in the Hans Sachs square and remarked that the synagogue visible there was so "ostentatious."*[39] *Doesn't this reflect your anti-Jewish sentiments all too well?*

I didn't mind the synagogue at all. Besides, it was a mistake to have Cosima's diary published. It said so many things that were not worthwhile writing down. I want to be judged only on my music dramas. I was an artist and put my art before politics, even when I was concerned about German identity. I simply referred to the very meaning of *Deutsche* (Germans) as "those Germanic races which, upon their natal soil, retained their speech and customs."[40] Today, you call it ethnic and/or cultural identity. The fact that the Nazis established their tyrannical racial dictatorship in Germany and elsewhere in Europe does not mean that the question of cultural identity is gone or will go away.

I did not and do not want to imply that. However, the problem is that in Die Meistersinger *you favor a kind of national identity based on exclusion and thus you promote the specter of at least ethnic if not racial purity.*

You are as stubborn as I am. The phrases you use to argue against me and my political point of view from the 1860s emphasize the power of art. Look, this opera is set in the early sixteenth century, when the Holy Roman

---

39. Cf. Katz, *Darker Side*, 109.
40. Wagner, "What is German?" 159.

Empire was already more a fiction or farce than reality. When I chose this topic in the nineteenth century it was to show that what really matters is the belief in the power of art to provide a national identity that truly unites a people.

Funny, now it is you who returns to cultural politics and not I.

But only to say, one more time, that the text reads that even if the Holy Roman Empire disappears what will be left is art. And the whole discussion of my artistic work proves this! Just look at this debate you mentioned earlier between the wonderful artist Mr. Barenboim and this scholar . . .

. . . Edward Said . . .

Whoever. Their conversation and other such debates . . .

Are you referring to the one between Marc Weiner and Hans Vaget?

These names mean nothing to me; you should know by now that I don't like to be interrupted. In any case all these scholarly debates show time and again that art in the long run overrides any politics. Otherwise, why have these debates at all about my genius?

I assumed that sooner or later we would disagree or would not be able to resolve the thorny issue of your underlying xenophobia. And maybe we should leave it up to the reader whether the historical context of nineteenth-century European nationalism absolves you of the strident nationalism within Die Meistersinger.

Look, it was not my intention, either back then or today, to write what people like you would probably call a "politically correct" opera. You might know, for example, that the Prussian court refused my ideas to write appropriate music after the Franco-Prussian War because they still regarded me as a revolutionary from 1848![41] That's how difficult it was for me to promote my concept of cultural politics! Painful as that was, I did not alter my position. When I look at *Die Meistersinger* today, I think of it in two ways. First, the opera indeed meets at the intersection of many different historical moments in German history, some aspects of which we have discussed. But in spite of your attempt to slander me with its politically questionable content, the opera is also proof of the very statement made, i.e.,

---

41. Ibid., 168.

that art in and of itself is above and beyond political rancor. How could you otherwise explain that this opera is still of interest in Germany and in other parts of the world?

I could agree on that, if I were allowed to invert the order of your thinking. If I can sum up by referring to Hans Mayer: A politically dubious piece like Die Meistersinger *can be autonomous only to the extent that it does not shy away from its manifold contradictions. As long as the Nuremberg of the opera reflects the political and economic tensions of the sixteenth century, and as long as this Nuremberg does reflect somehow the Nuremberg of the Nazis, only then can one begin honoring this art as an autonomous entity.*[42] *Only then can one honor the master who created the opera.*

D'accord.

Ignoring these aspects in a production of Die Meistersinger *would turn it into a folkloristic and naive Nuremberg or, worse still, kitsch. And as far as I know, you never were a friend of kitsch, however close you sometimes get.*

You open a whole new topic. Why don't we leave it for now. It seems you are not only as stubborn as I, but also as self-righteous. I also think that that this will be my first and last interview.

Somehow, I doubt it.

---

42. Hans Mayer, *Anmerkungen zu Richard Wagner* (Frankfurt/M: Suhrkamp, 1966), 82, 86.

Part III

Representation and/in Die Meistersinger

8

Die Meistersinger as Comedy: The Performative and Social Signification of Genre

Klaus van den Berg

Nothing is really serious without humor.
—Heiner Müller

I. *Die Meistersinger* and the Question of Genre

The chapter titled "Meistersinger-Staat" in Joachim Köhler's controversial book *Wagner's Hitler* examines how Nazi ideologues appropriated and enlarged upon the utopian potential embedded in Wagner's comic opera *Die Meistersinger von Nürnberg* by exploiting its material to turn public occasions such as party rallies into cultural performances.[1] Notwithstanding the grand sweep of *Der Ring des Nibelungen*, the revolutionary musical power of *Tristan and Isolde*, and the mysticism of *Parsifal*, Köhler insists that it was the utopian vision of *Meistersinger* as comedy that most inspired Hitler and the Nazis to make it the centerpiece of their social and cultural thinking.[2] This appropriation seems curiously anticipated—given his Marxist leanings—by Ernst Bloch, who contended that the "happy ending" of the comic genre, although perhaps the result of intrigue, deceit, and illusion, nevertheless had the power to release forces that would move society in a utopian direction.[3] The following will explore the ways in which

---

1. Joachim Köhler, *Wagners Hitler: Der Prophet und sein Vollstrecker* (Munich: Blessing Verlag, 1997); in English as *Wagner's Hitler: The Prophet and his Disciple*, trans. Ronald Taylor (Malden, Mass.: Blackwell Publishers, 2000).
2. Köhler produces a wealth of evidence of how Hitler and his circle used allusions to *Die Meistersinger* at many private and public occasions.
3. Ernst Bloch, *Das Prinzip Hoffnung* (Frankfurt a.M.: Suhrkamp, 1959) 514–15.

the dynamics of comedy infuse *Die Meistersinger* with a cultural and social potential at once so useful to the Nazis and troubling to later scholars.

Richard Wagner is rarely considered in terms of "comedy" or "humor" and, although originally conceived as a "satyr play" to his opera *Tannhäuser,* by the time of its premiere in 1868, *Die Meistersinger von Nürnberg* had evolved into a substantially more sophisticated work with decidedly "serious" content. This evolution is reflected in the change in Wagner's description of the genre from "Komische Oper" and "Große komische Oper" in the prose drafts to simply "Oper" in the final version. An early review by Eduard Hanslick of a production at the Vienna State Opera in 1870 complained that Wagner's talents as a writer were "inadequate, particularly with respect to humor."[4] Hanslick was even harsher about the comic qualities of the music, calling it "stilted, profuse, even repulsive."[5] More recently, Carl Dahlhaus noted that *Die Meistersinger* "is the brainchild of an untrustworthy sense of humor."[6] It seems few would agree with Martin Gregor-Dellin who labeled *Die Meistersinger* "the richest and wittiest libretto in the whole world of opera," a view strongly challenged by Martin von Amerongen.[7]

Contemporary critics and audiences, especially in the wake of studies by Theodor W. Adorno, Marc Weiner, and David Levin,[8] have been confronted by claims that the work is riddled with an anti-Semitic subtext that further inhibits acceptance of the opera as a comedy. This problem is only intensified when coupled with the history of the work's performance and reception during the Nazi era, reports that Hitler viewed *Die Meistersinger* as both the model "deutsche Volksoper" and the quintessential "komische Oper,"[9] not to mention Köhler's claims of troubling similarities between

---

4. Eduard Hanslick, "*Die Meistersinger* von Richard Wagner," in *Die moderne Oper: Kritiken und Studien* (Berlin: Hofmann, 1875); reprinted as *Collected Musical Criticism of Eduard Hanslick,* vol. 1 (Westmead: Gregg International, 1971), 300; also cited in Charles Osborne, *The Complete Operas of Richard Wagner* (London: Mara Books, 1996), 161.

5. Hanslick, "*Die Meistersinger* von Richard Wagner," 301; Osborne, *The Complete Operas,* 162.

6. Carl Dahlhaus, *Richard Wagner's Music Dramas,* trans. Mary Whittall (Cambridge: Cambridge University Press, 1979), 65.

7. Martin von Amerongen, *Wagner: A Case History,* trans. Stewart Spencer and Dominic Cakebread (London: Dent, 1983), 71. Amerongen refers to Gregor-Dellin without citing a source; the quote could not be independently verified.

8. Theodor W. Adorno, *Versuch über Wagner* (Frankfurt /M.: Suhrkamp, 1974); Marc Weiner, "Reading the Ideal," *New German Critique* 69 (1996): 53–84; David J. Levin, "Reading Beckmesser Reading: Antisemitism and Aesthetic Practice in *The Mastersingers of Nuremberg,*" *New German Critique* 69 (1996): 127–46.

9. Köhler, *Wagners Hitler,* 416. Theodor W. Adorno characterized Wagner's humor as "cruel" and considered Shakespeare's Malvolio and Shylock as models for Beckmesser: Adorno, *Versuch über Wagner,* 17.

the Nazis' and Wagner's "murderous humor."[10] If laughter depends on "how we remember,"[11] laughter in *Die Meistersinger* arises from a kind of remembering which seems morally untenable today.

Despite the fact that the genre classification of *Die Meistersinger* remains an unsettled and unsettling issue, there has been little effort to address the question despite the impressive amount of scholarship devoted to the work. Dieter Borchmeyer considers *Meistersinger* to be a comedy as part of his overall strategy of sealing off Wagner's music dramas from the anti-Semitism in his "unrelated" essays.[12] Borchmeyer rejects the notion that Beckmesser is a Jewish caricature by creating a forced syllogism: he places Beckmesser within the traditions of the "learned pedant" of European comedy and the *dottore* in the *commedia dell'arte,* and draws the conclusion that if Wagner were pursuing a "witch-hunt against intellectuals . . . we must therefore [. . .] regard every comedy of intrigue ever written as representing part of a pogrom against the Jews."[13]

In the following analysis of *Die Meistersinger,* however, I argue that the comic discourse of the work cannot be fully grasped without acknowledging its implied anti-Semitism or at least taking it into account, and that, conversely, the effectiveness of the work's anti-Semitism cannot be fully grasped without reference to its comic discourse. Comic discourse can be defined as the complex dynamic that occurs among various elements of a work and its context, meaning the comic situation and character constellations, the social and political vision implied by the victorious character or group of characters, expectations created by performance traditions and historical conventions, and the manner with which the audience becomes inscribed into the dramatic action. Unlike Borchmeyer, who derives his conception of comedy from a narrow eighteenth-century paradigm using the theories of Lessing and Schiller, I examine Wagner's *Meistersinger* by looking at it against historical paradigms of comedic conventions stretching back to Greek antiquity combined with consideration of the social nature of comedy. The notion of comedy as an expression of social values has

---

10. For example, Köhler shows how one of Wagner's anti-Semitic comments resurfaces as pure hate in Nazi ideology. In 1878, according to a conversation reported by Nietzsche, Wagner said "there are fleas and there are bugs. All right—they are there. But we fumigate them. And the people who don't are dirty pigs," Köhler, *Wagner's Hitler,* 294.

11. Herbert Blau, *The Eye of Prey: Subversions of the Postmodern* (Bloomington: Indiana University Press, 1987), 39. This is particularly reflected in the debate between those who advocate perceiving Beckmesser as a Jewish caricature and those who consider this interpretation as "eccentric." See, for example, Dieter Borchmeyer, *Richard Wagner: Theory and Theatre,* trans. Stewart Spencer (Oxford: Clarendon Press, 1991), 271.

12. Borchmeyer, *Richard Wagner,* 404–10.

13. Ibid., 272.

been developed by a number of twentieth-century theorists beginning with Sigmund Freud, who considered comedy as an unintentional discovery of human social relations, arguing that comedy may be a defense against the enemy and a victorious assault on him.[14] Similarly, in his celebrated essay on comedy, Henri Bergson argued that laughter has "a social signification."[15] Laughter is a group phenomenon inviting complicity and transforming theatrical actions into "social gesture[s]."[16] The social dimension of laughter is important in our investigation of Wagner's work, because comedy thus becomes a means of expressing dissatisfaction with or anxiety about social circumstances. According to Bergson, there are two essential situations of comedy: "unsociability in the performer and insensibility in the spectator."[17] What I will call the (mal)function of laughter plays out at the conclusion of *Die Meistersinger* with devastatingly cruel consequences.

Approaching this study from the more formal question of "genre," I will make reference to Roland Barthes's argument that genres are not fixed, but instead should be understood as loose sets of conventions which author and audience constantly renegotiate. Only through a negotiation between the author's manipulation of traditional conventions and the audience's social and cultural expectations do genres become intelligible. The typology of literature depends on the rereading or rewriting of texts, so Barthes envisions the text (also the audience, as I will argue) as a "multidimensional space in which a variety of writings, none of them original, blend and clash."[18] Barthes describes the reader—and by extension I would argue, the audience—as the "total existence of writing." A text's unity lies not in the origin of the text—for example, in the author's intention or in the strategies the author uses to create the text as an independent work of art—but in its destination, i.e., the reader or the audience.[19] If comedy is a socially negotiated construct, attitudes and values—ways of remembering—become clear through the author's manipulation of certain conventions. Appreciating how Wagner "manipulates" and deviates from standard comedic conventions and structures is vital in deriving a clearer conception of the social signification of the opera. Below I focus on two aspects of the comic discourse in *Die Meistersinger*: first, the social and cultural implica-

---

14. See Sigmund Freud, "Jokes and the Comic," in *Jokes and Their Relation to the Unconscious,* ed. and trans. James Strachery (New York: Norton and Routledge & Kegan Paul, 1960), 188–221.

15. Henri Bergson, "Laughter," in *Comedy,* ed. Wylie Sypher (New York: Doubleday, 1956), 61–190, here 65.

16. Ibid., 78.

17. Ibid., 155.

18. Roland Barthes, "The Death of the Author," in *Image, Music, Text,* trans. Stephen Heath (New York: Hill and Wang, 1977), 142–48, here 146. See also Roland Barthes, *S/Z,* trans. Richard Miller (New York: Hill and Wang, 1974), 3–4, 11–16.

19. Barthes, "The Death of the Author," 148.

tions of Wagner's scripting of the action, and second, Wagner's use of the theatrical tableau as a device for conveying a troubling social agenda, specifically in the finale of act two. There is also a musical dimension to this issue which I cannot explore here, but which Dahlhaus has addressed in terms of the orchestra's dramatic moments, exits, entrances, and critical commentary; this orchestral commentary not only facilitates the performative power of the comedy but also plays a primary role in the construction of the tableaux.[20] Ultimately, I argue that comedy in *Die Meistersinger* is a mode of performance, a "structured experience," which constructs and conveys meaning and gives expression and form to specific values and beliefs.[21]

II. Wagner's "Renegotiation" of Comedic Conventions

Northrop Frye's model of comic discourse, read as social and ritualistic action, is particularly useful for a genre analysis of *Die Meistersinger*. Rather than focusing on what have traditionally been considered the defining aspects of comedy, such as themes or character types, Frye analyzes how comic perspective is achieved by shaping situations, observing that the plot structure of comedy from Roman theatre to the twentieth century is "less a form than a formula."[22] This comic formula he describes as follows: "What normally happens is that a young man wants a young woman, that his desire is resisted by some opposition, usually paternal, and near the end of the play some twist in the plot enables the hero to have his will."[23] Despite their different approaches, there is a connection here between Frye and Barthes in that both stress the looseness and pliability of the convention, especially given that the social signification of comic action emerges in what Frye calls its "complex elements."[24] The first complex element is that the plot moves from one social center to another: at the beginning, the

---

20. Dahlhaus, *Richard Wagner's Music Dramas*, 75. Dahlhaus contends that Wagner's style in *Die Meistersinger* depends on "the infusion of archaism in modernity" (73, 75–79). This musical treatment echoes the manipulation of comic strategies by Wagner that I will discuss.

21. The notion of performance played out as a social drama was initially developed by Victor Turner in his essay "Frame, Flow, and Reflection: Ritual and Drama as Public Liminality," in *Performance in Postmodern Culture*, ed. Michel Benamou and Charles Caramello (Madison, Wisc.: Coda Press, 1977): 19–32.

22. Northrop Frye, *Anatomy of Criticism* (Princeton, N.J.: Princeton University Press, 1957), 163. See also Robert Corrigan, ed. *Comedy: Meaning and Form,* 2nd ed. (New York: Harper and Row, 1981), 7.

23. Frye, *Anatomy,* 163. Erich Segal has shown how the pimp sometimes takes the place of the father as blocking agent in Roman comedy since he is the guardian of the woman the comic hero desires. Erich Segal, *Roman Laughter* (Cambridge, Mass.: Harvard University Press, 1968), 79–84.

24. Frye, *Anatomy,* 163.

obstructing character(s) and their questionable values—the target for laughter—are socially or politically dominant. The comic hero, often with the help of a clever servant or friend, effects a change from one social center to the other, and this change is marked by a festival celebrating a marriage or some other formal ceremony in which the hero's new values become dominant. The second complex element is the retarding or hindering force, an impostor, a disguise, or a misunderstanding that threatens to thwart the hero's intentions. The ascension of the new value, represented by the hero's victory, is achieved by public exposure of the impostor(s) at the drama's climax. The new value is generally presented via the happy ending in a final tableau, which presents the dynamics of the new order.

It is, I would argue, instantly apparent that these basic plot devices are applicable to the dramatic structure of *Die Meistersinger,* but this does not diminish the legitimate debate concerning the content and focus of the gestures inscribed into the action of the opera. For example, Martin von Amerongen and Carl Dahlhaus read *Die Meistersinger* narrowly as a commentary on Wagner's musical politics: Beckmesser here is a representation of Eduard Hanslick, and Hans Sachs a romantically idealized synthesis of natural creativity and normative poetics.[25] By contrast, Peter Uwe Hohendahl considers the opera in terms of nineteenth-century German nationalism and, in the wake of Adorno, there have been a series of readings which argue the existence of an anti-Semitic agenda.[26] However, a dramaturgical analysis of Wagner's plot pattern using Frye's formula of comic performance provides additional perspective concerning the inscription of cultural values into the opera's fabric, especially in terms of (nineteenth-century) audience expectations. The opera's basic plot, which remained consistent through the numerous drafts, may be summarized as follows: the knight Walther von Stolzing, in the earliest draft called simply "a young man," comes to Nürnberg to participate in the Mastersingers guild. He falls in love with Eva, daughter of the respected Veit Pogner. The young man may marry her if he can win her approval in a public song contest. The primary obstacle to their union is Beckmesser—in the first draft simply called the Marker, later renamed Hanslich after Eduard Hanslick—who also has designs on Eva and thereby threatens the couple's union. However, through the schemes of Hans Sachs, who, in the earliest version, is not highly developed, the young man participates in the contest, ultimately winning the heart of the bride and the blessing of the whole town, which collectively demands the happy ending.[27]

---

25. Amerongen, *Wagner,* 72; Dahlhaus, *Richard Wagner's Music Dramas,* 69.

26. For overview see the Introduction to this volume as well as Hans Vaget's chapter on the Beckmesser debate.

27. For a detailed discussion of how Wagner's conception of *Die Meistersinger* changed over two decades, see Richard Turner, "Wagner's *Die Meistersinger*: the

Taking Frye's model as our starting point, the completed opera indicates that Wagner was confronted with two dramaturgical tasks: first, to establish the dominant social center at the beginning and, second, to transform his potentially insubstantial—even farcical—initial conception into a sophisticated comedy, with complex characters engaged in important aesthetic conflicts out of which a regenerated cultural order could emerge. As Hohendahl has shown, Wagner does indeed establish the social structures of his mythic Nürnberg: a harmonious society where the mastersingers were significant cultural leaders, a construction which of course deviates substantially from historical fact.[28] As we know, Wagner's cultural vision of Nürnberg draws on a variety of nineteenth-century German historical, political, and artistic sources, and is a cultural construction which, as Hohendahl argues, "position(s) Wagner within the development of the Nuremberg myth, which found its final articulation in the *Parteitage* of the 1930s."[29] From a strictly political perspective, Wagner's multi-dimensional yet sanitized image of Nürnberg was remarkably appealing to conservative and liberal readers alike.[30] Thus, while the world Wagner presents in *Die Meistersinger* appears to be the most "realistic" amongst his oeuvre, his Nürnberg is nevertheless a utopia with art at the center of its social order. It is, moreover, a highly calculated utopian image using stage effects designed to impress and engage audiences of his own time and, evidently, well into the future.[31]

But, despite its debt to nineteenth-century German fantasies, Wagner's Nürnberg is populated with slightly modified versions of character constellations traditional to comic discourse, a tradition including Shakespeare, Molière, and Goldoni as well as contemporaries like Scribe and Sardou, with which Wagner's audiences would have been familiar. My point is not only to stress how deep and broad Wagner's borrowings were but, from

---

Conceptual Growth of an Opera," in *Wagner 1976: A Celebration of the Bayreuth Festival* (London: The Wagner Society London, 1976), 83–97.

28. Peter Uwe Hohendahl, "Reworking History: Wagner's German Myth of Nuremberg," in *Re-Reading Wagner*, ed. Reinhold Grimm and Jost Hermand (Madison: University of Wisconsin Press, 1993), 49.

29. Ibid., 42.

30. Ibid., 56. This political ambiguity actually lends *Die Meistersinger* some subversive power, but may also have provided critical space for the Nazi appropriation of the work. For a discussion of how "conservative" comedies can nevertheless be "subversive"; see the analysis of *A Midsummer Night's Dream* in Louis Montrose, *The Purpose of Playing* (Chicago: University of Chicago Press, 1996), 109–205.

31. So effective that even the reformer of modernist stage space, Adolphe Appia, who reconceptualized *Parsifal* and the *Ring*, did not seek new visualizations for Wagner's detailed descriptions of scenes in *Die Meistersinger*. See Frederic Spotts, *Bayreuth: A History of the Wagner Festival* (New Haven: Yale University Press, 1996).

the point of "reception," that his contemporary audience would have been sensitive to this traditional discourse and to Wagner's modifications to it and deviations from it, thereby understanding the social implications embedded in such change.

One important alteration concerns the replacement of traditional parental opposition as the hindering force with a broader social and cultural marker. Eva's father, Veit Pogner, is in fact delighted at and supportive of the prospect that a young knight with an excellent, if impoverished, family background would join the mastersingers' circle and vie for his daughter's hand. Instead of the parent, it falls to the town clerk and high-ranking guild member Sixtus Beckmesser to become the obstacle. This takes the conflict from the private to the public sphere, even if aspects of the more conventional generation-gap motif remain. Beckmesser's rigidly conservative application of the Mastersingers' rules becomes the means not only of dismissing Walther on aesthetic grounds but, more importantly, keeping his musical and sexual rival at arm's length. The shift in formulaic comic structure thus transfers the emphasis both from private to public, as well as from the purely sexual pursuit of Eva—more pronounced in the first draft— to Walther's aesthetic victory staged as "cultural performance." Walther's performance succeeds according to the comic mode as a free-spirited and unmediated song presentation intuitively recognized and approved by the people; the performance stands in stark contrast to Beckmesser's distorted reading of the song.[32] So Beckmesser's aesthetic opposition de-emphasizes the more traditional sources of conflict in comedy—sexual and economic tensions between the generations—and sublimates them onto the social and aesthetic plane. This is not to say that there are no sexual tensions in the opera, e.g., in the allusions to *Tristan and Isolde*, not to mention both Sachs and Beckmesser as competitors for Walther, but it is the cultural debate which drives the dynamic of the opera.

There are numerous markers in the comedy to identify Beckmesser as the oppositional force. Within theatrical tradition, he is a descendant of both the *dottore* of the *commedia dell'arte* and the older characters in Molière's comedies who are funny because of their empty learnedness and overblown sense of their appeal to the opposite sex. As such, they appear both as figures depicting social values, classes, and ideals and equally as "timeless human characters."[33] Most recently James McGlathery's com-

---

32. David Levin shows how Beckmesser "is unable to" read the text. Levin, "Reading," 137.

33. See the classic study on the *commedia dell'arte* by Pierre Ducharte, which traces the social heritage of its stock characters: Pierre Ducharte, *The Italian Comedy*, trans. Randolph Weaver (New York: Day, 1929). Most prominently, Molière scholarship has recently emphasized the concrete social and political traces of Molière's characters. See Jürgen Grimm, *Molière* (Stuttgart: Metzler, 1984).

prehensive, if ultimately restricted, study claims that all of Wagner's works, including *Die Meistersinger,* are drawn from stock characters of the *commedia dell'arte.* While McGlathery reveals the economic and social elements of *commedia dell'arte* characters in *Die Meistersinger,* he has difficulty reducing the complexities of Wagner's dramatic structures to the standard *commedia dell'arte* scheme.[34]

This traditional type-casting of Beckmesser is augmented by the more controversial and, if correct, disturbing traits that set him apart as a figure with Semitic attributes. Marc Weiner argues—convincingly, I believe—that Wagner's vocal phrase structure and instrumentation typify Beckmesser as a Jewish character, hence making him a cultural outcast, by using devices of the synagogue—or, in Wagner's divisive terms, "gurgling," "yodeling," and "blabbering."[35] Furthermore, Weiner interprets Beckmesser's miserable failure in presenting Walther's song on the festival meadow as "the fantasy of retribution which Wagner will visit upon his object of anti-Semitic ridicule."[36] In this context, the choice of Nürnberg seems hardly coincidental, since the town had successfully barred Jews from its city limits for centuries.[37] Again, such a reading raises the stakes of the implications contained in Beckmesser's disappearance within the crowd after his failed musical performance.[38] Ultimately, whether we accept the anti-Semitic reading or not, Beckmesser still satisfies perfectly Frye's model of the "complex element" by functioning as the traditional comedic "blocking character" for marriage.[39]

Wagner further stacks the deck against Beckmesser by using two dramatic devices that elicit laughter. One of them is to invoke the late medieval and early modern concept of *Fastnachtspiel* (Shrovetide play), which, Helmut Prang has argued, was designed to purge hate and envy by using peasants and Jews as targets of humor.[40] Hate in the *Fastnachtspiel* was typically directed at outcasts, foreigners, Jews, or lower class people, thus bolstering middle-class self-confidence.[41] Since the historical Hans Sachs

---

34. James McGlathery, *Wagner's Operas and Desire* (New York: Peter Lang, 1998), 201–33. For example, McGlathery acknowledges that at least three characters—Beckmesser, Pogner, and Sachs—share traits and functions of Pantalone (202).

35. Marc Weiner, *Richard Wagner and the Anti-Semitic Imagination* (Lincoln: University of Nebraska Press, 1995), 121.

36. Ibid., 69.

37. In fact, Nürnberg was one of the first cities to convert to the Lutheran faith and successfully reject the location of Jews within its city limits. Köhler, *Wagners Hitler,* 352.

38. See Levin, "Reading," 145; and Köhler, *Wagners Hitler,* 372.

39. Frye coined the term "blocking agent" in his analysis of comic strategies: Frye, *Anatomy,* 166.

40. Helmut Prang, *Geschichte des Lustspiels: Von der Antike zur Gegenwart* (Stuttgart: Kröner, 1968), 47.

41. Ibid., 48.

was well-known as an author of the *Fastnachtspiel* genre, Wagner implicitly weaves the dramaturgy of the genre with its anti-Semitic overtones into his opera by making Sachs its hero.

Beckmesser is further typified and vilified by use of repetition—in Bergson's comic theory the quintessential tool for turning a character into an object of ridicule. Beckmesser is repeatedly humiliated, first during his supposed serenade of Eva in Act II, which renders him not only the object of Sachs's demeaning critique, but ultimately the objective of David's fist, and ultimately, in Act III, the victim of the crowd's thundering laughter. The repeated and jeering humiliation not only confirms Beckmesser as the opera's main target but, again more disturbingly, breeds an insensitivity which erodes audience empathy for the character's qualities as a human being. As I will show in greater detail later on, the onstage folk in Act III—from the perspective of phenomenological performance theory—functions as a stand-in for the theater audience, not only to further underscore and even direct the "intended" response to Beckmesser, but to magnify its effect.[42]

Beyond the shift from parental to cultural, and from private to public "obstacle" which Beckmesser enables, Hans Sachs turns out to be an important addition to the comedic dimension in *Die Meistersinger*. Surprisingly perhaps, this popular sixteenth-century Nürnberg poet and cobbler who was a cultural figurehead already in his own time, not to mention his virtual sanctification in later centuries, assumes the dramaturgical role traditionally taken by the slave in classical comedies or the servant in their seventeenth- and eighteenth-century counterparts. As Richard Beacham observes, the slave (servant), although socially and politically powerless, was a fantasy character through whom the audience could enjoy the utopia of social and political transformation.[43] Comedies, where the slave could successfully manipulate the proceedings, could thus become a safe haven, a pressure valve, for the albeit temporary realization of realistically unfulfillable desires.[44] Thus, in Roman plays, wily servants create delightful occasions for social critique out of the most absurd situations, even though there was little real chance for social reform. Similarly, servants of the Renaissance *commedia dell'arte* often brought potentially disastrous situa-

---

42. From a phenomenological perspective, the actor "stands in" for a representative number of people and the audience "authorizes" him to do so: Bruce Wilshire, *Role Playing and Identity* (Bloomington: Indiana University Press, 1982), 6–7.

43. Richard Beacham, *The Roman Theatre and Its Audience* (London: Routledge, 1991), 37–38.

44. Freud, "Jokes," 188–221. Compare also Segal, *Roman Laughter,* 123. However, as Segal points out, in Roman comedy, much like in Freud's Oedipal complex, the father prevails in many cases (18).

tions to harmonious resolution.[45] In *Meistersinger,* the traditional and popular function of the servant role is split: Hans Sachs is the facilitator of the happy ending, while other functions of the traditional servant are assigned to Sachs's apprentice David. Wagner also reconfigures the romantic component by making Sachs withdraw as Eva's suitor and, instead, pairs David with Magdalene, the traditional servant couple. However, it is dramaturgically significant that, while Sachs takes on the role of "facilitator" traditionally assigned to the "servant with common sense," his actual social standing is not as servant but rather as respected citizen and cultural figurehead. As opposed to the "powerless" servant who cannot actually effect change, Sachs is every bit in the social position to do so. The transformation depicted at the conclusion of *Meistersinger* is thus no longer utopian in the spirit of earlier servant-driven comedies, but plausible and even possible, and thus immensely more significant and powerful in effect.

The Sachs character is a combination of so many elements, from the historical person to the highly constructed folk hero of nineteenth-century Germany—what Wagner famously termed "die letzte Erscheinung des künstlerisch produktiven Volksgeistes" (the last manifestation of the artistic-productive spirit of the people)—that it is possible to read a variety of concurrent gestures into his dramatic role.[46] If we isolate the historical Sachs, author of didactic and, from a contemporary perspective, politically troubling *Fastnachtspiele* that targeted peasants and Jews, the more sinister meaning of "künstlerisch produktiven Volksgeist" becomes apparent.[47] Here we must keep in mind that both the *Fastnachtspiel* and *commedia dell'arte* conventions assume an ideological alignment between audience and performers. This becomes the basis for the type of "communal" laughter and

---

45. In these historical forms of comedy, the craftiness of the servant and the complexity of the intrigue were very often the significant criteria that made a comic role successful or even desirable for an actor to perform. Prang, *Geschichte des Lustspiels,* 61–67.

46. Richard Wagner, "Eine Mitteilung an meine Freunde," in his *Dichtungen und Schriften,* ed. Dieter Borchmeyer (Frankfurt/M: Insel, 1983), 6:259.

47. There seems to be anecdotal agreement concerning the anti-Semitic content of Sachs's carnival plays; however, I have found no detailed analysis of specific plays supporting such claims; see, e.g., Prang, *Geschichte des Lustspiels,* 45–56; Randall Listerman, *Nine Carnival Plays by Hans Sachs* (Ottawa: Dovehouse Editions, 1990), 9–25, and Klaus Ridder and Hans-Hugo Steinhoff, eds. *Frühe Nürnberger Fastnachtspiele* (Munich: Schöningh, 1998), 156–67. Keri Bryant's recent dissertation modifies this claim by showing that the presentation of German Jews in the sixteenth century was less extreme than formerly claimed. She acknowledges that writers such as Hans Sachs portrayed Jews, but that anti-Semitism was refracted by myth, folklore, and superstition. Keri Bryant, "Mixed Messages: The Role of the Jew in Sixteenth-Century German Fiction" (Ph.D. diss., University of Pennsylvania, 1994).

scorn against a common target which exemplify both genres.[48] Sachs, the "popular" sixteenth-century author of (anti-Semitic) *Fastnachtspiele,* is thus reborn as the main character in Wagner's nineteenth-century didactic *Fastnachtspiel.* The audience both on and off stage can identify with this hero and his goal to save German art from an enemy who is, once again, the Jew.

All of this prepares the way for the greatest departure from traditional comedic discourse. Frye's model stipulates that the individuals or group of characters in charge at the happy end usually mark the new ideological center. Hohendahl's reading of *Die Meistersinger* however suggests that there is a power vacuum at the conclusion waiting to be exploited. While Lortzing's opera *Hans Sachs* (1840) served to some extent as a model for Wagner, their respective endings mark an important difference. In Lortzing's work, the monarch who transcends all class distinctions arrives as a quasi *deus ex machina* at the conclusion to resolve the tensions.[49] But this monarch is absent from Wagner's libretto, thus necessitating a different solution for social and cultural rejuvenation during the final scene on the festival meadow. Departing from the traditional comic ending, it is not the happy couple Walther and Eva who define the new society, but Sachs, whom Wagner provides with an extensive aria ("Verachtet mir die Meister nicht"), addressed to Walther and the people, in which he describes the role of the artist and art.[50] Sachs's simultaneously forward- and backward-looking speech celebrates the importance of the "ordinary" mastersingers in sustaining a characteristic German art form. Beckmesser's absence from the final tableau—following his miserable failed performance—implies his failure as mastersinger and, more devastatingly, that his absence is necessary for the survival and further growth of German art.

In this sense, Sachs becomes the *deus ex machina* by functioning as the restorative and harmonizing figure, the formal authority accepted by the people.[51] Sachs embodies a dramaturgical gamut stretching from beloved,

---

48. Prang, *Geschichte des Lustspiels,* 47. Wieland Wagner's second Bayreuth production of *Die Meistersinger* in 1963 was instrumental in creating a performance approach that transformed the opera into a play within the play. In this approach, Sachs becomes the director of the action, leads the intrigue, and authors the happy ending. Bauer, *Stage Designs,* 189–90.

49. Hohendahl, "Reworking History," 55.

50. Martin Gregor-Dellin has argued that Wagner—who had planned the speech's inclusion from the initial prose draft—felt a dramaturgical need to conclude the work with a strong vision of art rather than with Walther's aria emphasizing love and happiness. Since Wagner's original version lacked the weight for such a dramaturgical move, he accepted Cosima's advice to adopt the specifically German nationalistic tone of the address in its final form. See Martin Gregor-Dellin, *Richard Wagner: Sein Leben, Sein Werk, Sein Jahrhundert* (Munich: Piper, 1980), 576–77.

51. Hohendahl, "Reworking History," 55–56.

popular, wily "slave/servant" to solid burgher and tradesman to regal and divine authority. In addition, Wagner's move to set a cultural icon rather than a political figure at the center of the new society privileges artistic over legal authority, a move confirmed visually when Eva takes the laurel from Walther's head and, instead, crowns Sachs while Pogner humbly kneels before him. Of course, Sachs's call for the sacred ability of German art to maintain an authentic culture even in the face of political cataclysm in the guise of French (literally *wälsch*) hegemony clearly infuses art with a political dimension. Hohendahl argues that this ending invites a political reading not only because of the intensity of the message, but also because there is no controlling political authority at the opera's conclusion. The artist assumes political leadership—albeit unsaid, albeit utopian. Joachim Köhler suspects that Hitler saw himself reflected in the implicit message of the opera's final moments, assuming himself to be none other than the sought-after artist-politician, possibly explaining why every major event of the Nazi party was transformed into an artistic performance designed to cement the political substance of the Führer.[52]

III. Tableau and Spectation in *Die Meistersinger*

Die Meistersinger stands in the nineteenth-century tradition of Eugene Scribe's so-called "well-made play," where tableaux at the end of each act are designed for powerful theatrical effect. The thematic thread linking the three tableaux that conclude the three acts in Wagner's opera connect art and politics by emphasizing that the mastersong is not just a self-contained artistic achievement but that the artist's expression must be rooted in the community.[53] Significantly, each tableau is also based on performance: in Act I, Walther performs his trial song; in Act II, Beckmesser performs his serenade and, finally, Act III concludes with the dual performances by Beckmesser and Walther. The recurring tableaux are a crucible for cultural negotiations. John MacAloon and other cultural anthropologists have seen performance as a mode of dramatizing shared stories and myths and providing alternatives to the governing models of politics and culture. Performances may lure audiences into participating in a cultural practice—and

---

52. Köhler, *Wagners Hitler*, 278–79.
53. The widespread use of tableaux in nineteenth-century melodrama is evident in the elaborate historical settings for theatrical productions by Charles Kean in London and the Meininger troupe in Germany, and in the conclusions to acts in Eugene Scribe's influential plays. The tableau often illustrates and, sometimes, substitutes for verbal narratives, thus de-emphasizing the narrative and foregrounding vivid situations. See Michael Booth, *Victorian Spectacular Theatre, 1850–1910* (Boston: Routledge, 1981); and Martin Meisel, *Realizations: Narrative, Pictorial and Theatrical Arts in Nineteenth Century England* (Princeton, N.J.: Princeton University Press, 1983).

may suggest possibilities for restructuring, even revolutionizing, cultural norms. At the end of Acts II and III, Wagner creates performance tableaux that ridicule the cultural model presented by Beckmesser—and advocate the model presented by Walther's song and Sachs's address. Walther's performance, evidently conjured up at the spur of the moment and performed without text and score, fascinates his audience and entices them to join in. Walther's performance eliminates the clear boundary between performer and audience and places the performance in a context where the opportunity for cultural awareness and, subsequently, social and political change, exists.[54]

Robert Scholes's analytical approach toward the "pragmatics" of complex comic situations is useful in understanding the mechanics of Wagner's finales.[55] Scholes's analysis of the famous screen scene from Richard Sheridan's eighteenth-century comedy *The School for Scandal* demonstrates that the success of comic situations depends on the construction of multiple onstage audiences that consequently allow for the "discharge of ironic perspective."[56] The more skillful the dramatist and the more complex the situation, the more pleasure the real audience will gain from the ironic discharge. This technique of creating a charged theatrical tableau where several characters function as audience not only serves to confirm the "impostor," but underscores the comedy's ideological perspective. For Scholes, it is "the fundamental irony of spectation [that] is at the bottom of it all—the fact that different viewpoints produce different feelings and that surfaces never tell the whole story."[57]

Many authors of comedy, including Molière, Goldoni, Beaumarchais, and Sheridan, have employed the technique of gradually drawing the targets of laughter into situations where their values and actions are disclosed as harmful, immoral, or plainly unacceptable. It is precisely at this point, as Bergson notes, that comedy operates not merely in the aesthetic realm but presents a social gesture that either restrains eccentric behavior or, more importantly in the context of *Die Meistersinger,* defends against a cultural threat. In the screen scene of Sheridan's *School for Scandal,* in the letter scene in Act IV of Molière's *Misanthrope,* and in the discovery scene at the conclusion of Mozart's *Marriage of Figaro,* tableaux express social values. In the case of *Die Meistersinger,* Wagner amplifies the social gesture through repetition, making Beckmesser fail not once but twice—which, in Bergson's

---

54. John J. MacAloon, ed. *Rite, Drama, Festival, Spectacle: Rehearsals toward a Theory of Cultural Performance* (Philadelphia: Institute for the Study of Human Issues, 1984), 1. See also Levin, "Reading," 142.

55. Robert Scholes, *Semiotics and Interpretation* (New Haven, Conn.: Yale University Press, 1982), 76.

56. Ibid., 79.

57. Ibid., 80.

theory, heightens the audience's comic response and desensitizes them to the physical and psychological anguish of the ridiculed character.

If we consider the lengthy process of writing and rewriting that characterized the creation of *Meistersinger*, we note Wagner's own concerns about the dramatic insufficiency of the 1845 outline. In *A Communication to My Friends* (1851), Wagner explains that the missing element he needed in order to transform what he called "the spirit of life" into comic form was one of the traditional tools of comedy: irony, here understood as a formal framing device that facilitates the disclosure of life's core without really touching it.[58] In the first prose sketch of *Die Meistersinger*, Wagner employs irony primarily to mark particular aspects of Beckmesser, the protoypical "hinderer" according to Frye's model. Hans Sachs is also a conduit for ironic posturing. For example it is Sachs, not Kothner, who announces the mastersinger rules to Walther, doing so "with irony" according to Wagner's directions, suggesting that Hans Sachs already here advocates aesthetic innovation.[59] Sachs also observes "with irony" how the Marker notes all of Walther's mistakes, thereby also making Sachs a vehicle to undermine the Marker.[60] But the full extent to which irony becomes a central component in the opera, and Sachs a quasi embodiment of "irony," is evident only in the final version.

Let us start by analyzing the conclusion of *Die Meistersinger* Act II (scenes 5–7) using Scholes's particularly handy concept of "ironic spectation." In many respects, the entire act can be viewed as an extended tableau, built over time through the introduction of ever-increasing layers of audiences (or spectators) on stage until, in the end, the entire town is present. The multiple spectation is initiated early on when Sachs forces Eva and Walther to abort their planned elopement and, instead, to watch Beckmesser's serenade. Sachs emerges as the key player, guiding an unknowing Beckmesser into performing in front of Eva and Walther. This dynamic places the audience in a position to identify with the hero and heroine by enjoying Beckmesser's humiliation—thus creating the kind of link between audience and performer common to the *Fastnachtspiel* and *commedia dell'arte*.

One of the immediate "ironies of spectation" is that, by watching Sachs interact with Beckmesser, Eva, and Walther—along with the audience—discover that Sachs is actually their ally. This also heightens attention to the rivalry between Sachs and Beckmesser rather than that between Walther and Beckmesser. Sachs becomes Beckmesser's marker, making the serenade

---

58. Wagner, "Eine Mitteilung an meine Freunde," 6:261–62.

59. Wagner, "1. Entwurf: *Die Meistersinger von Nürnberg*, Komische Oper in 3 Akten," in his *Dichtungen und Schriften*, 4:223–26.

60. See also Linda Hutcheon's *Irony's Edge: The Theory and Politics of Irony* (London: Routledge, 1994), 2, which considers irony as a strategy of identifying a target and a victim.

even more like a public test, while also allowing Walther—Beckmesser's former victim—the "ironic spectation" of witnessing Beckmesser's humiliation. An additional, often overlooked dynamic, is the comic "competition" between Sachs and Magdalene for Beckmesser's attention: while Sachs increasingly discourages Beckmesser by hammering the shoes, Magdalene continues to encourage Beckmesser with alluring poses.[61]

At the peripeteia of Beckmesser's despair—and in preparation for the ironic discharge—David becomes the last layer of onstage audience. However, since he is not interested in becoming yet another spectator but rather in exacting revenge on Beckmesser, David's entrance cuts through the carefully woven balance of the scene's multiple spectation. This is the traditional climax of tableau construction. With David, the layers of spectatorship simultaneously discharge the multiple layers of irony as they unravel. From a purely dramaturgical perspective, the moment of recognition achieves the automatic discharge of ironies, making David's fight with Beckmesser and the subsequent riot scene rather gratuitous. Although it is admittedly common in the *commedia dell'arte* for the servant/apprentice to be involved in a fight and physical mayhem, the attack on Beckmesser and the brawl are unusual. The pleasure derived from the moment of comic recognition becomes instead an occasion for physical punishment and thus a loaded social gesture. Beyond further ostracizing Beckmesser, the brawl also serves the overall comic framework to further desensitize the audience to the cruelty aimed at the "hinderer." Not only is this scene famously difficult to stage and perform, it has given rise to critical observations like those of Adorno, who provocatively argued that the scene was merely an anticipation of the pogroms of the Third Reich.[62] The problematic nature of the opera is, of course, underscored by such recontextualized, even anachronistic readings, and contributes to the current difficulties in classifying the work as a comedy.

Critics' unease notwithstanding, the "irony of spectation" allows a number of ideological issues to be addressed. First, the tableau framework draws the figure of Beckmesser into starker relief than the trial scene in Act I allowed by placing him in the broadest possible social and cultural context. Marc Weiner's analysis of Beckmesser's Act II serenade which "is based on a preference for florid, melismatic, high-pitched singing that, characteristically, shows little feeling for the German language"[63] is already described by Wagner, who conceived Beckmesser's high tessitura as an "impassioned, screeching tone of voice" to create a comic part that was unusual musically for the nineteenth century—compared to the basso buffo role of the Italian

---

61. Wagner, "1. Entwurf: *Die Meistersinger,*" 4:161 and 164.
62. Adorno, *Versuch,* 19.
63. Weiner, *Richard Wagner and the Anti-Semitic Imagination,* 121.

tradition—but quite logical within the discourse of comedy.[64] Weiner's point, of course, is that Beckmesser's excessively high tessitura had ideological significance for Wagner by identifying a foreign, non-German influence.[65] Thus, Wagner stacks the deck against Beckmesser by making him corrupt to the core (as manifest in his voice), so that when he awakens the entire town with his "screeching," Beckmesser is revealed not only as a failed singer (cultural reject) and failed lover (gender trouble), but also can legitimately be called a public nuisance (social outcast).

The tableau also provides Sachs an effective situational framework for "unmasking the impostor." Here again, Wagner draws on the ancient Greek comedy where "there was a struggle, or agon, with the Imposter (or alazon) who looked with defiling eye upon the sacred rites that must not be seen. The alazon was put to flight after a contest with either the young king or with a character known as the eiron, 'the ironical man.'"[66] According to Corrigan, at the heart of old comedy was this ritual comic combat between alazon (intruder), "who appeared to know more that he actually did" and the eiron (ironist), whose function it was to reduce and confuse the intruder.[67] The impostor who profanes the rites of the tribe or society must be beaten and driven out. Along the same lines, Aristotle's *Ethics* identifies Socrates as a model character who, disguised as the understated inquirer, challenges the so-called wise men. Socrates, as eiron, appears in an understated manner while leaving it up to the impostor to expose himself. It does not seem far-fetched to see in the Sachs-Beckmesser contest a transcription of the ancient eiron-alazon relationship.[68] Sachs slips often and easily into the role of eiron, for instance during the serenade scene of Act II, where, in a reenactment of the ancient rite of the eiron and alazon, he lets Beckmesser be the cause of his own doom.[69]

Building on long-standing and effective comic formulas, *Die Meistersinger* participates in a discourse of unmasking and punishment which endorses and confirms the values of a social and cultural order that is thus deemed superior.

---

64. "Drei unbekannte Schreiben Richard Wagners an Gustav Hölzel, mitgeteilt von Marie Huch in Hannover," in *Selected Letters of Richard Wagner*, trans. and ed. Stewart Spencer and Barry Millington (London: Dent, 1987), 222. Cited in Weiner, *Richard Wagner and the Anti-Semitic Imagination*, 118.

65. Weiner, *Richard Wagner and the Anti-Semitic Imagination*, 121.

66. Corrigan, ed., *Comedy*, 37. On the historical tradition of the eiron figure see Frye, *Anatomy*, 172–77.

67. Corrigan, ed., *Comedy*, 37.

68. A similar rivalry occurs in Act III when Walther and Beckmesser battle for Eva. Structurally this doubling of the "eiron" can be attributed to Wagner's sympathies, which are split between Walther and Sachs. Both reveal Beckmesser as an impostor, though the contest in Act III, while more formal, is less elaborate as comic discourse, since Walther demonstrates his mastery of poetry while Beckmesser fails.

69. Wagner, "1. Entwurf: *Die Meistersinger*," 4:161–68.

IV. The (Mal)Function of Laughter

Following the boisterous and lively finale of Act II, the third act opens with the melancholy prelude, which not only sets the stage for an act which is as long as the previous two combined, but which seems to further undermine classifications of the work as a comedy. Here, Wagner shifts the focus to a more reflective mood, where deeper philosophical and aesthetic questions are pursued and where the two couples Walther / Eva and David / Magdalene ultimately come together in the sublime quintet headed by the *pater familias* and general factotum Hans Sachs, presenting what in many respects can be regarded as the private conclusion of the opera.[70]

But the move from private, interior, and reflective moment of the quintet to the grand tableau on the festival meadow, which presents the new social and cultural order formed around Hans Sachs with Walther as the catalyst for the development of the new artist, serves to reestablish the work's comic structure according to Frye's model. I will defer discussion here of the extent to which, given more recent history, the opera's ending can legitimately be considered "happy," but within a nineteenth-century perspective such a claim would seem to be less problematic.

However, if we accept the anti-Semitic stereotyping, and perhaps even if we do not, the manipulation of laughter from the onstage audience directed at Beckmesser in the final scene smacks sour even without the experience of the Holocaust. In his essay on laughter, Bergson writes that "the art of the comic poet consists in making us so well acquainted with the particular vice, in introducing us, the spectators, to such a degree of intimacy with it, that in the end we get hold of some of the strings of the marionette with which he is playing, and actually work them ourselves."[71] In the case of *Die Meistersinger,* the "spectators" who "work the strings" in the final scene are not only in the auditorium but on stage as well. But the arguable purpose of comedy in the traditional sense goes horribly astray. For, if the ultimate goal of humor and laughter is to effect moral improvement of the malefactor—think especially of Count Almaviva at the conclusion of *The Marriage of Figaro*—this is cast aside in *Die Meistersinger.* The mocking, jeering crowd which forces Beckmesser to "lose himself" in their midst and effectively disappear from the action does not pursue improvement, but instead performs a scapegoat ritual: the disgrace and implied expulsion of an irreconcilable character.[72] Instead of improvement,

---

70. Michael Tanner, "The Tonal Work of Art," in *The Wagner Companion,* ed. Peter Burbidge and Richard Sutton (London: Faber, 1979), 204.

71. Bergson, "Laughter," 70–71.

72. Frye, *Anatomy*; Weiner has called attention to the scapegoat ritual without, however, placing it into the context of comedy. Weiner, *Richard Wagner and the Anti-Semitic Imagination,* 69.

Beckmesser experiences a continual slide from his moral and aesthetic high ground in Act I as the virtually all-powerful Marker to lowly thief in Act III—by attempting to steal Walther/Sachs's Meisterlied—following his artistic humiliation in Act II. When Beckmesser's total failure becomes apparent on the Festwiese, the crowd's laughter does not aim at correcting his manners so that he might end up as, in Bergson's phrase, "what we ought to be, what some day we shall perhaps end in being," but rather at casting him out.[73] Departing from the traditional ending of comedy, there is neither reconciliation with the blocking agent nor any indication that he might be reformed as a result of his experience. Laughter in *Die Meistersinger* does not function to restore and heal, but rather "malfunctions" to ostracize and wound.

V. Conclusion

Wagner exploited and modified traditional comic conventions in an attempt to create a unique and in the end uniquely successful music drama. This combination of dramaturgical borrowing and adapting corresponds in many respects to the compositional mode he developed for the opera, which Dahlhaus describes as a baroque musical style transformed into a "dreamlike diatonicism."[74] Similarly, the plot pattern and character constellation seem to echo traditional conceptions of the genre, but in fact radically extend the discourse of comedy, a notion embedded in the opera itself, when Sachs, thinking back on Walther's trial song notes the famous lines: "Es klang so alt,—und war doch so neu" (II, 3).

Marc Weiner has recently observed that Wagner critics often talk past each other because of deep methodological and ideological rifts.[75] He contends that there exists an interdependent dynamic between the two, in that critics accentuate methodological differences to conceal ideological differences while, at the same time, professing academic integrity to verify their results. To provide more insight into the *Meistersinger* dramaturgy, I have linked a traditional methodological concern, the concept of genre, with a more recent concern, the analysis of cultural content of Wagner's work. By focusing on the performative in *Die Meistersinger* I have shown that Wagner's comic dramaturgical strategies give expression to political and cultural intentions by taking advantage of the potential political and cultural implications inherent in historical comic traditions. From this perspective, the tableau, with its potential of discharging irony and of suggest-

---

73. Bergson, "Laughter," 71.
74. Dahlhaus, *Richard Wagner's Music Dramas*, 75.
75. Marc Weiner, "Über Wagner sprechen: Ideologie und Methodenstreit," in *Richard Wagner im Dritten Reich*, ed. Saul Friedländer and Jörn Rüsen (Munich: Beck, 2000), 343.

ing cultural practices, represents the most powerful strategy of performance through which Wagner promotes social and cultural signification. Linda Hutcheon has argued in a full-length study that irony—a primary function in the tableau and traditionally the focus of an aesthetic analysis—is political rather than poetic in nature; it is a means of isolating groups or individuals, and she particularly warns against a conflation of the concepts of irony and humor.[76] This may in fact point to the crux of the issue of comedy in *Die Meistersinger*. The most drastic example of "political" irony is that Sachs, a thoroughly cultural figure, becomes a medium through which a thoroughly political gesture can be made. If we consider Sachs's role in terms of political gesture, Borchmeyer's approach to the genre question of *Die Meistersinger* seems too limited, if not misdirected. While I would agree with Borchmeyer in classifying the opera as a comedy, it makes more sense to go beyond regarding it as a closed aesthetic construct. Instead, it should be understood in terms of the ways in which Wagner has infused and modified long-standing traditions of comedic discourse with cultural and historical elements that transform the genre's potential to deliver a series of stinging social gestures. However, while the dynamic created by this overlay of complex elements may loosen the work's genre classification in conventional terms, it does not nullify it. By the same token, the disturbing cultural and social messages of *Die Meistersinger* are not masked, but rather amplified by the work's comic discourse.

---

76. Hutcheon, *Irony's Edge*, 3.

9

Masters and their Critics: Wagner, Hanslick, Beckmesser, and *Die Meistersinger*

Thomas S. Grey

New Year's Day, 1869. In the very first entry of her voluminous diaries, Cosima Wagner reported on the progress of Richard's current projects, as she would continue to do faithfully for another fourteen years. Interspersed with prefatory remarks about her own great undertaking (the diaries) and a record of domestic details, we read that Richard is working on his fair copy of the now completed second act of *Siegfried* and "completing his essay on the Jews." "Before lunch (at one o'clock) my beloved read me what he had written. At table, he told me more of the range of his essay, and we discussed his position, that is to say, the position of art as laid down by the Jews, which made me see Mendelssohn for the first time as a tragic figure."[1]

What Richard and Cosima were discussing here was actually the now notorious article Wagner had published anonymously in the *Neue Zeitschrift für Musik* nineteen years earlier, "Judaism in Music." What Wagner had been working on that morning, on the other hand, and would finish over the next week or so, was a lengthy "afterword" to that essay intended to accompany its republication, now as an independent brochure under his own name. In the nineteen years since 1850, his situation had changed considerably. With the backing of King Ludwig II, he enjoyed a significant level of financial security, and, however controversial, his position as

---

1. *Cosima Wagner's Diaries,* ed. M. Gregor-Dellin and Dietrich Mack, trans. G. Skelton (New York and London: Harcourt, Brace, Jovanovich, 1977), 28. Throughout this essay, "Judaism in Music" refers to the original 1850 anonymous publication in article form (it actually appeared under the pseudonym "K. Freigedank"), while *Judaism in Music* refers to the 1869 republication in brochure form, under Wagner's name.

Germany's leading opera composer was by now unassailable. By 1869 he could afford to sign his own name to what had originally been a covert (and in fact largely ineffectual) piece of cultural terrorism. Just why he *wanted* to do so now, however, was (and has remained) a matter of some consternation. Whatever the reasons, it was at this point that the anti-Jewish rhetoric that had been percolating in his private and semi-private correspondence decisively spilled over into the sphere of public discourse.[2]

The psychological roots of Wagner's anti-Semitism are surely deep and twisted, and they are intertwined (of course) with those of nineteenth-century European and specifically German anti-Semitism, both above and below the surface of historical record. Leaving aside the root causes of Wagner's propensity to paranoia, persecution-complex, and general resentment, the more *immediate* impulses behind the original 1850 essay on (or rather against) "Judaism in Music," as well those behind its 1869 afterword, are not that difficult to discern. In 1850, struggling for a success and recognition he felt were long overdue (and still much too far from sight), Wagner was resentful of the artistic canonization of the recently deceased Felix Mendelssohn. Much more aggravating than that, though, was the continued popular success of Giacomo Meyerbeer, whose latest, long-delayed grand-opera blockbuster, *Le Prophète,* was just then starting out to conquer the European stage. (In contrast to Wagner's own dire professional situation in the wake of the 1849 uprisings, the success of Meyerbeer's opera seems to have driven him to distraction—or at any rate to extreme vituperation.) Mendelssohn was long gone by 1869, however, and Meyerbeer had died five years earlier, after a decade of declining productivity. While their positions in the repertoire were still secure, it would have been, at best, merely quixotic of Wagner to renew his attack on them as undeserving, aesthetically flawed, or bankrupt "competitors" at this point. And in fact, the 1869 afterword to *Judaism in Music* takes on a wholly new target: the "Jewish-dominated" press, specifically what Wagner maintained was a deliberate "Jewish" cabal or conspiracy to oppose him and his works—at every turn and at all costs. The motive for this journalistic conspiracy—which Wagner went so far as to call a case of "reverse discrimina-

---

2. Wagner returned to his "case" against the Jews most vehemently in journal entries of September 1865 documenting his current cultural and political concerns, recorded for the benefit of King Ludwig II and only later published in revised form in the *Bayreuther Blätter* of 1878 (as "Was ist Deutsch?"). Some hints of this return to anti-Jewish polemics were also contained in the articles, "Deutsche Kunst und Deutsche Politik," published in the *Süddeutsche Zeitung* in 1867 and 1868. These reached only a relatively limited readership, as compared to the reprinted *Judaism* brochure of the following year.

tion" [*die . . . gegen mich . . . umgekehrte Judenverfolgung*][3]—is said to be widespread antagonism towards the 1850 "Judaism" essay (this despite its anonymous publication and extremely limited circulation). And the ringleader of this alleged campaign against Wagner is identified, not surprisingly, as the leading Viennese music critic, Eduard Hanslick.

I.

Hanslick's name will remind us of the immediate context of the essay's republication: the premiere, less than one year earlier, of *Die Meistersinger,* in which Wagner secured for his nemesis a tarnished immortality by inscribing an unsubtle (and hence memorable) parody of Hanslick in the role of Beckmesser. (Not coincidentally, Hanslick had published a largely, though not exclusively, negative review of the *Meistersinger* premiere, six months before Wagner wrote his new "afterword"). Wagner vs. Hanslick is one of the most familiar chapters in modern music history. In revisiting it here, my purpose is to take a closer look at some of the historical particulars (especially in light of recent research on the "Judaism" essay by Jens Malte Fischer); to consider what a closer reading of Hanslick's role in that essay and in *Die Meistersinger* might tell us about the interrelation of the critic, the essay, and the opera; also, what light it might shed on Beckmesser's role as a possible anti-Jewish caricature (a claim subject to much debate, especially over the past decade). The case of Wagner vs. Hanslick furnishes significant material, furthermore, for an analysis of the relationship between composer and critic at this key moment on the brink of European modernism, as we might identify it, moving into the last three decades of the nineteenth century.

Before proceeding with all of that, though, I want to underline again a basic—and I think largely overlooked—point about this context. That is: while the original essay "Judaism in Music" was intent on attacking the credibility of Jewish musicians (specifically Mendelssohn and Meyerbeer), the 1869 afterword is wholly concerned with a different group, the "Jew-

---

3. Richard Wagner, "Aufklärungen über das Judentum in der Musik" [=afterword to 1869 brochure *Judaism in Music*], *Gesammelte Schriften und Dichtungen,* ed. W. Golther (Leipzig: Deutsches Verlagshaus Bong & Co., 1887–1911), 8:242; cf. *Richard Wagner's Prose Works,* trans. W. Ashton Ellis (London: Kegan Paul, 1895), 3:103. See also Wagner's embittered remarks about the press in the 1865 pamphlet on "A Music School for Munich," *Gesammelte Schriften,* 8:169, and *Prose Works,* 4:217, prefaced with an overt allusion to Hanslick in referring to "those flat [and misguided] assertions of our modern aestheticians in setting out their theories of the Beautiful in Music" (ibid.).

ish critic" (and more broadly, the "Jewish press").[4] Even if "innocently" conceived back in 1845, when Wagner first sketched a scenario on the *Meistersinger* material, the character of Beckmesser could ultimately be construed as an embodiment of *both* of Wagner's "Jewish" targets (in reverse chronological order, as it happens). In Act I Beckmesser is the hidebound pedant and tin-eared critic, i.e., the anti-Wagnerian Hanslick, the central target of the 1869 afterword. In Act II, the critic turns composer, and his rudimentary and bungled attempts at song are savaged by the sound critical judgment of Hans Sachs (and by the instinctive aesthetic good sense of the *Volk* in the final act). The inept fusion of would-be *volkstümlich* melody and classical formula (the bar-form) in Beckmesser's serenade might possibly be read to reflect Wagner's case against Mendelssohn, while the still more ludicrous and exaggerated infractions against language, music, and artistic sensibility perpetrated in Beckmesser's rendition of the purloined Prize Song resonate with Wagner's more vehement slander of Meyerbeer in the original *Judaism* essay, as well as in Part I of *Opera and Drama*. Either composer, however—Mendelssohn or Meyerbeer—is only a tentative background association by the time of the completed opera. Hanslick remains the critical target here (in two senses). That is no news, of course; but what *has* been overlooked, I think, is Hanslick's central position in the 1869 "afterword" to *Judaism in Music,* and how that reflects Wagner's ongoing preoccupations during the writing, composition, and production of *Die Meistersinger.* Let me now review briefly just what we know about the interaction of composer and critic up to this point.

II.

Eduard Hanslick began his critical career, in the later 1840s, as an enthusiastic advocate of "New Music," including Wagner's. On assignment for

---

4. Jens Malte Fischer does note the role of Hanslick's *Meistersinger* review as an immediate catalyst for the 1869 republication of the essay. Fischer sees a parallel to the circumstances of the original 1850 essay in that, in both cases, a longer-brewing period of rancor against supposed Jewish competitors and adversaries is finally ignited by a specific event or factor. In 1850, Fischer claims, it was the publication of an appreciative article on *Le Prophète* by Ludwig Bischoff in the first volume of his *Rheinische Musikzeitung* (Fischer, "Richard Wagners 'Das Judentum in der Musik': Entstehung—Kontext—Wirkung," in *Richard Wagner und die Juden,* ed. D. Borchmeyer, A. Maayani, and S. Vill [Stuttgart and Weimar: J. B. Metzler, 2000], 45). Elsewhere (pp. 39–40) Fischer discusses the role of articles in the *Neue Zeitschrift für Musik* by Theodor Uhlig and Eduard Krüger on Mendelssohn and Meyerbeer as catalysts for the essay. See also Fischer's commentary–edition–documentation: *Richard Wagners "Das Judentum in der Musik": Eine kritische Dokumentation als Beitrag zur Geschichte des Antisemitismus* (Frankfurt and Leipzig: Insel, 2000), 26–28.

the *Wiener allgemeine Musik-Zeitung* he reviewed the Dresden production of *Tannhäuser* in 1846, and his enthusiasm for the work found expression in a review of no fewer than twelve installments, hailing the composer as scarcely less than the great hope of German opera.[5] He did not encounter Wagner's next opera, *Lohengrin*, until 1858, at its Viennese premiere. In the meantime he had, of course, become aware of Wagner's theories about music, art, society, and his own brand of "musical drama" as the sole path to cultural salvation. All of this, along with the whole discourse of musical "progress" as it was developing around the nascent "New German School," was notably at odds with the more "pragmatic" aesthetics Hanslick had developed in *Vom Musikalisch-Schönen* [The Beautiful in Music], published in 1854. It has also been suggested that Hanslick may have taken offense at "Judaism in Music" when it was originally published in 1850.[6] This is certainly the explicit premise of Wagner's whole "Jewish conspiracy" theory in the 1869 afterword. But even if Hanslick *had* seen the original "Judaism" article of 1850 (which he explicitly denied), he would not likely have been aware of Wagner's authorship, which seems to have been known only to Wagner's immediate circle and, of course, to the editor Franz Brendel. At any rate, Hanslick was less than enthusiastic about the "new" opera (*Lohengrin*), which, he felt, got bogged down under stretches of quasi-naturalistic (but musically uninspiring) declamation, and lacked compelling musical and dramatic values. Compared to his nearly unbounded enthusiasm for *Tannhäuser* twelve years earlier, Hanslick's review of the first Viennese

5. The original text of the *Tannhäuser* review can be found in Hanslick, *Sämtliche Schriften,* vol. 1, *Aufsätze und Rezensionen 1844–1848*), ed. Dietmar Strauß (Cologne, Weimar, Vienna: Böhlau, 1993), 57–93. See also Strauß's discussion of the review "Hanslicks *Tannhäuser*-Aufsatz im rezeptionsgeschichtlichen Kontext," in his afterword, 315–22. The review is translated by Henry Pleasants III in his anthology, *Vienna's Golden Years of Music 1850–1900: Eduard Hanslick* (New York: Simon and Schuster, 1950).

6. Following Wagner's cue, Eric Sams proposed that it was knowledge of the original "Judaism" article and of Wagner's authorship that explained Hanslick's critical *volte-face* after the early *Tannhäuser* review; see his "Eduard Hanslick: the Perfect Anti-Wagnerite," *The Musical Times* 116 (1975): 867–68. Peter Wapnewski subscribes to this view in the afterword to his edition of Hanslick's memoirs, *Aus meinem Leben* (Kassel: Bärenreiter, 1987). In reviewing the 1869 edition of *Das Judentum in der Musik,* Hanslick denied that he had any notion of Wagner's original authorship, however, or even that he had ever seen the original essay in the *Neue Zeitschrift* (though that may be questionable). See also Fischer, *Richard Wagners "Das Judentum in der Musik,"* 233. Furthermore, there is no reason to suppose that Hanslick would have considered himself a target of the 1850 essay, which makes no mention of him or of any music critics. As discussed below, Hanslick identified himself as an Austrian Catholic (his Jewish mother, Karoline Kisch, converted upon marriage to his father). It was only Wagner's 1869 afterword that forced the issue of Hanslick as "Jewish critic."

Lohengrin in 1858 (by all accounts far and away the best performance the opera had yet received) adopts a strikingly waspish tone throughout.[7]

By the early 1860s, when Wagner and Hanslick crossed paths in Vienna, Hanslick's influence as a music critic had begun to solidify to the extent that in 1861 he quit his "day job" at the Ministry of Education to pursue journalism full time (and a nominal academic appointment at the University of Vienna). By then, Hanslick had occasion to write about *Lohengrin* a few more times in *Die Presse*, where he had also given *The Flying Dutchman* a somewhat tepid, though scarcely hostile, review (in 1860).[8] Wagner was clearly annoyed about what he heard regarding the recent state of Hanslick's opinion of him and his works. A greater concern, however, was the potential damage Hanslick might cause to Wagner's current project: the plan to realize the premiere of *Tristan und Isolde* at the Vienna Court Theater. Rather than ingratiating himself with the critic, however, Wagner made a point of treating him with studied rudeness on the few occasions they met in Vienna. Luise Dustmann, who had sung the first Elsa in Vienna and was being coached to create the role of Isolde, tried to bring about a reconciliation between the two. We have only Wagner's account of the evening, according to which he was timidly taken aside at one point by a teary and contrite Hanslick, begging forgiveness for his blinkered, regressive views and wishing for nothing so much as a chance to be properly enlightened by the Master himself as to the truth of this "new art."[9] Again according to Wagner, it was the magnanimous condescension he displayed towards his penitent critic on this occasion that eventually led to a revival of the *Tristan* rehearsals, abandoned some months earlier due to troubles with the tenor, Aloys Ander.[10] Whatever goodwill may have been generated between them—and from Wagner's own description of his behavior, it is hard to believe there could have been very much—was certainly dissolved on the famous occasion when Wagner read the *Meistersinger* libretto at the home of the well-connected (and presumably well-intentioned) physician Dr. Joseph Standhartner.

---

7. *Die Presse*, 9–10 November 1858. Translated in Pleasants, *Vienna's Golden Years of Music*, 51–64; reprintd in Hanslick, *Sämtliche Schriften*, vol. 4 (Vienna: Böhlau, 2002), 333–52.

8. Reprinted in A. Csampai and D. Holland, eds., *Richard Wagner: Der fliegende Holländer* (Reinbek bei Hamburg: Rowohlt, 1982), 140–44.

9. Richard Wagner, *My Life*, trans. Andrew Gray (Cambridge and New York: Cambridge University Press, 1983), 694–95.

10. Hanslick himself provides a good deal of information about the on-again-off-again Viennese rehearsals for this ultimately abortive *Tristan* production in his review of the belated Vienna premiere of 4 October 1883. See Hanslick, *Musikalisches Skizzenbuch* [*Die moderne Oper*, vol. 4] (Berlin: Allgemeine Verein für Deutsche Literatur, 1888), 3–28, here 3–11.

Masters and their Critics: Wagner, Hanslick & Beckmesser 171

The prose sketch of the scenario drafted late in 1861 gave to the malicious and pedantic "Marker" of the singer's guild the obviously pointed name [Veit] Hanslich. Whether Wagner was tactless enough to retain this name when reading the libretto in Hanslick's presence we do not know. He did, of course, think better of carrying over the name into the finished work; instead, he chose the suspiciously Latinate "Sixtus Beckmesser" from a list he had compiled of "authentic" Nuremberg masters' names.[11] It is impossible not to suppose that Hanslick registered the parodic intentions behind this character, with or without the original tendentious name. In this case, we do have accounts from both Wagner's and Hanslick's respective autobiographies. Not surprisingly, they offer rather different perspectives of the event.

In *Mein Leben* Wagner describes as follows the gathering at the home of Dr. Standhartner, one evening in late November 1862, just after his return to Vienna for the revival of the *Tristan* rehearsals. (If there is any truth to Wagner's claim, just mentioned, that this revived attempt to stage the premiere of *Tristan und Isolde* at the Vienna Hofoper was due in some part to Hanslick's intercession, Wagner's behavior during this episode is cast in an even more dubious light.) Wagner writes that he had promised the Standhartners a dramatic reading of the *Meistersinger* libretto, such as he had done for the Schotts in Mainz, and elsewhere:

> Since Herr Hanslick was considered to be on good terms with me now, it was thought to be doing me a favor by inviting him to this occasion, as well. In the course of the evening, the much-feared critic grew ever paler and more out of sorts [*verstimmter*]. And no one could help but notice how it was impossible to prevail upon him to remain a moment longer after the end of the reading, when instead he took his leave with an unmistakable tone of annoyance. My friends were all in agreement that Hanslick regarded the entire poem as a pasquinade directed at himself, and the invitation to this reading as a deliberate affront. Indeed, the critic's attitude towards me changed [again] markedly from this evening

---

11. The undated prose draft (probably from early November 1861) and the fair copy of the same, dated 18 November 1861, are reproduced in the first supplementary volume to the expanded edition of Wagner's writings: *Sämtliche Schriften und Dichtungen,* ed. R. Sternfeld (Leipzig: Breitkopf und Härtel, 1911–16), 11:356–94. In the first of these, the masters are identified only by their last names, and among them the "marker" as "Hanslich." The fair copy adds first names, "Veit" for Hanslich. Except for Pogner (here, "Thomas Bogler") none of the other masters' names were changed between this final prose draft and the full libretto.

forwards, turning to an embittered enmity, whose consequences we would soon have occasion to witness.[12]

Hanslick offers this account in *his* autobiography, written in the 1890s:

> The *Primarartzt* Dr. Standhartner—a Wagner enthusiast, but nonetheless an affable and tolerant character—invited me to a soirée at which Wagner read the complete text of his *Meistersinger*. I was not able to imagine just how one could set to music the long catalogue of [*Meister-*] *Weisen* rattled off by David [towards the beginning of Act I]. "Ah, as song [*im Gesang*], that will flow by so lightly that one won't even notice," Wagner assured me. Apart from this and some similar lapses of taste in the diction, the choice of material seemed to me a fortunate one, and very promising for Wagner in particular. I reported on this *Meistersinger* reading in *Die Presse*: "After the oppressive fires of the 'Nibelungen,' we have here an appealing, sometimes merry and sometimes moving picture of life and customs [*Sittenbild*] of [old-] German town life, founded on simple circumstances and motivated by the joys and sorrows of ordinary people. With *Die Meistersinger* Wagner will do the German theater a greater service than with [the whole of] his 'Nibelungen' project. While the latter awaits a still dreamt-of future, the operatically undernourished present eagerly anticipates the former. Wagner has opened up for himself two divergent paths. It can be no matter of indifference to German art which of these paths he will choose to follow—whether he will choose to be to his nation a Mastersinger, or a Nibelung."[13]

The invidious comparison with the *Ring* project was scarcely calculated to please Wagner, but otherwise Hanslick maintains a discreet silence on the role of Beckmesser, and for that matter, on the whole glorification of Wagnerian *Worttonkunst* so unmistakably inscribed in the new work. Even though the reissued *Judaism in Music,* with its provocative denunciations of Hanslick in the new afterword, had not yet appeared when he was called upon to review the completed opera in June 1868, Hanslick's tolerance for Wagner—as personality and as cultural phenomenon—had certainly not

---

12. Translated from original text in *Mein Leben,* ed. M. Gregor-Dellin (Munich: List-Verlag, 1976), 720–21; cf. *My Life,* 704. Several pages later Wagner recalls how he was persuaded to publish the text of Act I of his new libretto in the new Viennese journal, *Der Botschafter,* edited by Friedrich Uhl and Julius Fröbel. After this, he adds, "My friends insisted they noticed Hanslick growing more and more venomous" (*My Life,* 706).

13. Eduard Hanslick, *Aus meinem Leben,* ed. P. Wapnewski (Kassel: Bärenreiter, 1987), 217–18.

increased. For now, it was Hanslick's turn to provoke. His review of *Die Meistersinger* at its Munich premiere clearly played a role in Wagner's decision to reissue the *Judaism* essay with the new diatribe against the press, and Hanslick in particular. Wagner in fact admitted this explicitly in a letter to Carl Tausig written some months after the reissue: "[T]he unheard-of shamelessness of the Viennese press in connection with *Die Meistersinger,* the ongoing campaign of slander and lies [*freche Lügenschneiderei*] against me, and the truly destructive consequences of these . . . finally convinced me to take this reckless step."[14]

III.

Having been so tactlessly forewarned (back in 1862) of the revenge Wagner was planning to exact on his critics in *Die Meistersinger,* Hanslick found himself in a strange position when the time came to review the completed opera in 1868. The unsubtle persiflage of the composer's critics so deeply embedded in the details of the drama was not very likely to convert Hanslick—already alienated on both aesthetic and personal terms—to the Wagnerian cause. But the only alternative for Hanslick was to step right into Beckmesser's notorious shoes and continue the very critique that Wagner's opera was designed to explode. Disdaining to complete the conversion to Wagnerism, then, that he had been ready to undertake back in Luise Dustmann's salon (according to Wagner's *Mein Leben*), Hanslick accepted the role of Beckmesser, so to speak, while trying to maintain as much dignity as possible.

In Hanslick's review of *Die Meistersinger,* small concessions to the work (praising its turn from mythical bombast to a human-scale comedy in a "picturesque" historical setting, some nicely imagined stage effects, and isolated moments of musical beauty) are offset by renewed denunciations of the larger Wagnerian project and its implementation here. A charming

---

14. Letter to Carl Tausig, April 1869, reprinted in *Sämtliche Schriften und Dichtungen,* 16:102–3. The larger context here reads: "Dieses alte Stück [the "Judaism" article of 1850] noch einmal zu sehen, mag für viele—namentlich gänzlich unschuldige—sehr schmerzlich gewesen sein; es hätte mir erspart und diesen erspart werden können, wenn der *latente* Erfolg jenes Artikels [i.e., the alleged "secret" influence manifested in the ongoing "cabal" against Wagner] endlich auch auf jener Seite sich verloren hätte. Ich erwartete dies auf lange Zeit, aber die unerhörten Unverschämtheiten der Wiener Presse bei Gelegenheit der 'Meistersinger', die fortgesetzte freche Lügenschneiderei über mich, und die wahrhaft zerstörenden Erfolge hiervon, haben mich endlich, da ich durch eine Frage hierüber veranlaßt war [?], zu meinem rücksichtslosen Schritte bestimmt." Wagner was responding to a telegram from Tausig reporting that the Jews in Vienna were reconciled to him, even after the stir cause by this publication, thanks to the effects of the current successful production of *Lohengrin* there.

but exiguous plot has, he feels, been inflated by an impossibly prolix text, with its "endless discourses and counterdiscourses, domestic conversations, and dry instructional treatises."[15] A few agreeable songs or song-like passages (Walther's "Am stillen Herd" and the Prize Song, Pogner's address, the apprentices' Waltz-Ländler, and some other details from the final scene) or a small core of attractively conceived "leitmotives," as he already identifies them here, are not enough to compensate for vast stretches of tedious, awkward, semi-intelligible, semi-melodic musical declamation. Even the most attractive of the leitmotives offer no more than a "feeble life-preserver amidst the raging ocean of endless melody."[16]

Much of his criticism is certainly consistent with what Hanslick had begun to take issue with in *Lohengrin* (or in what he knew of the other music dramas to date: mainly *Das Rheingold* and *Tristan*). Still, it is surprising how complacently he walks into the trap of self-identification with the critic-villain Beckmesser. Hanslick commends the deliberately "conciliatory" gestures in Walther's role ("Am stillen Herd," the Prize Song) while, as if on cue, he complains of the "inordinate restlessness of accompaniment and modulation"[17] in the Trial Song—Walther's first, ill-advised attempt to win admittance to the guild through a flight of improvisatory poetic-musical fancy, and the number deliberately calculated (by Wagner) to excite the deepest opposition from the Masters. A comparison of Beckmesser's reaction to the "Trial Song" with what Hanslick describes as the "peculiar, foundational principles" of Wagner's music drama suggests that Wagner understood his target well indeed.

Walther's "Trial Song" ("Fanget an!—So rief der Lenz in den Wald") is merely a rather mild, affectionate parody of the advanced Wagnerian language in *Tristan und Isolde*. At the point where Beckmesser interrupts it ("Seid ihr nun fertig?"), he has heard a quite clearly shaped song in F major

---

15. "Von der zähen Weitschweifigkeit aller dieser Reden und Gegenreden, häusliche Gespräche und trockenen Belehrungen, bei stetem festsitzen der Handlung, läßt sich schwer eine Beschreibung geben" ("Dr. Ed. Hanslick über Richard Wagner's 'Meistersinger,'" *Allgemeine musikalische Zeitung* 3.29 [1868]: 225). This source reproduces most of Hanslick's original review of *Die Meistersinger* (in *Die Presse* [June 1868]). The body of this review (most everything related to the work as such, as opposed to the performers) was reprinted in his review of the 1870 Vienna premiere, with minor changes. The text available in Hanslick's collected reviews (*Die moderne Oper*, vol. 1, 1875) is based on the 1870 review. The translation in Henry Pleasants's anthology, *Vienna's Golden Years of Music,* 116–31, is based on the later text, noting some of the deviations from the original.

16. "Dr. Ed. Hanslick über Richard Wagner's 'Meistersinger,'" 227.

17. At least, this remark appears in the text of Hanslick's review of the first Vienna production (27 February 1870), as reprinted in *Die moderne* Oper [vol. 1]: *Kritiken und Studien* (Berlin: A. Hoffmann & Co., 1875), 295.

consisting of two parallel strophes with a short "improvised" interlude apostrophizing Beckmesser as "Winter" lying in wait, in the thorny underbrush, in hopes of ambushing the lyrical aspirations of youth and springtime as celebrated in Walther's two strophes or *Stollen*.[18] The chromatic passing tones and sequential "surging" of the accompaniment to these strophes function as signifiers of the *Tristan* style, without undermining the rather simple, songlike phrase structure and largely diatonic melody of the vocal line. Here, as throughout the opera, the most angular, anti-melodic, and chromaticized music is that depicting the bitter enmity of the critic himself (here, the interlude "In einer Dornenhecken, von Neid und Gram verzehrt"), a chromaticism paradoxically inscribing the pedantic-conservative anti-Wagnerian Beckmesser/Hanslick with the very music he is meant to oppose. By interrupting where he does, Beckmesser "scans" the song as a fairly conventional A B A' structure. By the time Walther completes his song, amid the chaos of the Mastersingers' voluble resistance, it turns out to project a kind of embellished Bar-form (A–B A'–B' C), the interpolated "B" contrasts being Walther's "improvised" allusions to his opponent and judge, Beckmesser.[19]

Beckmesser's indignant response to Walther's song is cleverly compounded—like so much in the opera—of archaic and modern discourses, in this case the language of the old Nuremberg singing-school (as cribbed from Wagenseil's chronicle) and that of contemporary Wagner criticism as practiced by Hanslick and others (F.-J. Fétis and Pierre Scudo in Paris, or

---

18. The notion that this passage in Walther's Trial Song alludes to the Grimm brothers' tale of the "Jew in the Thornbush" is discussed at length by Hans Rudolf Vaget in "'Der Jude im Dorn' oder: Wie antisemitisch sind *Die Meistersinger von Nürnberg?*" *Deutsche Vierteljahrsschrift für Literaturwissenschaft und Gesitesgeschichte* 69, no. 2 (1995): 271–99. While Vaget does not view the Hanslick/Beckmesser connection as evidence of an intended "Jewish" portrait of Beckmesser (see p. 289), his argument in support of the Grimm allusion would nonetheless strengthen the web of associations between Beckmesser and Wagner's "Jewish critics," chief among them being Hanslick (in Wagner's mind). For my part, however, I find the textual and situational basis of the allusion too tenuous to suppose that Wagner could have expected his audience to register it at all (as opposed to the very obvious topicality of Hanslick's critical opposition to the composer). It is worth recalling that Adorno, who first mentioned the Grimm tale in connection with Wagner, did not claim to hear a textual allusion in these "asides" interpolated into Walther's Trial Song. Rather (as Vaget himself notes: ibid., 293), he perceived a more general analogy between the plight of the "villainous" Jew in the fairy tale, dancing despite himself in the thornbush at the sound of the boy's fiddle, and the villains of Wagner's operas (Beckmesser among them), who are manipulated by the score like hapless marionettes at the hands of a malicious puppet-master.

19. See Thomas Grey, *Wagner's Musical Prose: Texts and Contexts* (Cambridge: Cambridge University Press, 1995), 303–4.

Ludwig Bischoff in Germany, to name just a few). "'Twill be a rough task," complains Beckmesser, to tally all the faults of this performance; "Where to begin, where there's not even a clear start or finish" ("Zwar wird's 'ne harte Arbeit sein: wo beginnen, da wo nicht aus noch ein?")

> Von falscher Zahl und falschem Gebänd—
> schweig ich schon ganz und gar:
> zu kurz, zu lang—wer ein End da fänd?
> Wer meint hier im Ernst eine Bar?
> Auf 'blinde Meinung' klag ich allein:—
> Sagt, konnt ein Sinn unsinniger sein?
> . . .
> Und dann die Weis', welch tolles Gekreis
> aus 'Abenteuer-,' 'blau Rittersporn'-Weis,'
> 'hoch-Tannen-,' 'stolz-Jüngling'-Ton!

> Of false meter and phrase.
> I'll not even speak:
> here too short, there too long—and
> no end to be found.
> Who can call this a Bar form?
> Enough to cite 'obscurity'—
> Could any sense be more senseless?
> . . .
> And then the tune, what a mad jumble
> of 'adventure,' 'blue knightsspur' tunes,
> 'high fir-tree' and 'proud youth' styles.

The alleged mixture of *Tönen* and *Weisen* (hypothetical poetic and melodic templates) alludes to the hybridization of genre that was seen as a hallmark of the whole "New German" school. Before that, Beckmesser objects to the missing outlines of "Bar" form (though Walther has already explained that he's not finished yet), but at the same time alludes unmistakably to the recently coined and much ridiculed idea of "endless melody." And in the final couplet of his critique, Beckmesser likewise echoes the fundamental terms of Wagner's modern critics, with just the thinnest of historical disguises in the archaic spelling of *Melodei*:

> Kein Absatz wo, kein Koloratur,
> von Melodei auch nicht eine Spur!
> No 'periods,' no coloratura,
> and not a trace of melody!

Again, in his irritation, Beckmesser paradoxically adopts the sequential fragmentation and nervous, twitchy chromaticism of the very Wagnerian

Zukunftsmusik (starting at "Hier habt ihr verthan! Ihr Meister, schaut die Tafel an") scorned by conservative critics. And to complete this inversion of critics and criticized, immediately as Beckmesser concludes his catalogue of Walther's shortcomings and transgressions ("von Melodei auch nicht eine Spur!"), the rest of the masters express their collective indignation to the very same musical material, breathlessly repeated, that had expressed the swelling accents of youthful love and the bursting-out of spring in Walther's own Trial Song (Masters: "Wer nennt das Gesang? Es ward einem bang!" etc.).

Hanslick acknowledges that one must at least admire the "consistency" with which the composer applies his "new principle" of musical-dramatic composition, even if *Die Meistersinger* has not converted this particular critic to the new gospel of Wagnerian music drama.

> This [principle] is the deliberate dissolution of all fixed form into a shapeless, sensually intoxicating 'sounding' [*Klingen*], and the substitution, in place of independent, articulated melodies, of a vague and formless melodizing [*Melodisiren*]. We might as well accept Wagner's dubious phrase [*schiefes Wort*] "endless melody" as the technical term for this [procedure], since by now everyone has some notion of what that suggests. This "endless melody" is the leading, which is to say undermining force [*musikalisch unterwühlende Macht*] in *Die Meistersinger,* just as in *Tristan.* We hear a short motive; and before it has a chance to be worked into a regular melodic theme, it is tweaked and twisted through continual modulation or enharmonic changes, [sequenced] up or down, drawn out by some decorative accretion, then once more broken into pieces, repeated by this or that instrument. Conscientiously avoiding any full cadence, this boneless and tendon-less organism, this tonal mollusk continues to replicate itself, oozing forwards into infinity.[20]

Unlike many of Wagner's early opponents, Hanslick was at least able to identify with some accuracy what it was he objected to in the music and its "application to the drama."

Wagner's (in some respects very clever) attempt to preempt these criticisms through parody in *Die Meistersinger* does not prevent Hanslick from posting some successful strikes of his own. "Wagner knows exactly what he wants," writes Hanslick. "His conscious aims are expressed by every note in the score; nothing is accidental." Hanslick is quite clear about

---

20. This translation conflates details from both 1868 and 1870 texts. The phrase *knochenlose Ton-molluske* replaces the original phrase "diese knochen- und muskellose Gestaltung" in the 1870 text (*Die moderne Oper*, 302–3; cf. "Dr. Ed. Hanslick über Richard Wagner's 'Meistersinger,'" 226). Perhaps the original "muskellose" later suggested the near-anagram "Molluske," as an appropriately related image (though in fact Hanslick's description would sooner imply something like a snail or a slug).

Wagner's aim to capture all levels of utterance in tone (as well as gestures, facial expressions, etc.), not content with reducing a few key expressive moments into arias or ensembles. "But then," objects Hanslick, "no room [is left] for the kind of happy coincidence that [often] gives products of artistic imagination, no less than those of nature, their ultimate appeal."[21] As the victim of Wagner's vengeful humor in the figure of Beckmesser, Hanslick could appreciate all too well the obsessively "scripted" character of Wagner's art. He is remarkably astute in his perception of what is impressive as well as limiting in Wagner's micro-management of the *Gesamtkunstwerk*. (Hanslick's perception of Wagner as a kind of artistic "control freak" anticipates the composer's greatest grudging admirer of the next century, Theodor W. Adorno, who, in a certain paradoxical way, himself sometimes comes across as a kind of high-modernist Beckmesser.)

For Hanslick, the overweening contrivance (or simply heavy-handedness) of the "humor" in Wagner's comedy invites resistance. (He was of a mind with Liszt and Nietzsche in this, both of whom took exception to Wagner's sense of humor in real life, as well.)[22] Of course, Hanslick had good reason to feel "unamused" by the merciless lampooning of Beckmesser throughout the second and third acts of the opera. And yet he makes no overt attempt at rescuing the character from Wagner's ridicule. Obviously, Hanslick does recognize the "set-up," as demonstrated by one brief aside in his review, though one that refers to the masters as a group, rather than to the "marker" in particular. ("A genial poet stands in opposition to a dozen pedantic guild-members, who cannot understand him, yet dare to judge him. Do you notice something up here, my perspicacious reader?")[23] But Hanslick does not try to reinvent Beckmesser in a positive light, or otherwise excuse him. For instance, he first introduces Beckmesser to the reader as "a malicious old fop who exercises the role of 'Marker.'"[24]

Instead, Hanslick distances himself from the semisadistic "fun" that Wagner grants his other characters at Beckmesser's expense. Of the relentlessly misaccented serenade in Act II, with its grotesquely exposed lute accompaniment, Hanslick remarks simply that "it begins quite characteristically, though soon becomes artificial [*verkünstelt*]." As if instinctively assuming Beckmesser's point of view, he takes aim at Sachs's mischievous ditty: "Hans Sachs competes against him [Beckmesser] with a cobbling-

---

21. "Dr. Ed. Hanslick über Richard Wagner's 'Meistersinger,'" 226.
22. For more on "comedy" in *Meistersinger*, see Klaus van den Berg's essay in this volume [N.V.].
23. "Dr. Ed. Hanslick über Richard Wagner's 'Meistersinger,'" col. 1; *Die moderne Oper*, 300. "And in fact, the superiority of the genial personality who dictates his own rules, over and against the confining rules of the School, is defended with especial zeal and excessive prolixity [*Redseligkeit*] through every act."
24. Hanslick, *Die moderne Oper*, 294.

song ("Jerum, Jerum, Hallo hallo he!") that, while ostensibly comic, sounds more like an angry hyena than a merry cobbler." Sachs's joke of marking the errors of Beckmesser's song with hammer-strokes on the soles of the shoes he's finishing for the Marker himself is "squeezed relentlessly dry by the composer, leaving us with a tedious and tasteless impression." Still more telling is the way Hanslick registers an underlying "brutality" behind the musical and dramatic tactics of this seemingly harmless comedy. The prelude is dismissed as a "composition of painful artifice and downright brutal effect." Then Hanslick twice mentions his discomfort with the massive "riot" ensemble that forms the climax to Act II. From what he had seen in the score, his curiosity had originally been piqued by the ingenious complexity of the ensemble writing; but in performance, he was put off by an effect of merely "brutal shouting and screaming."[25] Musical humor is a tricky thing, notes the veteran aesthetician. Wagner miscalculates the necessary means—those "gruesome dissonances" of Beckmesser's own gestural music, throughout the opera, being a case in point. Further along these same lines, Hanslick asks: "If peaceful burghers and craftsmen must express their dissatisfaction in such raging tones" as these (speaking of the masters' condemnation of Walther's Trial Song and Beckmesser's attempted prize song), "what accents are left for a composer to depict the French Revolution? Not to speak of the riot scene of Act II, less comic than it is merely ugly and coarse."[26]

The excess, indeed violence of this "riot scene" at the end of Act II has elicited qualms from later critics, Adorno notable among them. Adorno was not willing to pass off this scarcely provoked outbreak of mass hysteria as merely a somewhat drastic theatrical figure of the "poetic frenzy" apostrophized by Sachs in his Act III monologue. For him, it had too much disturbing resonance with more sinister exhibitions of popular violence in the Nazi era.[27] Other critics sometimes balk at this as an oversensitized and anachronistic reaction, turning the glorified neighborhood pillow fight of Wagner's good-natured (if frenetic) finale into a symbolic pogrom. However, at least one reviewer of Wagner's pamphlet on *Judaism in Music,* reissued the year after the *Meistersinger* premiere, thought to identify this anti-Semitic polemic precisely as "a literary pendant to the *Prügelszene*" in the new opera.[28] Though an isolated instance, this connection between the essay and the opera brings us back to my starting point: the question of

---

25. Ibid., 296–97 (all foregoing quotations in this paragraph).
26. Ibid., 301–2.
27. See Theodor W. Adorno, *In Search of Wagner* [Versuch über Wagner], trans. Rodney Livingstone (London: NLB, 1981), 121.
28. See Fischer, *Richard Wagners "Das Judentum"*, 314 (citing an anonymous brochure, *Richard Wagner und das Judentum. Ein Beitrag zur Kulturgeschichte unserer Zeit, von einem Unparteiischen*. Elberfeld, 1869).

whether, and in what ways, the case of Hanslick vs. Wagner at the time of *Die Meistersinger* may have been inflected by the reissue of *Judaism in Music* in 1869.

IV.

The debate over whether Beckmesser might have been intended by Wagner (at least covertly) as a Jewish caricature has, reasonably enough, looked to the essay "Judaism in Music" for evidence of what traits the composer particularly identified, and thus may have thought to parody, as "Jewish." Citing corroboration from the anti-Jewish stereotypes limned in that text, those arguing the case of Beckmesser as anti-Semitic caricature have identified especially these aspects of the role as evidence:[29]

1. the nervous, disjunct, and irascible qualities of Beckmesser's vocal lines;
2. the emphasis on notes "unnaturally" high for the prescribed bass voice (frequently jumping to a tenor f' or g') meant to suggest a querulous cracking of the voice;
3. the prosodic abuses and melodic poverty of his abortive "serenade" in Act II;
4. its awkward decorative melismas, thought to mirror Wagner's tendentious description of "cantorial singing" in the essay;
5. Beckmesser's attempted "theft" of Walther's Prize Song in Act III and his inability to interpret it (symbolizing the Jews' unsuccessful appropriation of European languages and musical traditions inherently "alien" to them); and
6. Beckmesser's ludicrous garbling of Walther's poetry, further distorted by its mismatching to the tattered shreds of his own failed serenade

---

29. See, e.g., Barry Millington, "Nuremberg Trial: Is There Anti-Semitism in *Die Meistersinger?*" *Cambridge Opera Journal* 3.3 (1991): 247–60; Paul Lawrence Rose, *Wagner: Race and Revolution* (New Haven and London: Yale University Press, 1992), chaps. 5 and 7; Marc Weiner, *Richard Wagner and the Anti-Semitic Imagination* (Lincoln and London: University of Nebraska Press, 1995), chap. 2. Following the example of Jacob Katz (*The Darker Side of Genius: Richard Wagner's Anti-Semitism* [Hanover N.H.: University Press of New England, 1986]), Dieter Borchmeyer has become the most outspoken proponent of maintaining the ideological "purity" of the works, over and against Wagner's personal and political views on the subject of the Jews. See, for example, his afterword to *Richard Wagner: Theory and Theatre*, trans. Stewart Spencer (Oxford: Oxford University Press, 1991), "A Note on Wagner's Anti-Semitism" (pp. 404–10), or more recently, the concluding section of his chapter "Nürnberg als ästhetischer Staat: *Die Meistersinger*—Bild und Gegenbild der Geschichte," in his *Richard Wagner: Ahasvers Wandlungen* (Frankfurt and Leipzig: Insel Verlag, 2002).

(again, an allegory of the Jews' alleged inability to understand truly the languages of their "host" cultures from within).

Reading the original 1850 essay alongside the text and score of the opera does highlight many of these suggested parallels.

As mentioned earlier, the principal individual targets of the 1850 essay were Mendelssohn and Meyerbeer. However, the original ideas for an opera on the Nuremberg "mastersingers" had already been drafted back in 1845, and there is no specific evidence that Wagner might have viewed it, either then or later, as a vehicle for "artistic revenge" on these two maligned Jewish competitor/adversaries, as he came to see them. And when he did at last return to the "mastersingers" scenario and develop it into a complete libretto, in 1861–62, competition from these (or any other) "Jewish musicians" was no longer much of a concern.[30] Precisely in the period of 1861–62, however, Wagner was several times confronted by the person he regarded as his most influential *critical* opponent, Eduard Hanslick. To judge by the afterword appended to *Judaism in Music* in 1869, Wagner had become increasingly preoccupied over the preceding years with the notion of a "conspiracy" of Jewish critics bent on ruining him and his whole cause. Their secret motive was (allegedly) revenge on the author of "Judaism in Music"—never mind the fact that it was published anonymously, and rather obscurely, nineteen years earlier, and had received nothing like the attention attracted by the theoretical writings published under Wagner's own name back at that time. And, again according to the 1869 afterword, the ringleader of this "Jewish conspiracy" was Eduard Hanslick—never mind the fact that Hanslick regarded himself as an Austrian Catholic, by birth and upbringing.[31]

Hanslick's mother, Karoline, was in fact the daughter of Salomon Abraham Kisch, a well-to-do Jewish merchant in Prague. She had converted to Catholicism when she married Hanslick's father (of German-speaking Bohemian peasant background), who was in a position to propose to Karoline ("Lotti"), thanks to a windfall brought his way by a winning

---

30. The possibility mentioned above, in passing (p. 168), that Beckmesser's own performances in Acts II and III might resonate with the composer's critique of Mendelssohn and Meyerbeer (and "Jewish musicians" more generally) does follow from the idea that Beckmesser might have been realized, in the final instance, as a more general embodiment of Jewish "unmusicality" as construed by Wagner. But for this supposition, unlike the association with Hanslick, we have no particular circumstantial evidence.

31. Cf. *Richard Wagner's Prose Works*, 3:104, where W. A. Ellis gives in a footnote the text of Hanslick's disclaimer regarding his alleged Jewishness, which speaks only of his father's side of the family. This disclaimer is taken from a piece in the *Deutsche Rundschau*, Jan. 1894 (p. 56), and it was reiterated in the autobiography *Aus meinem Leben* (see p. 221 of the 1987 edition by Peter Wapnewski).

lottery ticket.[32] It appears that Hanslick may have confided to Wagner information about his family background during one of their brief encounters in the early 1860s. A diary entry by Cosima from 27 June 1870 strongly suggests this, as well as suggesting that Wagner was quite deliberately aiming to "out" Hanslick's Jewish background in the 1869 afterword, in a gesture he regarded as well-deserved retribution:

> At lunch he [R. W.] tells us about Hanslick (his mother a Jewess) and Herr Ambros, who allowed himself to be bought by the *Neue freie Presse* (against R.), how both of them had approached him, made admissions to him, and then, reckoning on his good manners like the miserable creatures they are [!!], had no fear that he would one day tell what he knew.[33]

In any case, Hanslick is the only individual Wagner identifies in the whole diatribe against his alleged "Jewish" critics in the 1869 afterword (that is, aside from Ludwig Bischoff, who was not Jewish, and Ferdinand Hiller, who was not a critic). The chief tactic of these nebulous "conspirators" has been, Wagner asserts, to scare the public away from any contact with his more recent works by associating them with his wild and easily discredited "theories." The first stage of this "tactic" was to prejudice the "educated classes" against Wagner. That job, writes Wagner, fell to "a certain Viennese lawyer, a great musical *amateur* and a connoisseur of Hegelian dialectics [i.e., Eduard Hanslick]," whose "Jewish origins, however discreetly disguised, made him especially receptive to this cause."[34] "This man now penned a pamphlet [*Libell*] on 'the beautiful in music,'" Wagner continues, "in which he advanced the cause of musical Judaism with astonishing skill." The gist of this, it is explained (however implausibly), was to establish a canon of classical "beauty" in music based on the works of Haydn, Mozart, and Beethoven, and then to propose Mendelssohn as the proper heir to the tradition. (In this exalted position he was strategically "propped up by a few Christian notables, such as Robert Schumann.") Having persuaded the Viennese intelligentsia that a great aesthetic prophet had emerged from its midst, Hanslick was able to insinuate himself as a highly respected music critic. In that capacity he could lead the campaign against Richard Wagner

---

32. See Hanslick, *Aus meinem Leben*, 8 and 512 (Wapnewski, afterword).

33. *Cosima Wagner's Diaries*, 1:239. Wagner must have been alluding to the attempted reconciliation of Hanslick with Wagner as engineered by Luise Dustmann recounted in *Mein Leben* (though not in Hanslick's autobiography). The reference to A. W. Ambros (whether regarding the Wagner-Hanslick enmity, or any confidential confession to Wagner) is not clear. By the time in question, Ambros was little engaged in criticism of contemporary music.

34. Wagner, *Gesammelte Schriften*, 8:243.

"in widely read daily papers," declaring the composer and his newest works for null and void.[35] (And in fact, it is probably the aura of intellectual authority vouchsafed by *Vom Musikalisch-Schönen* that Wagner aims to satirize in Beckmesser's egregious incompetence as a judge of "authentic" musical and poetic value, more than the authority that accrued to Hanslick by virtue of his journalism *per se*).

V.

Wagner had already begun fomenting publicly against the "Jews" and the press in the series of writings executed during the mid-1860s under the aegis of Ludwig II. But it is above all the afterword to the 1869 reissue of *Judaism in Music*—with its repeated attacks on Hanslick as the mastermind of an international (indeed "interdisciplinary": aesthetic and journalistic) anti-Wagnerian Jewish conspiracy—that presents the most conspicuous evidence of a link between Wagner's notion of his perceived "Jewish" critics and the figure of Beckmesser. Yet for whom would this network of associations be legible? For Wagner himself, obviously. And presumably for Hanslick, who reviewed the *Judaism* pamphlet soon after it (re-)appeared in 1869.[36] Neither one, however, cared to raise the associations between Hanslick, *Judaism,* and Beckmesser to the level of public discourse. Hanslick, for obvious reasons, did not want to dignify Wagner's parody of his critics by engaging in any vocal counteroffensive. Wagner, for his part, was not inclined to compromise the enduring dignity of his own works by publicizing personal, topical allusions in them that would contradict his and others' Romantic notions of a "pure" and timeless art-work. (And music dramas could aspire to that status, too, if on a broader level than "absolute" instrumental composition.) These concerns, rather than any sensitivity to the feelings of his "enemies," were surely behind the decision to substitute "Sixtus Beckmesser" for "Veit Hanslich" when developing the prose drafts into a full libretto.

---

35. Ibid., 8:243–44. Wagner returns to Hanslick and *Vom Musikalisch-Schönen* (finally identifying the author by name) on p. 251, where he complains of how Hanslick's theories of musical *Judenschönheit* were insinuated into the aesthetic system of the otherwise upstanding, "thoroughly blond German aesthetician, Herr Vischer," and thereby acquired an undeserved credibility under the aegis of this *ganz christlich-deutsche Berühmtheit*. Thus Hanslick's "Jewish" theory of the musically beautiful was raised to the status of a dogma. (In fact, as several reviewers of Wagner's 1869 brochure pointed out, Hanslick among them, the musical chapters in Vischer's *Ästhetik* were provided by Karl Köstlin, not by Hanslick.)

36. *Neue freie Presse,* 9 March 1869. Reprinted from *Wilhelm Lübke und Eduard Hanslick über Richard Wagner* [(Berlin 1869)] in Fischer, *Richard Wagners "Das Judentum,"* 232–38.

To what extent Hanslick would have read in Beckmesser's role a parody of himself specifically as a "Jewish" critic—complemented by a parody of the modern "Jewish" composer (Mendelssohn, Meyerbeer, Offenbach?) in Acts II and III—it is impossible to say.[37] By republishing the original text of the "Judaism" essay just as *Die Meistersinger* was poised to debut throughout Germany and Austria, Wagner must have been aware that he was providing a possible "key" to such a reading of Beckmesser, at least to those who cared to avail themselves of it. Few did, apparently—at least, considering the evidence of both the opera's and the reprinted essay's early reception. To judge from the generous sample of reviews of the 1869 *Judaism* brochure recently reprinted by Jens Malte Fischer, there is scant evidence that anyone—to begin with, at least—was reading the content of the essay into the text, or subtext, of the opera. (The remark cited earlier, comparing the essay to the *Prügelszene* of Act II, is an exception, and even it proposes only an analogy, not a conscious *thematic* link.)

As another reviewer (Karl Gutzkow) suggested, opposition to the *Judaism* essay *was* likely to have an impact on the reception of the new opera, given the timing of the two things; "and it might be well advised to avoid such Jewish *fora* as Frankfurt-am-Main, or else the cobbler Hans Sachs is liable to meet with a tarring."[38] Thus, for example, several protests against early productions of *Die Meistersinger* can be linked to anti-Wagnerian sentiment stirred up by the *Judaism* pamphlet (Cosima cites such an incident in Mannheim, for instance, in her diary entry for 4 July 1869). In most of these cases there is no evidence that audiences were reading any thematic link between the opera itself and the content of the *Judaism* brochure (a point that is frequently overlooked in recent writing on this topic). One apparent exception, interestingly, occurs in the case of the first Viennese

---

37. In his review of the brochure Hanslick does dismiss, in passing, Wagner's error in identifying him as a Jew ("seine zierlich verdeckte jüdische Herkunft . . ."), though more casually than in *Aus meinem Leben*. Here he passes it off with a joke: "This one falsehood [in addition to that about Hanslick's supposed contribution to Vischer's *Ästhetik*], my alleged Jewishness, I will credit to the blind rage of a man who, like the rabbi in Heine's 'Disputation,' goes about at all times with an unsheathed dagger in hand so as to treacherously circumcise unsuspecting Christian passers-by" (for original text, see Fischer, *Richard Wagners "Das Judentum,"* 235).

38. Cited from Fischer, *Richard Wagners "Das Judentum,"* 273. Karl Gutzkow, "Literarische Briefe: An eine deutsche Frau in Paris. IV" (*Die Gartenlaube* 20 [1869]: 310–12). Cf. also p. 287 in Fischer.

production, in February 1870. A notice in the *Neue Zeitschrift für Musik* from the arch-nationalist Wagner-acolyte, Ludwig Nohl, reports a local rumor that Wagner was ridiculing a "traditional Jewish song" in Beckmesser's Act II serenade.[39] Neither Nohl nor Cosima Wagner (who also mentioned this notice in her diary some days later) offers any confirmation that these protesters were "on to something," or that any such musical parody had been intended by the "Master." While the ungainly melismas of Beckmesser's serenade obviously do parody Italian coloratura, the basic melodic *ductus* of the song is surely meant to sound *alt-deutsch*, and it is difficult to imagine what sort of "traditional Jewish song" these Viennese listeners had in mind (unless of course it was a textual allusion they were reacting to). Even if these Viennese protesters were reading the right message for the wrong reasons, Nohl and Cosima, no less than Richard, were not about to sanction public protests of this sort.

VI.

Whether or not Wagner had meant to parody "Jewish music" in any aspects of his score, *Die Meistersinger* itself was subject to a number of musical-theatrical parodies soon after its 1868 premiere (and continuing into the early twentieth century). One might well turn to these for evidence of connections between the opera and Wagner's newly publicized anti-Semitic attitudes. Here again, the evidence is equivocal. Some of these allude quite overtly to the *Judaism* brochure, but again as a current topical reference, not as something thematically linked to the opera. The reference is most explicit in an 1869 Berlin parody with the title *Die Meistersinger, oder: Das Judentum in der Musik* (printed 1871), and it is also clear enough in an 1872 parody, *Hepp, Hepp! oder, Die Meistersinger von Nürnberg. Große konfessionell-sozialdemokratische Zukunftsoper in 3 Aufzügen*. In the latter case (as in a 1917 Viennese parody, *Die Meistersinger von Ottakring*), it is actually the *Walther* figure who is exposed as "a Jew"—a tactic paral-

---

39. L. Nohl, "Die Meistersinger in Wien," *Neue Zeitschrift für Musik* 66.11 (11 March 1870): 104. Specifically, Nohl reports (but does not confirm) the rumor that Beckmesser's serenade was "based on a Jewish melody, chosen by the composer in order to mock the Jews and their music." Millington relates this episode to his thesis that the melismas and accompanimental style of the serenade allude to Jewish cantorial singing styles ("Nuremberg Trial," 251–54).

lel to numerous contemporary caricatures of Wagner that portray him in the guise of his own demonized Jewish enemy. (Similarly, the critic and novelist Gustav Freytag ridiculed Wagner's arguments in the *Judaism* brochure by concluding that they merely served to define Wagner himself as "the greatest Jew of them all.")[40]

In the first of these parodies, the Walther/Wagner figure ("Richard von Wahnsing") is confronted by four "Jewish musicians," faintly disguised under the names Felix Mandelbaum, Jacob Meyerbach, Jacob Offenbeer, and Jacob Haltevieh [= Halévy]. One after the other they pop up out of a box where a certain musical "Don Quixote" has packed them away with the help of a certain "brochure." They mock their young opponent to tunes from their respective oeuvres. But the actual Beckmesser figure in this skit—"Wahnsing's" rival and the arbiter of the mastersingers' trial-singing—is a foreign musician who speaks in a heavily Italianized pidgin-German and goes by the name of "Werda." This "Werda" appears on the scene costumed *als Troubador* and singing a ditty with this familiar rhythm (à la "La donna è mobile") and suggestive text:

Ich bin der Größte
Ja aller Meister,
Denn alle Geister
Beherrsche ich ja.
. . . .
Auf den Drehorgeln
Hört ihr die Lieder,

---

40. "Im Sinne seiner Broschüre erscheint er selbst als der größte Jude" (G. Freytag, "Der Streit über das Judenthum in der Musik," *Die Grenzboten* 28 [1869]: 336). As evidence, Freytag submits the following list of Wagnerian traits: "Striving for effect by pretentious and coldly calculating means (but unregulated by true artistic feeling); inability to give full and pure melodic and harmonic expression to musical feeling; exaggerated nervous unrest; delight in the unusual and the contrived; the effort to conceal the weaknesses of his melodic invention through clever effects (*witzigen Einfall*) and external artifice; thus also the greatest talent for a refined stage-direction (*Regie*) of effects. And finally and fundamentally: in place of any secure artistic feeling in which form and content are effortlessly merged, we find the unrefined pretension of a willful dilettante who strains beyond the limits of his art and thereby offends the laws of beauty, which he is incapable of following—an experimenting frame of mind that seeks satisfaction in the grotesque, unconcerned whether or not these experiments wreak havoc on singers, orchestra, and the very organism of the musical drama." Freytag's review is also reprinted in Fischer, *Richard Wagners "Das Judentum,"* 267–71.

Ja meine Lieder
Nur ganz allein.[41]

Wagner's *real* competition, in other words, is not primarily identified with those "Jewish musicians," but with a higher authority in matters of popular melody and vocal display, Giuseppe Verdi (and the Italian tradition).

The full title of the second of these parodies translates as: "Hepp, Hepp! The Mastersingers of Nuremberg. A grand denominational/social-democratic opera of the future in three present-day acts, composed for the past by Richard, text also by Richard (but a different one)." Here the Walther/Wagner figure, going under the pseudonym Adam Walther Holzing, is exposed as a Jew by the Beckmesser figure (Sixtus Aufmesser, writer for a social-democratic weekly paper) when Walther (real name, Adam Meyersohn) seeks to infiltrate their singing-club. But the Sachs-figure defends him, telling the orchestra to play a bit of Mendelssohn's "Spring Song" as evidence that "Jews can, after all, succeed with musical notes as well as bank notes."[42] The later *Mastersingers of Ottakring* (a relatively new working-class Vienna neighborhood) similarly presents a "Jewish" Walther seeking admittance to an exclusive men's choral group. Again, it is Walther who is exposed (by the Beckmesser character) as a Jew, ineligible for membership ("Walther Isidor Goldzink, of Goldzink & Son, wholesale suppliers of goose-fat, tel. 34034—out of order.") The joke in this case seems to be that the Beckmesser character is likewise a Jew, at best faintly disguised ("Simon Beck-Messer, a *rachsüchtiger Schnittwarencommis* at the Gerngroß department store, *Plüschabteilung*"), who perhaps adopts an exaggerated *Judenfeindschaft* as part of his cover. His first name and hyphenated last name would seem intended as clues to his disguised identity, as would such lines as these from the serenade he presents to the Eva figure ("Resi"):

---

41. "I am the greatest, / yes greatest of masters; / for I am the ruler / of all the spirits. . . . On the barrel-organs / you hear my songs, / yes all my songs / and nobody else's." Franz Bittong, *Die Meistersinger, oder: Das Judentum in der Musik. Parodistischer Scherz in 1 Akt* (Berlin, 1871). Cited from Fischer, *Richard Wagners "Das Judentum,"* 338. The text of the parody was published anonymously in 1872 (Spremberg: W. Erbe); the author's name appears to have been Richard Schmidt-Cabanis. There is no mention of the composer/arranger, however.

42. See Andrea Schneider, *Die parodierten Musikdramen Richard Wagners: Geschichte und Dokumentation Wagnersche Opernparodien im deutschsprachigen Raum von der Mitte des 19. Jahrhunderts bis zum Ende des Ersten Weltkrieges* (Anif-Salzburg: Müller-Speiser, 1996), 373. The author of the parody was Robert Weil (publication: Vienna: Doblinger, 1917); the arranger of the music was Fritz Recktenwald.

"O du kleine, O du feine Nixe
ich hab mir schon heute gebadet
die Füße zu dein Namenstag, O Schickse!"[43]

Playing on the baptismal motif central to Wagner's opera, the "Jewish" Walther has himself baptized a Catholic at the Paulanerkirche in the Wieden, thus entering the contest and winning the girl.

Beckmesser's apparent Jewishness in this late parody of 1917 comes across only as an incidental comic counterpoint to the principal idea—also evident in "Hepp! Hepp!"—of casting Walther (i.e., Wagner) as a Jew. (And Beckmesser's "disguised" Jewish identity is in any case not entirely clear: cf. n. 43.) The earlier parodies, from the immediate orbit of the *Judaism* brochure and the *Meistersinger* premiere, make no allusion to the alleged "Jewishness" of Wagner's critics at all. Wagner's parodists, no less than his "serious" critics (like Hanslick), were willing to ridicule his fanatic anti-Semitism without necessarily trying to detect its traces in the operas. If Wagner *himself* identified Beckmesser—as I believe he probably did—with traits he attributed to his Jewish musical as well as critical adversaries (as he saw them), did he fail in his attempt to make these associations manifest to his audience? The answer, I think, is no: simply because he did not in fact attempt this. That is, Beckmesser may well have manifested negative traits Wagner himself could read as "Jewish" (in his behavior and the musical expression of this behavior). But if so, I believe he was satisfied for these to remain a kind of private subtext, at least for the time being, a subtext that need not interfere in the popular dissemination of his opera.[44]

---

43. Ibid., 380. Andrea Schneider assumes that this character is *not* meant to be a Jew, despite the characteristically hyphenated name, but on the contrary, "a pan-Germanist tradesman from the provinces" who speaks in a Carinthian dialect and expresses vehement anti-Jewish and anti-Slavic sentiments. A reference to him as a *rother Schuft* (red rogue) does not allude to left-socialist labor sympathies, she argues, but identifies his position as a "non-citizen or also a non-Christian" [i.e., an atheist, but not Jewish?] (ibid., 204). Another reading, however, might be that that character disguises a Jewish identity behind exaggerated displays of nationalist pan-Germanism.

44. Hans Rudolf Vaget makes a similar claim regarding the possible allusions in Beckmesser's role to the Grimm fairy tale "The Jew in the Thorn Bush" ("The 'Metapolitics' of *Die Meistersinger*: Wagner's Nuremberg As Imagined Community," in *Searching for Common Ground: Diskurse zur deutschen Identität 1750–1871*, ed. N. Vazsonyi [Cologne & Weimar: Böhlau, 2000], 279–80). Given the rather tenuous status of this particular allusion, it is indeed likely to be present only for those who have been alerted to it (and I am not convinced that Wagner himself ever intended it to begin with). More important to realize, I believe, is the status of a broader "allegorical" discourse of anti-Semitism in the operas that, while it so far eludes any positive proof, could easily have been available to a sizeable audience subgroup receptive to such nuances.

The ongoing debates over the question of anti-Jewish subtexts in Wagner's operas may find an instructive parallel in the controversy over the presence of dissident anti-Soviet attitudes "encoded" in the music of Dmitri Shostakovich, a controversy that has likewise exercised many critics and listeners over the past two decades. As Richard Taruskin has insisted in the case of Shostakovich (primarily with reference to instrumental music, without text), the "doubleness" of the music—its potential to be heard and read to different, seemingly opposite ends—is an essential characteristic, a product of the composer's personality, his musical vocabulary and technique, and above all the fraught and fractured historical context in which he lived.[45] Granted, the temptation has been to read Shostakovich as a victim and a hero, while the debated subtexts of Wagner's operas would necessarily paint him as an oppressor and a villain, an ideological ancestor of a criminal Nazi regime. Since it is impossible to exculpate Wagner fully here, as regards the written record (the *Judaism* brochure first and foremost), the impulse to cordon off the artistic oeuvre is understandable. As I see it, however, the nexus of *Die Meistersinger* and the 1869 *Judaism* brochure with its new afterword undoubtedly opened up the door to associations between Beckmesser as a dramatic, and indeed musical, figure and Wagner's rejection of the Jews, first as musicians and now as critics. Having opened that door, however, Wagner himself did not cross the threshold and point out the associations thus made available. (And one could choose to exculpate him on these grounds.) The potentially insidious "doubleness" of Beckmesser, along with those other suspects—principally Mime and Alberich, less so Klingsor and Kundry—remains all the same. Beckmesser fulfills his function as a pseudo-historical German mastersinger, town clerk, comic-opera pedant, and foolish, avaricious suitor. None of that prevents one from noting the ways in which the character and his music may have been designed to embody Wagner's well-documented attitudes towards the Jews, and as a vehicle for a kind of semiprivate revenge against one in particular (by Wagner's lights, if not by his own): Eduard Hanslick.

No doubt the historical truths hardest to accept are those that are fundamentally ambiguous. The role of Wagner's anti-Semitism in the conception, or in the effect, of his operas seems to me to be just such a case. Whether Wagner would have thought to highlight such subtexts for a later generation, were he still around some sixty or seventy years later, is impossible to say, any more than what Wagner would have done if he had still been alive to accept the accolades of Hitler and his government. For Wagner's sake, we can probably assume it's lucky he never had the chance.

---

45. See, for example, Taruskin's review of publications by Anthony Philips and Esti Sheinberg ("Double Trouble") in *The New Republic*, 24 December 2001, 26–34.

10

"Du warst mein Feind von je": The Beckmesser Controversy Revisited

Hans Rudolf Vaget

No opera takes us to the dark heart of the matter that we associate with German history more directly than does *Die Meistersinger von Nürnberg*. Of the many questions posed by that history, the thorniest may well be the role played by high culture, and specifically by music, in the rise of National Socialism. In the immediate aftermath of World War II and long thereafter, most commentators on the "German problem" tended to argue that Adolf Hitler and Nazism marked a complete break with the great cultural achievements of Germany's past. In the last two decades, notably since 1986, when the "Historikerstreit" helped focus the debate about the place of the Holocaust in German history, notions of discontinuity have begun to give way to a growing awareness of fateful continuity. Today, we are prepared to read the emplotment of what Friedrich Meinecke famously termed the "deutsche Katastrophe" in the narrative of German culture quite differently from the essentially exculpatory sense in which that narrative was constructed in the post-war period.[1]

This shift of perspective was by no means as pioneering as it may have seemed at first, for it was anticipated in the debates of the late 1930s, when there began in the United States, in particular among the exiles from Nazi Germany, a painful process of self-examination and a painstaking search for antecedents. In April of 1938, Thomas Mann, the most prominent of the exiles and a dyed-in-the-wool Wagnerian, penned a series of unsparingly self-critical reflections, some of which he published under the provocative title "Bruder Hitler."[2] In this essay, Mann courageously views Hitler as a fellow

---

1. Friedrich Meinecke, *Die deutsche Katastrophe: Betrachtungen und Erinnerungen*, 5th ed. (Wiesbaden: Brockhaus, [1946], 1955).

2. Thomas Mann, "Bruder Hitler," *Achtung, Europa! Essays 1933–1938*, ed. Hermann Kurzke and Stephan Stachorski (Frankfurt/Main: Fischer, 1995): 305–12. First published in English under the title "That Man is My Brother," *Esquire* 11 (March 1939): 132–33.

artist in the Wagnerian mold—a chip off the same old block from which Mann traced much of his own artistic lineage. A few years later, in *Doctor Faustus,* he undertook to unfurl on a grand scale the fateful concatenation of "German" music and German history, suggesting that Germany took the road to barbarism not despite, as the familiar cliché would have it, but rather because of the German idolatry of music.

At about the same time that Mann wrote "Bruder Hitler," Theodor W. Adorno embarked on his seminal *Versuch über Wagner* with the aim of mapping the "Urlandschaft," the primordial topography, of fascism.[3] Shortly thereafter, invoking the example of Mann, the young Harvard historian Peter Viereck sought to identify and expose the "roots of the Nazi mind."[4] In an article of 1939, entitled "Hitler and Wagner," Viereck pointed to Wagner, the "politically most influential artist of modern history," and identified him as "the chief well-spring of Nazi ideology."[5]

It seems necessary to recall these pioneering interventions in order to throw into relief the marked change that has occurred since that time. In their examination of the Hitler-Wagner nexus, Mann, Adorno, Viereck, and others highlighted a whole range of ideological affinities, among them nationalism, megalomania, the substitution of myth and fairy tale for history, the totalitarian mind-set, demagoguery, self-praise, love of pomp, the rejection of liberalism, the espousal of revolutionary dynamism for its own sake, and the obsession with racial purity. In their view, anti-Semitism constituted but one of many factors. Today, however, it seems fair to say, that the topic of anti-Semitism virtually monopolizes the debate about the historical legacy of Richard Wagner in general and of *Die Meistersinger von Nürnberg* in particular.

Undoubtedly, this shift was caused by the growing and now widespread awareness of the significance of the Holocaust as a historical marker of the human capacity for inhumanity. Does it follow that the Holocaust must be regarded as "the central event" of German history, "the event toward which every text, every moment in German history and, yes culture moved inexorably?"[6] What we call History results from a far-flung web of contingencies; it does not move with inexorable purposefulness toward one goal,

---

3. Theodor W. Adorno, "Selbstanzeige des Essaybuches 'Versuch über Wagner,'" *Gesammelte Schriften,* ed. Gretel Adorno and Rolf Tiedemann (Frankfurt/Main: Suhrkamp, 1971), 13:504.

4. This is the subtitle of the 3rd edition of Peter Viereck, *Metapolitics* (New York: Capricorn Books, 1965), for a long time the most widely used introduction to the study of Nazi ideology in American colleges.

5. Peter Viereck, "Hitler and Wagner," *Common Sense* 8 (November 1939): 3–6.

6. Sander L. Gilman, "Why and How I Study German," *German Quarterly* 42 (1989): 192–204, here 200.

even though the monstrosity of a particular event may appear to justify such a notion. Plausible though it may at first appear, a Holocaust-centered preconception of German history must be regarded as unsound. It encourages, and is itself based on, a tunnel vision of the German past that draws a direct line from anti-Semitism to the Holocaust at the expense of other, equally relevant considerations. And it encourages, because it is itself based on, a highly questionable historiographical practice—"backshadowing"—which Michael A. Bernstein has defined as "a kind of retroactive foreshadowing in which the shared knowledge of the outcome of a series of events [. . .] is used to judge everything that went before."[7] Nowhere, it seems to me, has the temptation to backshadow proved more irresistible than in the case of Wagner's writings about Jews and Jewry. If, for instance, a critique of Wagner is undertaken for the express purpose of making the world "understand the true necessity of continuing the ban on Wagner's music" in Israel, as Paul Lawrence Rose has done, we can be sure that the author practices backshadowing and is intent upon linking Wagner to the Holocaust.[8] Or, to cite another example, if Wagner's relationship to Hitler is defined as that of prophet and disciple, and if Hitler is presented as merely the eager, brainwashed executioner of Wagner's prophecies, we can be equally sure that the author is offering a tunnel vision of German history in which, with inexorable logic, Wagner's hostility toward the Jews is said to lead inevitably to the Holocaust.[9]

The controversy over Sixtus Beckmesser took its cue from Theodor W. Adorno's famous assertion that "all the rejects of Wagner's works are caricatures of Jews."[10] This pronouncement, although part of a comprehensive argument about the nexus of aesthetics and ideology in Wagner's operatic works, has by now taken on a life of its own. As soon as the debate about Wagner began to focus on his anti-Semitism, which, remarkably, occurred long after the complete edition of Adorno's book on Wagner first appeared in Germany in 1952, two warring camps began to form. One group of Wagner scholars—among them Hartmut Zelinsky, Barry Millington, Paul L. Rose, and Marc A.

---

7. Michael A. Bernstein, *Foregone Conclusions: Against Apocalyptic History* (Berkeley: University of California Press, 1994), 16.

8. Paul Lawrence Rose, *Wagner: Race and Revolution* (New Haven, Conn., and London: Yale University Press, 1992), 181. For a comprehensive history of the ban on Wagner in Israel, see Na'ama Sheffi, *The Ring of Myths: The Israelis, Wagner and the Nazis,* trans. Martha Grenzeback (Brighton: Sussex Academic Press, 2001).

9. Joachim Köhler, *Wagner's Hitler: The Prophet and His Disciple,* trans. Ronald Taylor (Oxford: Polity Press, 1999).

10. Theodor W. Adorno, *In Search of Wagner,* trans. Rodney Livingstone (London: NLB, 1981), 21.

Weiner[11]—became devoted to the task of substantiating Adorno's assertion. The most extreme cases for the prosecution were presented by Zelinsky, who argued in 1978 that the "Jewish theme" was, at bottom, Wagner's only theme, and by Weiner, who argued in 1995 that Wagner's operas, when properly decoded, must be regarded as "documents of hatred."[12] Another group—among them Peter Wapnewski, Dieter Borchmeyer, Udo Bermbach, Hermann Danuser, and Owen Lee—became equally devoted to the task of refuting Adorno's verdict. The most determined brief for the defense was submitted by Borchmeyer, who argued "that to foist his [Wagner's] anti-Jewish ideology on to his artistic oeuvre was as remote from his field of interest as it was beneath him as an artist. There are no Jewish characters in his music dramas, still less any anti-Semitic tendencies. His hatred of the Jews was excluded from the inner sanctum of his artistic personality."[13]

Before we examine the merits of these arguments with respect to *Die Meistersinger*, we must take note of a number of recent developments that have brought additional pressure to bear upon the question of what to make of Beckmesser. Paramount among them is the intensification and globalization of the discourse on the Holocaust during the last decade and a half. Saul Friedländer has recently noted a rapidly growing awareness of the "centrality of the Holocaust in present-day historical consciousness."[14] And Yehuda Bauer has observed that the Holocaust discourse now extends far beyond the fields of German and Jewish history and has in fact become an issue of global concern: "The Holocaust has become a symbol of evil in what is inaccurately known as Western civilisation, and the awareness of that symbol seems to be spreading all over the world."[15] Inevitably, this has further upped the stakes of the ongoing debate about Wagner, who is deeply implicated precisely because the man who set the Holocaust in motion claimed that the sword he was wielding was forged by Wagner.[16] If, as

---

11. Hartmut Zelinsky, "Die 'Feuerkur' des Richard Wagner oder die 'neue Religion' der 'Erlösung' durch 'Vernichtung,'" in *Musik-Konzepte 5: Richard Wagner: Wie antisemitisch darf ein Künstler sein?* (München: text und kritik, 1978), 79–112; Barry Millington, "Nuremberg Trial: Is There anti-Semitism in 'Die Meistersinger'?" *Cambridge Opera Journal* 3 (1991): 247–60; Rose, *Wagner: Race and Revolution*; Marc A. Weiner, *Richard Wagner and the Anti-Semitic Imagination* (Lincoln and London: University of Nebraska Press, 1995).

12. Weiner, *Wagner and the Anti-Semitic Imagination*, 347.

13. Dieter Borchmeyer, *Richard Wagner: Theory and Theater*, trans. Stewart Spencer (Oxford: Oxford University Press, 1991), 408.

14. Saul Friedländer, *Nazi Germany and the Jews*, vol. 1: *The Years of Persecution, 1933–1939* (New York: Harper Collins, 1997), 1.

15. Yehuda Bauer, *Rethinking the Holocaust* (New Haven, Conn. and London: Yale University Press, 2001), x.

16. Letter to Siegfried Wagner, 5 May 1924, in *Hitler: Sämtliche Aufzeichnungen, 1905–1924*, ed. Eberhard Jäckel and Axel Kuhn (Stuttgart: DVA, 1980), 1232.

again Friedländer has remarked, Hitler has become "the ultimate standard of evil, against which all degrees of evil may be measured,"[17] then everything with which Hitler associated bears an indelible stain and is rendered suspect. This applies with special force to what he cherished most: Wagner and *Die Meistersinger,* his favorite opera.

Two major international conferences have recently been held in order to sort out the multiple strands that link Wagner to Hitler. In 1998, at Bayreuth, the topic was "Richard Wagner und die Juden"; the following year, at Schloß Elmau, the topic was "Richard Wagner im Dritten Reich." The two conferences yielded some unexpected results that further complicate the issue. Dina Porat and Saul Friedländer surprised the gathering in Bayreuth when they pointed out, independently, that contrary to widespread assumptions, Hitler never invoked Wagner's hostility toward Jews to justify his own murderous hatred or the anti-Jewish policies of Nazi Germany.[18] Several speakers noted that Hitler's cult of Wagner was grounded not in the theories and the ideology of the composer, but rather in the aesthetic character of his operatic works. Young Hitler, it was suggested, long before he turned to politics, began to internalize Wagner's operas, which, in turn, colonized his imagination.[19] The crucial formative experience appears to have been the encounter of the fifteen-year-old Hitler with Wagner's *Rienzi*; in what might be called a case of Wagnerian self-fashioning, he began to harbor fantasies of one day becoming, in the manner of Cola di Rienzi, the dictatorial "tribune" of the German people. As for Beckmesser, no consensus emerged at the Bayreuth conference. Rose reiterated his thesis that some of Beckmesser's music represents a parody of synagogue chant, while Hermann Danuser argued that the hapless "Merker," drawn as he is according to comedic conventions of universal appeal, cannot and should not be read as the embodiment of Wagner's particular hostility toward Jews.

Of particular relevance to the issue at hand is Jens Malte Fischer's new "critical documentation" about Wagner's pamphlet, *Das Judentum in der Musik.* Fischer's book, which is indispensable, consists of three parts: a

---

17. Friedländer, *Nazi Germany*, 1.

18. Dina Porat, "'Zum Raum wird hier die Zeit.' Richard Wagners Bedeutung für die nationalsozialistische Führung," in *Richard Wagner und die Juden*, ed. Dieter Borchmeyer, Ami Maayani, and Susanne Vill (Stuttgart, Weimar: Metzler, 2000), 207–20; Saul Friedländer, "Bayreuth und der Erlösungsantisemitismus," in *Richard Wagner und die Juden*, ed. Dieter Borchmeyer, Ami Maayani, and Susanne Vill (Stuttgart, Weimar: Metzler, 2000), 8–18. Cf. also Saul Friedländer, "Hitler und Wagner," in *Richard Wagner im Dritten Reich*, Ein Schloß Elmau-Symposium, ed. S. Friedländer and Jörn Rüsen (Munich: C. H. Beck, 2000), 165–78.

19. Hans Rudolf Vaget, "Wieviel 'Hitler' ist in Wagner? Anmerkungen zu Hitler, Wagner und Thomas Mann," in *Richard Wagner und die Juden*, ed. Dieter Borchmeyer, Ami Maayani, and Susanne Vill (Stuttgart, Weimar: Metzler, 2000), 178–204.

lucid, securely contextualized analysis of Wagner's most notorious essay; an annotated presentation of the enlarged 1869 edition of that text; and a generous documentation of its contemporary critical reception, comprising some twenty-four rejoinders.[20] Fischer's main quarrel is with those who focus exclusively on the 1850 version of the pamphlet and align it, sometimes with exculpatory intent, with Wagner's contemporary writings on operatic reform, his "Zürcher Kunstschriften." Wagner's real fall from grace, according to Fischer, occurred when, reacting to the progress of Jewish emancipation in the 1860s, he republished *Das Judentum in der Musik* and, crossing a fine line, speculated that the ejection by force of "the corrosive foreign element" that the Jews represent might be the best way to halt the decline of German culture.[21]

Although Fischer does not directly comment on the Beckmesser controversy, it should be obvious that his findings have a direct bearing on it. He rejects the position of Borchmeyer and others, who hold that Wagner's enmity to Jewishness is to be viewed not as anti-Semitism in the racial and political sense but as the expression of a more traditional form of anti-Judaism, by stressing the "proto-racial" character of Wagner's essay.[22] The proximity in purely chronological terms of *Die Meistersinger*, which premiered in 1868, to Wagner's reopening of the "Jewish issue" in 1869, suggests that his obsessive hostility could not have been far from his mind as he completed the opera. Ominously, Wagner considered naming the only "reject" in this opera Veit Hanslich—a crude and all too overt allusion to his most prominent critic, Eduard Hanslick, whom he took to be Jewish.[23] It seems significant, though, that Wagner rejected this clumsy idea, and if we believe Danuser, he did so in order not to compromise the "universalistische" character of his operatic works.[24] Even so, Fischer suggests that Hanslick's hostile review of *Die Meistersinger* was the straw that broke the camel's back and prompted Wagner to go on the attack.[25] It appears then that by reintroducing his pamphlet in a significantly augmented form, Wagner wanted to make up for what he wisely had refrained from doing in the opera—vent his ad hominem hostility.

---

20. Jens Malte Fischer, *Richard Wagners "Das Judentum in der Musik": Eine kritische Dokumentation als Beitrag zur Geschichte des Antisemitismus* (Frankfurt/Main: Insel, 2000).
21. Ibid., 108.
22. Ibid., 83.
23. Hanslick's Jewish mother had in fact converted to her husband's Catholic faith.
24. Hermann Danuser, "Universalität oder Partikularität? Zur Frage antisemitischer Charakterzeichnung in Wagners Werk," in *Richard Wagner und die Juden,* ed. Dieter Borchmeyer, Ami Maayani, and Susanne Vill (Stuttgart, Weimar: Metzler, 2000), 79–100.
25. Fischer, *Richard Wagners "Das Judentum,"* 101.

Fischer has to concede, however, that Wagner's hostility originated not in the musical controversies of Germany, but rather in the cosmopolitan center of France, from 1839–1842, during a period of failure, frustration, and poverty. Fischer refers to this as the "incubation period" of Wagner's hatred of the Jew.[26] Other critics, notably Borchmeyer,[27] have also stressed the French connection of Wagnerian anti-Semitism, but all tend to emphasize the personal dimension of the problem: Wagner's frustration with musical life in Paris, which, he convinced himself, was dominated by Jewry—personalities such as Meyerbeer, the enormously popular composer, and Maurice Schlesinger, the influential music publisher. On closer inspection, however, it turns out that Wagner's anti-Jewish obsession may well have been sparked by the experience of being rejected, but equally, if not more so, by the very air he breathed in Paris, where certain criticisms made of Meyerbeer in the French press "mesh uncannily with later derogatory stereotypes of the Jewish composer," notably in Wagner's infamous pamphlet.[28] Unlike their German coreligionists, the Jews of France had been enjoying full legal equality since 1791, but appearances to the contrary notwithstanding, criticism of Meyerbeer during the July monarchy, at least on certain occasions, was expressed in terms foreshadowing Wagner almost verbatim: the composer of *Les Huguenots* lacked melodic invention; he was a skilled imitator but not an original creator; he sought out effects, mostly of a scenic nature, purely for the sake of effect; like the Wandering Jew, he lacked national roots; and that—as Hector Berlioz registered with chagrin—he was adept at manipulating the press. This seems to indicate that Wagner's anti-Jewish animus originally sprang less from a championing of German art than from a transnational objection to the direction opera had taken under the wildly successful Meyerbeer.

As with all knotty problems, it seems advisable to disentangle the different threads of the seemingly intractable Beckmesser controversy. Those threads may be reduced, essentially, to four.

1. Beckmesser's covert Jewishness is said to be revealed through his music. This argument was first made by Millington and has since been endorsed and expanded by Weiner. Millington's chief point concerns Beckmesser's Act II serenade, which is said to be a parody of the "cantorial style" of Jewish sacred music.[29] Weiner argues that Wagner's use of pitch carries

---

26. Ibid., 59.
27. Borchmeyer, *Wagner: Theory and Theater*, 405.
28. Kerry Murphy, "Berlioz, Meyerbeer, and the Place of Jewishness in Criticism," in *Berlioz: Past, Present, Future*, ed. Peter Bloom (Rochester, N.Y.: University of Rochester Press, 2002). I am very grateful to both the author and the editor for graciously making this paper available to me.
29. Millington, "Nuremberg Trial," 251.

ideological meaning and that Beckmesser's distinct vocal line, which for the purpose of caricature was placed "impossibly high," is indicative of racial difference.[30]

Neither Millington's nor Weiner's thesis has found favor with the experts. Long before Millington, Egon Voss, author of a magisterial study of Wagner's symphonic style,[31] had shown convincingly that Beckmesser's serenade, with its disregard for the basic laws of musical prosody, and with its schematic ornamentation, is to be viewed as a parody of Italian opera.[32] Beckmesser is indeed marked as the embodiment of an un-German conception of art, not on account of his putative Jewishness but rather on account of his adherence to foreign styles. Furthermore, Danuser has reminded us, significantly, that Wagner did not know synagogue chant nearly well enough to parody it convincingly.[33] It is fair to conclude, then, that the supposedly unassailable musical argument for Beckmesser's Jewishness has failed to produce a consensus, based as it is on the dubious proposition that "for Wagner, sounds reflect national essence," and that "the tessitura of speech, like that of song, also provides a sign of national identity."[34]

2. Wagner's opera is said to be a kind of "scenic representation of the ideas he had expressed in *Das Judentum in der Musik*" and elsewhere.[35] In the literature that takes its inspiration from Adorno, this notion is treated as a foregone conclusion. David Levin, who finds much to endorse in Weiner's analyses, takes the argument a step beyond Weiner's assumption of an "anti-Semitic imagination" by arguing that "we can define an *aesthetics* of antisemitism in Wagner"; that he "invests certain characters not just with vile qualities"; and that "those qualities are in turn associated with vile *aesthetic practices.*" Jews in Wagner's works are "dogged by aesthetic qualities that the composer loathed."[36] Remarkably, this notion of an "aesthetics of antisemitism" does not include Beckmesser's music; here Levin parts company with Weiner and Millington. Rather, the chief char-

---

30. Weiner, *Richard Wagner and the Anti-Semitic Imagination*, 110, 123.

31. Egon Voss, *Studien zur Instrumentation Richard Wagners* (Regensburg: Gustav Bosse Verlag, 1970).

32. Egon Voss, "Wagners 'Meistersinger' als Oper des deutschen Bürgertums," in *Richard Wagner: Die Meistersinger von Nürnberg: Texte, Materialien, Kommentare*, ed. Attila Csampai and Dietmar Holland (Reinbek: Rowohlt, 1981), 9–31; English translation by Stewart Spencer, *Wagner* 19 (1991): 39–62, here 56f.

33. Danuser, "Universalität oder Partikularität?" 97.

34. Weiner, *Richard Wagner and the Anti-Semitic Imagination*, 114.

35. Ibid., 71.

36. David J. Levin, "Reading Beckmesser Reading: Anti-Semitism and Aesthetic Practice in 'The Mastersingers of Nuremberg,'" *New German Critique*, Special Issue on Richard Wagner, ed. David J. Levin and Mark M. Anderson, 69 (Fall 1996): 127–46, here 129; cf. also Levin's "Reading a Staging/Staging a Reading," *Cambridge Opera Journal* 9 (1997): 47–71.

acteristic by which Beckmesser's Jewishness is supposed to become manifest is his incapacity "to render the text; [. . .] he cannot read it." This observation refers by no means to the final scene alone; it applies to Beckmesser's entire intellectual physiognomy, because he is unable to read Walther's, and by implication, Wagner's aesthetic project as a whole: "For the Jew is invariably assigned to a social and aesthetic position that the *Gesamtkunstwerk* is assigned to annul."[37] In order to give this argument some semblance of plausibility, Levin boldly assumes that the threat of the "welsche" influence in Sachs's concluding address "is structurally interchangeable with that of the Jew,"[38] thereby substituting a racial distinction for what in the opera and in Wagner's essays is clearly a national distinction between Italian and French opera on one hand and Wagner's own, self-consciously German artwork of the future on the other.

The inability to "read" in the comprehensive sense that Levin suggests is, of course, by no means restricted to Beckmesser. With the exception of Sachs, none of the other masters is at first either willing or able to follow Walther. If Beckmesser were so uniquely handicapped, he could hardly have achieved the position of preeminence among the masters that he in fact occupies. His failure to make sense of Walther's songs can be explained far more plausibly in light of the comic perilousness of his situation, which is that of an old bachelor possessed by the desire for a much younger woman, and in light of the desperation he feels as a public official who knows in his heart of hearts that he is fraudulently trying to win the prize with a poem of which he is not the author. If there is anything here by which Beckmesser could be tied to Wagner's argument in *Das Judentum in der Musik*, it is his overt lack of originality. But Levin does not make this argument. Instead, he invokes Slavoj Žižek's *The Sublime Object of Ideology* to maintain that in "Wagner's commitment to [. . .] a program of seamless aesthetic totalization, the Jew functions as the structural guarantor of that totality by representing [. . .] that which does not belong, which must be exorcised."[39] Why that structural element must be a Jew remains unclear, which may explain why, in his essay of 1997, Levin no longer insists on Beckmesser's Jewishness.

Plausible though it may appear that Wagner's most self-conscious opera should be expressive of his anti-Jewish obsession, the entire attempt to read an aesthetically so multilayered and complex opera as *Die Meistersinger* as the translation of the author's political beliefs leads us, as especially Michael Tanner and Danuser have reminded us, into the murky waters of the intentional fallacy.[40] Wagner's pamphlet, *Das Judentum in der Musik*,

---

37. Levin, "Reading Beckmesser Reading," 138.
38. Ibid., 145.
39. Ibid., 131.
40. Michael Tanner, *Wagner* (Princeton: Princeton University Press, 1997), 16f; Danuser, "Universalität oder Partikularität?" 99f.

is a text very different from *Die Meistersinger*; it derives from a different level of his creative personality and articulates a very particular concern that is not *eo ipso* part of the universal vision of Wagner's operatic works, which originate in a distinct region of the creator's psyche. It is simply erroneous to argue, as Weiner and Levin appear to do, that we can and in fact ought to distill from the polyvalent and equivocal language of the music dramas a message as narrow and simplistic as the hatred of Jews.

3. *Die Meistersinger* is said to have an affinity to the Grimms' anti-Jewish fairy tale, "Der Jude im Dorn" (The Jew in the thornbush). Here we are confronted with a different and more difficult assertion, which does not presuppose authorial intention but interrogates, instead, the signifying potential of the poetic and musical text, which may be activated through an open or oblique echo of other texts.

Once again, the direction of the debate was set by Adorno's observation in the opening chapter of his study, "Social Character," that Wagner's sense of humor is an ugly one, for it is based on ridicule, humiliation, and cruelty, and serves as a "device for rationalizing the worst." In other words, "The use of laughter to suspend justice is debased into a charter for injustice."[41] With Beckmesser, Adorno believes, Wagner revived certain Renaissance traditions of representing the Jew on stage, as exemplified by *The Merchant of Venice*. Other precedents he names are "the fairy tales of the German tradition," of which "none is more apposite than the story of the Jew in the bramble-bush." Adorno then suggests that the spirit of "Der Jude im Dorn" informs Wagner's creative imagination and shapes his treatment of "rejects" such as Beckmesser. Like the German lad in the tale, who has traded his money for a magic fiddle and who mischievously makes the Jew dance upon thorns, so, too, does Wagner mischievously send Beckmesser into the thicket of things and make him dance, excruciatingly, to his tune. Adorno adds: "Wagner's music, too, is a worthy lad that treats the villain in like manner"—which leads him to claim, as quoted above, that "all the rejects in Wagner's works are caricatures of Jews."[42] The desire to torture the "rejects" is said to be a basic feature of the operas' social character. Adorno leaves open the question of Wagner's knowledge of the fairy tale, but he certainly seems to presuppose it.

This point was taken up in 1991 by Millington, who identified in Walther's Act I Trial Song an explicit and "indisputable" allusion to the fairy tale that is reinforced by certain textual echoes elsewhere in the opera. This is presented as proof positive of Adorno's claim that "anti-Semitism is woven into the ideological fabric of *Die Meistersinger*."[43] Millington locates the allusion in the lines starting with "In einer Dornenhecken," sung

---

41. Adorno, *In Search of Wagner*, 21.
42. Ibid., 23.
43. Millington , "Nuremberg Trial," 247.

immediately after we hear the "Merker's" first scratchings of chalk. To Millington, this is "perhaps the clinching piece of evidence."[44]

In an attempt to problematize Millington's interpretation, and to make further distinctions, I have adduced additional evidence in an earlier study of Beckmesser that would appear to support a Grimm-inspired reading of Walther's Trial Song, while at the same time disputing Millington's claim that this clinches the case for an anti-Semitic coding of the entire opera.[45]

In the fairy tale, the Jew is constructed from the familiar stereotypes about appearance, language, and money-mindedness, and, beyond that, by his opposition to music. He wants to put an end to the jubilant singing of the songbird, which he is listening to when the German lad first encounters him; he "cannot bear it," just as he, literally, cannot stand the music of the magic fiddle; and he maligns the lad's music-making every chance he gets. In fact, it seems plausible to assume that the lad immediately regrets having killed the bird, and that it is for this reason that he tortures the Jew by making him dance on the thorns. This is presented as just payback—explicitly, for the Jew's stereotypical fleecing of Christian Germans, and implicitly, for the Jew's enmity to music. It should be noted here that in the third edition of the Grimms' *Kinder- und Hausmärchen* of 1837, the "Jewish" features, especially the resentment of music, are more pronounced than in previous editions[46]—a reflection perhaps of the then growing importance of music to the definition of the German identity as well as of the Other. Money and music stand in an inverse relationship; indeed, the entire story turns on the exchange of money for music. The Jew has money but lacks music; the German gives away his money and is rewarded with the magic gift of music.

There is, then, an obvious and striking similarity between the deep structure of the fairy tale and Wagner's argument in *Das Judentum in der Musik,* and both texts may serve as mirrors for Beckmesser, the true referent of Walther's asides about the "Dornenhecke." Just like Old Winter, he sits in his "Gemerk," his very own thornbush, consumed with envy of the bird's outpourings, and he plots to stop the "frohe Singen." Contrary to Adorno's suggestion, the appositeness of the fairy tale to *Die Meistersinger* rests not on any sadistic treatment of the "reject" by Walther, or Wagner, but rather

---

44. Ibid., 247.

45. Hans R. Vaget, "'Der Jude im Dorn' oder: Wie antisemitisch sind 'Die Meistersinger von Nürnberg?" *Deutsche Vierteljahrsschrift für Literaturwissenschaft und Geistesgeschichte* 69 (1995): 271–99; for a shorter English version, see Vaget, "Sixtus Beckmesser—a 'Jew in the Brambles'?" *Opera Quarterly* 12 (1995): 35–45.

46. This is evident from the useful parallel printing of the first and third editions of "Der Jude im Dorn" in Hermann Hamann, *Die literarischen Vorlagen der Kinder- und Hausmärchen und ihre Bearbeitung durch die Brüder Grimm* (Berlin: Mayer & Müller, 1906), 141–46.

on Beckmesser's opposition to Walther's natural genius. This removes the accent from the supposedly racial dimension, and places it on the vocal and aesthetic implications of the "Dornenhecken" image itself.

This entire passage is constructed with obvious deliberation and great circumspection in terms both of poetic and musical structure. The two references to the "Dornenhecken" mark the place at which Walther, on the spur of the moment, freely augments the traditional form of the stanza, or "Stollen"; in so doing he confuses not only Beckmesser, but the masters as well. Walther, on an improvising roll, adds to the highly lyrical twenty-one-line stanza he has already produced eight more lines of a contrasting, reflective character. The fact that his skill at improvising allows him to integrate into the song his irritation over Beckmesser's noisy marking of his "mistakes" may be seen as indicative of his innate synthesizing prowess as an artist. Musically, too, the two extended asides about the "Dornenhecken" stand out. The lyrical flow of the first twenty-one lines in each stanza is set in F major, a key long associated with pastoral scenes. The new material is harmonically indeterminate, the accompaniment considerably reduced; it appears to articulate growling and resentment against the intrusion of something alien and threatening. This foreshadows a similar musical gesture in Sachs's concluding address, starting at "Habt acht!" at which point there occurs an abrupt change from C major to C Minor, followed by further modulating.[47] Walther's Trial Song as a whole is clearly marked as a particularly privileged site of signification.

Dieter Borchmeyer, defending his conviction (previously cited) that anti-Semitism was "barred from entering" the inner sanctum of Wagner's creativity, denies any affinity between the opera and the fairy tale.[48] Pointing to the absence of documentary proof of Wagner's familiarity with this fairy tale, he asserts that before Adorno drew attention to it, "Der Jude im Dorn" had been practically unknown. This argument, strictly speaking, is immaterial to the argument laid out above (since it does not rest on authorial intent), and Borchmeyer's position is vulnerable on other grounds as well. The affinity of Wagner's operatic imagination to the world of the fairy tale has often been remarked upon by Nietzsche and Thomas Mann, among others, and this is hardly surprising, given the overlap between Wagner's entire project and that of early *Germanistik,* the new scholarly field the Grimm Brothers helped inaugurate. Both may be described, in the last analy-

---

47. Cf. Reinhold Brinkmann, "Lohengrin, Sachs und Mime oder nationales Pathos und die Pervertierung der Kunst bei Richard Wagner," in *Deutsche Meister—Böse Geister? Nationale Selbstfindung in der Musik,* in Zusammenarbeit mit der Staatsoper Unter den Linden, ed. Hermann Danuser and Herfried Münkler (Berlin: Edition Argus, 2001), 206–21, here 211f.

48. Dieter Borchmeyer, "Beckmesser—the Jew in the Brambles?" *Program Book: Bayreuther Festspiele 1996,* 100–109.

sis, as attempts to revive, and tap into, the oldest manifestations of the "Volksgeist"—language, myth, fairy tales—and thereby to define the cultural identity of the Germans as the necessary precondition for political unification.

What is more, there is proof of the affinity from Wagner himself: in a letter to Theodor Uhlig of 10 May 1851, he expresses his surprise at discovering the similarity between his *Young Siegfried* (later renamed simply *Siegfried*) and the Grimm "Tale about the Boy who Went Forth to Learn What Fear Was." In other words, Wagner himself appears to have been unaware of the extent of his own familiarity with the Grimm fairy tales, which, at least in this case, seem to have entered the inner sanctum of his creativity quite easily—by osmosis. If in addition we consider that the *Kinder- und Hausmärchen* rapidly became the most widely read book in Germany after the Bible, and that in 1860 Grimm fairy tales became obligatory reading in the primary schools of Prussia,[49] it seems more likely than not that "Der Jude im Dorn" was known both to Wagner and to his public. Still, as long as we cannot be certain of Wagner's familiarity with the tale—Borchmeyer admits this much—all claims that it could *not* have been on Wagner's mind when he wrote Walther's Trial Song rest on shaky ground.

In an attempt to invalidate the claim of an affinity between the opera and the fairy tale, Borchmeyer flatly denies that the elaborate treatment of the theme of music has anti-Jewish overtones and dismisses it as a retroprojection from Wagner's notorious essay onto the fairy tale. It seems to me, however, that the textual evidence—the Jew's opposition to the music of the bird and the lad's magic instrument, which, after all, are torture to the Jew—speaks for itself.

Where does all this leave us with regard to Adorno's assertion of Beckmesser's essential Jewishness? It seems incontrovertible that the image of the "Dornenhecken" in Walther's Trial Song and Wagner's elaborate treatment of it provide a strong intertextual link to the fairy tale. This constitutes a potentially anti-Jewish element whose presence in the text of *Die Meistersinger* simply cannot be denied. At the same time, it needs to be stressed that its textual import and its range of signification fall far short of the interpretive weight Millington has brought to bear on it. After all, not one of the masters present reacts to the "anti-Jewish" barb in Walther's song, nor does that barb have any palpable consequences in the dramatic action. Walther himself, of course, has no knowledge of the fairy tale; he is improvising and, in reaction to Beckmesser's markings, just "happens" to hit upon the image of the "Dornenhecken"—suggesting perhaps that he, too, has access to the source of the *Volksgeist,* from which the fairy tales supposedly sprang and which seems to be inaccessible to Beckmesser. In a sense, then, Beckmesser is characterized as the enemy of the new music, the

---

49. Vaget, "'Der Jude im Dorn,'" 281f.

"music of the future": first, through his reaction to Walther's Trial Song, then through his own serenade, and finally through his botched rendition of the Prize Song. How could this not evoke—over the heads of the protagonists on stage—associations with the most articulate critic of Wagner's music, Eduard Hanslick, whom the composer, in the 1869 printing of *Das Judentum in der Musik,* pointedly, though not quite correctly, took to be Jewish?[50]

To resume this explanation of the presence of a potentially anti-Semitic element in the text of *Die Meistersinger:* Like most ambitious creators, Wagner aspired to broad, even universal acceptance, and therefore took pains to keep any overt indication of his very particular anti-Jewish obsession out of his operatic work. By and large he succeeded in this. In two instances, however, with Beckmesser and with Mime in Acts I and II of *Siegfried,* he was unable or unwilling to mask completely the affinity of his portrayals to his publicized views on Jewry. In the case of Beckmesser, he was drawn, perhaps subconsciously, to the image of the "Dornenhecken," for the discursive strategies of both the fairy tale and his own pamphlet are similar. It is an arcane image, a distant allusion communicated to the cognoscenti in the way that the Wagnerian orchestra communicates with the audience: over the heads and behind the backs of the protagonists. The question of Beckmesser's Jewishness never becomes a recognizable concern of *Die Meistersinger.* It therefore seems rash and misleading to maintain, as Millington and Weiner do, that all accounts of the opera, on stage or in theoretical analysis, are incomplete, or invalid, if they do not foreground the implied Jewishness of Wagner's comic protagonist.[51]

4. Given the widely diverging readings of Wagner's portrayal of Nuremberg's formidable "Merker," it is hardly surprising that critics should so disagree. How are we to imagine Beckmesser's future role after his humiliation in the singing contest before all his fellow citizens? Wagner's relevant stage direction is famously indeterminate: "Er stürzt wütend fort und verliert sich unter dem Volk" (He rushes away in fury and is lost in the crowd). What precisely does this mean, and how should it be staged?

---

50. Cf. Fischer, *Wagners "Das Judentum,"* 106; Thomas S. Grey, "Selbstbehauptung oder Fremdmissbrauch? Zur Rezeptionsgeschichte von Wagners 'Meistersingern,'" in *Deutsche Meister—Böse Geister? Nationale Selbstfindung in der Musik,* in Zusammenarbeit mit der Staatsoper Unter den Linden, ed. Hermann Danuser and Herfried Münkler (Berlin: Edition Argus, 2001), 303–23, here 319ff.

51. Cf. M. Owen Lee, "Wagner's Influence: The First Hundred Years," in *Wagner: The Terrible Man and His Truthful Art,* The 1998 Larkin-Stuart Lectures (Toronto: University of Toronto Press, 1999), 33–64, here 46: "It is a measure of the arrogance of the new Wagner critics that one of them, who thinks he has conclusively proven Beckmesser to be a Jewish caricature, now insists that henceforth no production of *Die Meistersinger* can be valid unless it depicts his so-called findings on stage."

Some stage directors have opted for the worst case scenario prescribed by Millington and endorsed by a number of other critics.[52] Christoph Nehl in Frankfurt (1993) and Hans Neuenfels in Stuttgart (1994) have presented Wagner's treatment of Beckmesser as, in a nutshell, an ominous prelude to the Holocaust.[53] Their underlying assumption seems to have been that *Die Meistersinger* must be read as the theatrical analogue to Wagner's anti-Jewish pamphlet and the anti-Jewish fairy tale, both of which end with the annihilation of the Jew—literally, by hanging, in "Der Jude im Dorn," and figuratively, through assimilation, in *Das Judentum in der Musik*. Weiner, choosing highly charged language, offers the most extreme reading: "Though Beckmesser does not die in the course of the drama, he is beaten and expelled, and his public execution is sublimated into the horrific phantasy of ritual exclusion contained in this, Beckmesser's final song."[54]

Other stage directors followed the growing tendency to arrange for a more or less good-natured reconciliation between Sachs and Beckmesser and thereby suspend the "Merker's" ambivalent assessment of their relationship: "Du warst mein Feind von je." Apparently, this tendency was launched by Joachim Herz's Leipzig production in 1960:[55] here, Beckmesser (portrayed sympathetically throughout), does not rush off but rather stays and listens to Walther's correct rendering of the Prize Song. When Sachs then offers him his hand, Beckmesser, after some inner struggle, grasps it.[56] In this and many similar stagings, in a studied manner, Beckmesser is neither marginalized nor expelled, for Nuremberg "needs him," as Walter Jens wrote in an oft-cited and obviously Holocaust-inspired justification for a conciliatory production of this history-laden opera.[57] Similarly conciliatory productions have been presented by Götz Friedrich (Stockholm 1977, Deutsche Oper Berlin 1979), Wolfgang Wagner (Bayreuth 1984 and 1996), Francois Rochaix (Seattle 1989), and Michael Hampe (Australian Opera 1985). These have now, it seems, become the norm.

---

52. Aside from the critics already mentioned, see Gerhard Scheit, *Verborgener Staat, lebendiges Geld: Zur Dramaturgie des Antisemtismus* (Freiburg: ca ira, 1999), 301–7.

53. See Patrick Carnegy, "Stage History," in *Richard Wagner: Die Meistersinger von Nürnberg*, ed. John Warrack (Cambridge: Cambridge University Press, 1994), 135–52.

54. Weiner, *Richard Wagner and the Anti-Semitic Imagination*, 71.

55. See Joachim Herz, "Der doch versöhnte Beckmesser," in *Richard Wagner: Die Meistersinger von Nürnberg: Texte, Materialien, Kommentare*, ed. Attila Csampai and Dieter Holland (Reinbek: Rowohlt, 1981), 213–15.

56. Cf. Carnegy, "Stage History," 147.

57. Walter Jens, "Ehrenrettung eines Kritikers: Sixtus Beckmesser," in *Richard Wagner: Die Meistersinger von Nürnberg: Texte, Materialien, Kommentare*, ed. Attila Csampai and Dietmar Holland (Reinbek: Rowohlt, 1981), 249–57.

Rejecting such conciliatory readings, which he attributes to a collective "will to fun," Levin surely has a point when he observes: "There is no evidence of such a reconciliation in the score, the correspondence, or the text."[58] But does it follow from this that Wagner's stage direction carries a sinister meaning? Levin takes Wagner's words to mean "he loses himself beneath them"[59] and interprets them as marking the beginning of Beckmesser's "ghettoization;" Nuremberg's "Merker" is said to be " left in in order to be left out."[60] But this, obviously, is far-fetched and untenable philologically speaking.

There is a more plausible way of imagining Beckmesser's future place in Nuremberg society, it seems to me, that does not twist Wagner's words, squares with the action on stage, and does not derive from backshadowing. "Sich verlieren" carries many different nuances of meaning, as any good dictionary will show. The definition that seems most appropriate here is "to disappear from sight" and become invisible—either because of growing distance or because an obstacle, such as the crowd on stage, blocks the view. If we read "sich verlieren" in this way, we may conclude that, after having disgraced himself as a "Meister," Beckmesser will cease to be the "Merker" of the Mastersingers' guild; but he will not cease to exist as a person, and he will remain a fully accepted member of the citizenry of Nuremberg.

It is time, it seems, to step back from the controversy that hovers over Beckmesser and remind ourselves that the question of his "Jewishness" is but one of several issues that have fueled the historically necessary debate about the role of Wagner in the prehistory of National Socialism. Let us remember that the issue of Beckmesser's "Jewishness" would not have gained the prominence it did had it not been for the intensification of the Holocaust discourse starting in the late 1970s. And let us concede that critics on both sides of the issue have been engaged to a greater or lesser extent in backshadowing, which may well account for much of the passion that has characterized this controversy.

If we look at the entire history of *Die Meistersinger* in Germany, with its entanglements in the political agendas of the most diverse regimes, it becomes evident that anti-Semitism was not a major, let alone a determining factor in its political appropriation—not even in the Third Reich. Contrary to expectations, including my own, the evidence does not seem to be there.[61]

---

58. Levin, "Reading a Staging," 68.
59. Levin, "Reading Beckmesser Reading," 146.
60. Ibid.
61. Cf. *Die Meistersinger und Richard Wagner: Die Rezeptionsgeschichte einer Oper von 1868 bis heute*. Katalog einer Ausstellung des Germanischen Nationalmuseums, ed. Gerhard Bott (Nuremberg: Germanisches Nationalmuseum, 1981); Grey, "Selbstbehauptung oder Fremdmissbrauch?" 324.

Just as Hitler refrained from invoking Wagner's well-known views about the Jews to justify his own, much more radical, hatred, the Nazis, too, in their pronouncements on *Die Meistersinger* and in the quasi-official productions at Bayreuth, at Nuremberg, and at the Staatsoper in the capital, did not bother to play the card of anti-Semitism.[62] Such behavior differs from that of some of the most prominent Wagnerians, from Alfred Lorenz and Otto Strobel to party hacks such as Hans Alfred Grunsky and Hans Severus Ziegler, who welcomed the arrival of Hitler in gushing panegyrics and hailed the promise of renewal in what they took to be the spirit of Wagner. But it accords fully with the ideological function of the cult of Wagner in Nazi Germany, which was focused less on the ideology, useful though this might have seemed, than on the aesthetic aura of the opera.[63] The Nazis understood that it would be a mistake to use Wagner's highly auratic art for propaganda in the crude sense, for it might then lose its irreplaceable value for the ubiquitous aestheticization of political life. From what we know about the Führer's cult of Wagner,[64] this general policy decision was most likely taken by Hitler himself.

Thus, at its core, the Nazi cult of Wagner was a cult of genius. And here we must remember that a near-religious reverence for the artist-genius had been deeply ingrained in German culture ever since the "Genie-Kult" period of the 1770s.[65] Such reverence lends itself all too easily to political exploitation. In Nazi Germany, where the use of the superlative was a staple of propaganda, panegyrics to Wagner and panegyrics to Hitler became interchangeable; both were represented as the greatest Germans the German people had brought forth and the most German of the geniuses produced by the Aryan race. The appeal was to the seemingly natural, politically innocent pride in the accomplishments of German culture—a core element of nationalism. This is why Beckmesser and his putative Jewishness

---

62. See David Dennis's essay in this volume for a detailed investigation of this question.

63. Cf. Udo Bermbach, "Liturgietransfer: Über einen Aspekt des Zusammenhangs von Richard Wagner mit Hitler und dem Dritten Reich," in *Richard Wagner im Dritten Reich,* Ein Schloß Elmau-Symposium, ed. S. Friedländer and Jörn Rüsen (Munich: C. H. Beck, 2000), 40–65; and Reinhold Brinkmann, "Wagners Aktualität für den Nationalsozialismus," in *Richard Wagner im Dritten Reich,* Ein Schloß Elmau-Symposium, ed. S. Friedländer and Jörn Rüsen (Munich: C. H. Beck, 2000), 109–41.

64. Cf. Saul Friedländer, "Hitler und Wagner," 165–78; Hans Rudolf Vaget, "Wagner-Kult und nationalsozialistische Herrschaft," in *Richard Wagner im Dritten Reich,* Ein Schloß Elmau-Symposium, ed. S. Friedländer and Jörn Rüsen (Munich: C. H. Beck, 2000), 264–82.

65. Cf. Jochen Schmidt, *Die Geschichte des Genie-Gedankens in der deutschen Literatur, Philosophie und Politik, 1750–1945,* 2 vols. (Darmstadt: Wissenschaftliche Buchgesellschaft, 1985).

played no prominent role in the Nazi appropriation of *Die Meistersinger* and why the spotlight was instead turned on the rousing "Wach auf" chorus and the apotheosis of "holy German art."[66]

One particular moment in the early phase of the Third Reich seems to be emblematic of what the Nazi appropriation of Wagner was all about. In a special performance of *Die Meistersinger* at the Berlin Staatsoper on 21 March 1933 that was to cap the famous Day of Potsdam—a propaganda spectacular and a prime exhibit of the aestheticization of political life, designed by Joseph Goebbels to create for the new regime the semblance of historical and cultural legitimacy, only two weeks after the no longer free election of 5 March—the people of Nuremberg on the stage of the Staatsoper were instructed, as they sang the "Wach auf" chorus, to turn to Hitler's box, thus transferring their rousing homage from Wagner's fictitious Hans Sachs to Germany's real Adolf Hitler.[67]

At first glance, *Die Meistersinger von Nürnberg* appears to be a completely depoliticized opera that culminates in the vision of an "aesthetic utopia," marking the end of politics as Wagner knew them.[68] But this is deceptive, because an opera that has for so long reverberated upon the political landscape of German history as this work indubitably did simply has to be inscribed with some basic political meaning. And indeed, as soon as we look at *Die Meistersinger* through the appropriate lens, the profoundly political character of the work is immediately thrown into relief. That appropriate lens is "metapolitics," a concept introduced by the political theorist Constantin Frantz and endorsed by Wagner himself, who, among other gestures of ideological solidarity, made Frantz the dedicatee of the second edition of *Oper und Drama* (1868). In order to be genuinely German, Frantz argued, "politics must be elevated to metapolitics. The latter

---

66. Cf. Brinkmann "Wagners Aktualität"; Vaget "Wagner-Kult."

67. Cf. the report concerning that special performance on the "Tag von Postdam" by Hugo Rasch: "Die Festvorstellung in der Staatsoper," in *Der Völkische Beobachter,* 23 March 1933.

68. This, in a nutshell, is the central motif of Udo Bermbach's commentary on *Die Meistersinger*; see "Die Utopie der Selbstregierung: Zu Richard Wagners 'Die Meistersinger von Nürnberg,'" in his *Wo Macht ganz auf Verbrechen ruht: Politik und Gesellschaft in der Oper* (Hamburg: Europäische Verlagsanstalt, 1997), 238–59; Bermbach, "'Die Meistersinger von Nürnberg.' Politische Gehalte einer Künstleroper," in *Deutsche Meister—Böse Geister? Nationale Selbstfindung in der Musik,* in Zusammenarbeit mit der Staatsoper Unter den Linden, ed. Hermann Danuser and Herfried Münkler (Berlin: Edition Argus, 2001), 274–85; cf. also Dieter Borchmeyer, "Nürnberg als Reich des schönen Scheins: Metamorphosen eines Künstlerdramas," in *Deutsche Meister—Böse Geister? Nationale Selbstfindung in der Musik,* in Zusammenarbeit mit der Staatsoper Unter den Linden, ed. Hermann Danuser and Herfried Münkler (Berlin: Edition Argus, 2001), 286–302.

is to ordinary politics what metaphysics is to physics."[69] Viewed from this elevated vantage point, our ostensibly nonpolitical opera clearly reveals its potent political content and its potential for long-term efficacy. Chief among the metapolitical characteristics of Wagner's opera are the notions, implicit in the poetic and musical text, of an archetypal national community ("Volksgemeinschaft"); of charismatic leadership; and of the marginalization of the lone "reject."[70] In this regard, the political ramifications of Wagner's treatment of Beckmesser cannot be overlooked. It provided a model for the marginalization of "rejects" in general, a model which, in an atmosphere filled with anti-Semitism, was likely to develop a dangerous dynamic of its own.

---

69. Constantin Frantz, "Offener Brief an Richard Wagner," *Bayreuther Blätter* 1 (1878): 169.

70. For a more detailed account of the metapolitical profile of *Die Meistersinger*, see my essay "The 'Metapolitics' of 'Die Meistersinger': Wagner's Nuremberg as Imagined Community," in *Searching for Common Ground: Diskurse zur deutschen Identität, 1750–1871*, ed. Nicholas Vazsonyi (Cologne: Böhlau Verlag, 2000), 269–82.

11

"I Married Eva": Gender Construction and *Die Meistersinger*

Eva Rieger

I

The German press recently reported on a study that examined whether or not equal rights had made it into the home. Although wives claimed that their husbands did half the housework, statistics revealed that, on the weekends, women took on these chores as a matter of course irrespective of any additional work they may have had. Thus women had a greater burden without even being aware of it. The fact that women have always been responsible for the household has effectively blurred their vision. Embedded traditions and ideologies also affect the objectivity of scholarly investigations and result in flawed studies.

This could also be why, within *Meistersinger* scholarship, so little has been written about Eva Pogner, "the purest of German maidens";[1] this is remarkable, considering the abundance of Wagner literature. As a female stereotype par excellence, she corresponds to all the stereotypes of the traditional bourgeois woman. The existing literature discusses her with evident satisfaction, since she so exactly fits the model of the ideal women, giving her a sacrosanct aura and protecting her from overly critical analysis. Max Josef Beer describes Eva as being, among other things, "lovely," "charming," having a "sweet simplicity," "naturalness," and a "special kindness."[2] Wilhelm Broesel also sees Eva as "modest," "charming," "winsome," "traditional," "virtuous," "natural," "innocent," "sweet," and "full

---

1. Marc A. Weiner, *Richard Wagner and the Anti-Semitic Imagination* (Lincoln: University of Nebraska Press, 1995), 307.
2. Max Josef Beer, *Eva Pogner: Ein deutsches Charakter-Frauenbild* (Vienna: Gutmann, 1882).

of genuine naïveté."[3] German musicologists still condescendingly use the diminutive "Evchen" as if they identified themselves with Sachs, who often addresses Eva as "child" and "Evchen" and who does not take her particularly seriously.[4]

In recent years, efforts have been made methodologically to loosen the rigid separation between biographical versus musical-aesthetic research. Achieving this goal would be particularly important in the case of Richard Wagner to effect a closer understanding of his works and thereby eliminate misunderstandings. For a long time, the biographical method was dismissed as being a merely hackneyed approach, and even the operas were considered exclusively in musical-political or musical-aesthetic terms. While it is true that, especially during the years he enjoyed the protection of Ludwig II, Wagner sought to transform art and musical-political creativity, it would nevertheless be a mistake to efface the erotic impulses driving his creations as Carl Dahlhaus does when he describes as "the" theme of *Die Meistersinger,* Wagner's thesis that art is the sole justification for life.[5] Dahlhaus thereby overlooks the many other layers and, as many others, ignores Wagner's erotic stimulus as a basis for his interest in the theme of the work. Bryan Magee also maintains: "*The Mastersingers* [. . .] was about the one subject that he regarded as of fundamental importance yet 'political,' namely the artist's relations to his art, and to tradition, and to society."[6]

"I pour out into my art the violent need I feel for love, a need which life cannot satisfy, and all I find in return is that people at best mistake me for an energetic—opera reformer!" (*SL,* 274)[7] These words are from Wagner's most productive creative period. Between 1852 and 1858, while the relationship with Mathilde Wesendonck was bringing him both torment and joy, he conceived and composed the most significant works of his career. To this period belong the completion of the *Walküre* text, the total revision of *Der junge Siegfried* and *Siegfrieds Tod,* the composition of *Das Rheingold,*

---

3. Wilhelm Broesel, *Evchen Pogner* (Berlin, Leipzig: Schuster & Loeffler, 1906).

4. E.g., Kurt Overhoff, *Die Musikdramen Richard Wagners: Eine thematisch-musikalische Interpretation* (Salzburg: Pustet, 1967); Hans-Joachim Bauer, *Richard Wagner* (Stuttgart: Reclam, 1992).

5. Carl Dahlhaus, *Richard Wagners Musikdramen* (Velber: Friedrich, 1971), 70.

6. Bryan Magee, "Wagner's Theory of Opera," in *Penetrating Wagner's "Ring": An Anthology,* ed. John L. DiGaetani (New York: Da Capo, 1978), 72f.

7. Richard Wagner to Luise Brockhaus, 11.11.1852, in *Richard Wagner, Sämtliche Briefe* (Leipzig: Deutscher Verlag für Musik, 1993), 5:106. [*Selected Letters of Richard Wagner,* trans. & ed. Stewart Spencer and Barry Millington (New York, London: W.W. Norton, 1987), abbreviated as *SL* with page numbers in parentheses following translation. Some of the translations have been slightly modified.—N.V.]

Die Walküre, Act I and a large part of Act II of *Siegfried,* both text and music of *Tristan und Isolde,* as well as a prose sketch of *Die Sieger.* In April 1857, he and his wife moved into the "Asyl" (Haven) on the Wesendonck estate. One year later, they had to leave because of the rift between Minna Wagner and Mathilde Wesendonck. Wagner proposed marriage, but was turned down: for Mathilde, leaving her family would have been "sacrilege."[8] The prose draft of the *Meistersinger* text still developed amidst the spiritual travails of this relationship. In December 1861, embittered, he wrote from Paris that he had hoped to be able to live close to her. "But I am by now totally resigned!" though for a long time he had "remained an incorrigible optimist" (*RW to MW,* 288–89).[9] One month later, the prose draft was complete and the musical composition ensued in the following five years.

Die Meistersinger von Nürnberg portrays a hierarchical world with a clear upper and lower stratum, and Wagner makes it apparent on different levels that this order had grown organically and is therefore "natural." To this order belong both the social classes as well as gender roles. The male roles claim an inordinate share of space, not only because of the length of the parts but also in terms of the music. Already in the prelude, one is struck by the monumental style of the two Meistersinger motifs. The music is square in structure, with calm note values and a diatonic style that would be reminiscent of Lutheran chorales, were there not also the rising triads, the strong presence of the wind and brass, and the martial rhythm (see example 11.1). Both motifs evoke connotations of a masculine world and suggest a mixture of celebration, steadfastness, and active male bonding.

Example 11.1

Egon Voss is incorrect in assuming that the third part of the prelude (where the middle section is thinly orchestrated and contains the markings *sehr kurz gestoßen*) represents a parody of the Mastersingers, because the identical section is heard when Beckmesser prepares to sing his *Preislied* in

---

8. Entry for 14.3.1873, in Cosima Wagner, *Die Tagbücher,* ed. Martin Gregor-Dellin and Dietrich Mack (Munich, Zurich: Piper, 1976), 2:653.

9. Letter from late December 1861, in *Richard Wagner an Mathilde Wesendon[c]k: Tagebücher und Briefe 1853–1871,* ed. Wolfgang Golther (Leipzig: Breitkopf & Härtel, [1904], 1914), 334f. [The English is in *Richard Wagner to Mathilde Wesendonck,* trans. William Ashton Ellis (New York: Vienna House, 1972), abbreviated as *RW to MW* with page numbers in parentheses following the quote. Some of the translations have been slightly modified.—N.V.]

Act III.[10] Thus this section of the prelude refers to Beckmesser, leaving the dignity of the Mastersingers *per se* unaffected.

The men are organized into guilds; they are the active ones whose work is recognized socially. Far less space is given to the women. They are hardly ever present, and when they are, then in their familiar roles as observers or peacemakers. As the street riot unfolds on stage, they pour buckets of water on the crazed men to bring them back to their senses. The two women of the opera, Magdalene and Eva, belong to different social classes and thus receive contrasting musical characterizations. In operatic tradition, women of lower social standing (e.g., Blonde from Mozart's *Die Entführung aus dem Serail* or Ännchen from Weber's *Der Freischütz*) are characterized by greater melodic intervals and a syllabic ductus, whereas the so-called "femme fragile" appears with a more legato, melismatic melody, usually with smaller intervals. In her conversation with Walther and Eva, Magdalene sings a seventh leap ten times; by contrast Eva sings this interval only once. Eva is mostly accompanied by sweet-sounding instrumentation, which consists largely of the "feminine" woodwind instruments. Assuming a leading role is the clarinet, which already in Mozart signals the realm of love.

Wagner combines the world of male representation and dominance with the female world of love already in the prelude. The second subject of the prelude (see example 11.3), which Barry Millington describes merely as "a more pensive idea," presents reduced instrumentation with a score marking *sehr zart und ausdrucksvoll* (very tenderly and expressively).[11] This is a legato motif paraphrased by the woodwinds, with clarinets the most prominent, which represents the erotic world. But also the transition motif from measures 27 to 40 (see example 11.2) of the prelude, characterized by Kurt Overhoff as the "divine idea of female beauty," depicts both Eva Pogner and the biblical Eve as well as the motif from the "Abgesang" of Walther's *Preislied* (see example 11.4), which extols both Eves.[12] Here also, the instrumentation is reduced to woodwinds and strings, and the marking reads *ausdrucksvoll* (expressive) and *piano*. It is not by accident that both of Eva's motifs descend, signifying "feminine" weakness, in contrast to the Meistersinger motif which, despite the opening drop of a fourth, surges upwards.

---

10. Egon Voss, "Wagners 'Meistersinger' als Oper des deutschen Bürgertums," in *Die Meistersinger von Nürnberg: Texte, Materialien, Kommentare*, ed. Attila Csampai and Dieter Holland (Reinbek b. Hamburg: Rowohlt, 1981), 22.

11. Barry Millington, "Die Meisteringer von Nürnberg," *The New Grove Dictionary of Opera*, ed. Stanley Sadie, (London: Macmillan, 1992), 3:312–16, here 313.

12. Overhoff, *Musikdramen*, 128; also described as "Wooing motiv," cf. Bauer, *Richard Wagner*, 331.

Beauty motif

Example 11.2

Love motif

Example 11.3

Abgesang from Preislied

Example 11.4

The biblical and worldly Evas are merged rather effectively at the start of Act I, where both motifs permeate the chorale as a quasi ritornello in the church. Walther makes eye contact with Eva, who alternates between looking down into her hymnal and returning his glances. Religious and sexual elements are blended in typical Wagnerian fashion.

Although the opera is filled with motif fragments and variations of all sorts, two additional motifs point to Eva, above all, the motif of longing (example 11.5), which is found in Act II, scenes 2, 4, and 5. Eva speaks alternately with Magdalene, Sachs, and Walther. The rising chromaticism signals impetuous desire, and it is not surprising that this motif is related to the "Abgesang" from Walther's aria in Act I, scene 3, "So rief der Lenz" (example 11.6), since Walther's song has an unconcealed eroticism: "my pulses beat with ardent heat of unknown feelings thronging; through sultry night, with potent might, tempests of sighs in tumult rise and tell my passion of longing [. . .] ." Sachs shows his desire for Eva by echoing Walther's beginning in his own soliloquy "Lenzes Gebot, die süsse Noth" (Act II, scene 3). The motif of longing is also heard when Eva wants to flee with Walther (Act II, scene 5), where, now diversely transformed, it determines the continuation of the dramatic action. These sequences and the suspension all point to her desire: when in love, Eva is strong and able to give of herself. Wagner's female figures are not at all asexual. However, indications of passion and the ability to give of oneself are only possible in connection with the male protagonist.

Longing motif

Example 11.5

"So rief der Lenz"

Example 11.6

The bridal motif (example 11.7) can be traced back to the *Preislied:* it is taken both from measure 7 (significantly at the word "Wonnen" [rapture]) of the *Preislied,* as well as from the introduction to the *Preislied* (Act III, scene 5). One also hears it in the conversations between Eva and Sachs (Act II, scene 4, and Act III, scene 4). It is thus more strongly connected to the nonsexual love between Sachs and Eva, and is reduced to three notes when Sachs says no to Eva's naive question whether he would be a possible candidate to marry her.

Bridal motif

Example 11.7

Shoe motif

Example 11.8

A periodically structured simple phrase in the dialog with Sachs (Act III, scene 4) takes on a decisive significance (example 11.8). It appears more than thirty times in the simple single-measure form and is subjected to multiple variation. Eva's shoe is too tight, but in reality she is talking both about her helplessness to affect the result of the competition and about her feelings for Sachs. The motif reflects her simple and small world; it perpetually winds around itself and becomes monotonous because of the frequent repetition. It is later ennobled when transformed into Eva's baptismal theme (Act III, scene 4).

Judging from the motifs which are accorded her, Eva has both an erotic (chromatic, rising) and an idealized (diatonic, descending) component. In the descending Meistersinger fourth, which appears throughout the opera and which is contained in her motifs (examples 11.2 and 11.7), lurks the possessiveness of the male world; the chromaticism of the motif of longing (example 11.5) presents the attractiveness she exudes for men. While Walther's erotic feelings break out without restraint in Act 1, only to become ennobled through idealization in the *Preislied* at the end of the opera—in other words, he undergoes a developmental process of maturation—Eva statically carries both aspects in her. She remains both the biblical and the worldly woman and is only ever seen in connection with her "femininity," where her sole value consists of a man's love for her and her reciprocation of his feelings. Thus her identity is composed of the love she exudes, which then determines the content of her life. She is a prize to be won, a projection surface reflecting male desire and idealization that is then reflected back onto her. Several motifs are allotted to her, but she has no autonomous motif that characterizes her as an individual, and instead is blended with Walther's image of the ideal woman. When, as late as 1967, Kurt Overhoff comments with evident self-satisfaction on this fact: "this is the essence of women, that only in love do they awaken to selfhood," it becomes apparent that the ideology of the loving woman who exists solely for her man persists stubbornly well into our own times.[13]

The love between Sachs and Eva, as well as his renunciation of it, is missing in the initial sketches from 1845 and 1851. They became important the moment Wagner experienced and suffered from his passion for Mathilde Wesendonck. Musicology has largely regarded this relationship as a matter for tabloid journalism and has thus underplayed its significance. A prototypical example of such an attitude is evident in the following statement from Hans Mayer: "the Wesendon[c]k episode [. . .] is, despite everything, more tragicomical than tragical. It was not an artistic transposition." As a result, a bas-relief of Mathilde reveals to him "idolization, but also hardness along with the ability to be hurtful."[14] Robert Gutman considers her to be "rather foolish."[15] Thus she is branded as a sadistic dominatrix and a fool. Such statements by profound Wagner experts reveal the benighted search for knowledge which, behind the mask of scholarship, compulsively continues to exclude the feminine.

In an 1854 letter to Liszt, Wagner wishes for "a female soul into which I can fully immerse myself, which would seize me completely—how little would I then need of this world."[16] At the same time, the emotional and

---

13. Overhoff, *Musikdramen*, 158.
14. Hans Mayer, *Richard Wagner in Selbstzeugnissen und Bilddokumenten* (Reinbek: Rowohlt, 1969), 93 and 89.
15. Robert Gutman, *Richard Wagner: Der Mensch, sein Werk, seine Zeit* (Munich: Heyne, 1970), 137. [Translated from the English *Richard Wagner: The Man, His Mind and His Music* (New York: Harcourt, Brace, 1968), 110.]
16. Letter of 9.4.1854; Richard Wagner, *Sämtliche Briefe*, 6:109.

erotic ties between him and Mathilde Wesendonck, with whom he became acquainted and fell in love while living in Zurich, intensified. She was the enthusiastic listener. Out of affection came love, which evolved into an almost unbearable desire. As a wife and mother, she resisted it on moral grounds. His sufferings became even more unbearable from the knowledge that she loved him. Since she was indecisive about the sexual union, he wanted to demonstrate how indispensable it was. Thus he turns to her in his diary from October 1858:

> I shunned men, since their contact pained me, and strenuously sought isolation and retirement; yet the more ardently did I cherish the yearning to find in *one* heart, in one specific individual, the sheltering, redeeming haven to harbor me entire and whole. By the world's nature this could only be a loving woman: even without having found her, that was bound to be clear to my clairvoyant poet's eye. [. . .] that you could hurl yourself onto every conceivable sorrow of the world in order to say to me "I love you"—that redeemed me, and won for me that solemn peace from which my life has now gained another meaning (*RW to MW*, 60).[17]

Time and again, he thought of Mathilde as the co-creator of his works: "Place no reliance on my art! I have discovered all about it now: 'tis no solace, no compensation for me; it is simply the accompanist of my deep harmony with you, the fosterer of my wish to perish in your arms. [. . .] *With* you I can do all things—*without* you, nothing, nothing! [. . .] Everything falls asunder with me, as soon as I sense the slightest absence of harmony between us; believe me, only one!—you hold me in your hands, and only with you can I—achieve."(*RW to MW*, 69–70).[18]

Mathilde Wesendonck played a decisive role as the model for Sieglinde and Brünnhilde, as well as for Eva and Isolde. One motivation for the composition of *Tristan und Isolde* was so that Wagner could free himself from the unfulfilled sexual love; another was to send Mathilde a message: "I shall now return to *Tristan* to let the deep art of the sounding silence there speak to you for me" (*RW to MW*, 64).[19] As different as the various female roles are in terms of essence and lifestyle, they have something in common: love overwhelms them without any effort on their part; they love unconditionally and suffer greatly. Although Wagner continually dealt with a panoply of themes and often changed his mind, it is equally evident that certain matters remained constant. Among these belong his relationship to

---

17. Entry from 12.10.1858: *Richard Wagner an Mathilde Wesendonck*, 115.
18. *Richard Wagner an Mathilde Wesendonck*, 1.11.1858, 119.
19. *Richard Wagner an Mathilde Wesendonck*, 125. Wagner subsequently sent the diary entry dated October 12 [1858] to her.

women. He looked for partners who would support him unconditionally, preferably financially, as the selection of Mathilde Wesendonck and Jessie Laussot shows—but equally important was their psychological support and the requisite enthusiasm for his work. His wife Minna was unable to produce the latter. For several years, Mathilde Wesendonck was the trigger and the driving force for his art. Wagner often calls her "the child"[20] and thus compares her to Eva Pogner: "Does the wicked child intend, perhaps, to let the Master know absolutely nothing more about her? I should have been so glad to hear how the *Meistersinger* pleased her. [. . .] If the Child would only write from the Green Hill!" (*RW to MW*, 297).[21] "Keep your heart secure against *Sachs*, or you'll fall in love with him!" (*RW to MW*, 290).[22] The extent to which he identified himself with Sachs is evident from the following sentence he wrote to her: "Think of me some time during the prelude to Act III."[23]

Forced to leave the beloved "Asyl" on the grounds of the Wesendonck estate, Wagner felt himself both homeless as well as bereft of a loving partner. With the help of his art, he wanted to bring Mathilde to the point of perceiving their love as an act of providence from which there was no escape because it was rooted in her womanly nature. It is no accident that the love for Eva which Hans renounces is still missing from the 1845 and 1851 text sketches of *Die Meistersinger*, and appears for the first time in the 1861/62 version, which he wrote after the love affair with Mathilde. The bourgeois maiden Eva Pogner suffers, like her predecessors, from the torment of love. In Act III, in an "outpouring of emotional complexity"[24] filled with tritones, she makes it clear to Sachs that she could not do anything else: "It was a necessity, a compulsion." Wagner was convinced that love overwhelmed people like a force of nature, and that for this reason couples were meant for each other without any effort on their part. Once, when he and Cosima were talking about Schiller's play *Wallenstein*, he saw a similarity between the unconditionality of Thekla's love and that of Eva Pogner: "It is magnetism which contrives, for example, that the sheep finds

---

20. *Richard Wagner an Mathilde Wesendonck*, 339. Letter of 13.02.1862. Cf. the letter of 10.04.1859: "So the child is teaching the master [. . .] only because there is no such thing as severance, for us, could we go through this re-meeting!" (*RW to MW*, 117); ibid., 168. The German original is in *Richard Wagner an Mathilde Wesendonck*, 168.

21. Letter of 13.02.1862; *Richard Wagner an Mathilde Wesendonck*, 339.

22. Letter of end of December 1861; *Richard Wagner an Mathilde Wesendonck*, 336.

23. Quoted by Hans Scholz, ed., *Richard Wagner an Mathilde Maier (1862–1878)* (Leipzig: Weicher, 1930), 8.

24. John Warrack, *Richard Wagner, Die Meistersinger von Nürnberg* (Cambridge: Cambridge UP, 1994), 125.

in the wide world the grass which is good for it, all the rest is shadowy show. Thus a woman in love—the whole world consists of phantoms, but she knows where *he* is" (*Diary*, 219).[25] The longing for love erupts—still fragmentary in form, but passionate in content—in Walther's first song before the Mastersinger guild. Sachs is the only one who recognizes this: "Springtime's command, that sweet need, they laid it in his breast, then he sang, as sing he must!" Similarly, Eva can only explain her choice of Walther in terms of a higher power. In Act III she says to Sachs:

> Aye, dearest Master, chide at will, my fancy was the right one still;
> and if I had a voice, and were my heart my own;
> 'tis thou would'st be my choice, the prize were thine alone.
> But now I feel a power that tears my will in twain;
> and were I wed this hour, all choice would be in vain;
> to stem the flood that surges here, ee'n you, my Master, would not dare.

The resigned-sublime instrumentation, which presents us with the pensive Sachs alone on stage, underscores perfectly the nobility of the renunciation. Even though Sachs can be violent and authoritarian, Wagner is committed to portraying him as goodly and noble. Typical for this is the Lied he sings vociferously in order to disturb Beckmesser's serenade. He complains that Eva has left paradise wantonly, and closes with the following strophe:

> Eve, my woes must wring thy heart, and make us mourn together!
> The world condemns the cobbler's art and treads upon his leather!
> Were not an angel there, to charm away my care,
> to Paradise oft calling me, I soon would let my cobbling be!
> But when enthroned in Heaven's seat, the world doth lie beneath my feet,
> then, born anew, I am a shoemaker and a poet too!

The "angel" beckoning him to paradise refers to the real Eva, with whom he communicates his longing through the darkness. Her love for Walther has caused her to forsake the "paradise" of twosomeness, thereby making it impossible for Hans to relate to her as a partner. Eva only half understands the message, but this suffices for her to call out: "His song doth pain me, I know not why!" Wagner fantasizes himself to be the wise Sachs who, though loved, voluntarily forgoes that love, thus transforming defeat into

---

25. Entry dated 13.05.1870, in: C. Wagner, *Tagebücher*, 230. [*Cosima Wagner's Diaries, Vol. I, 1869–1877*, trans. G. Skelton (New York: Harcourt Brace, 1978), abbreviated as *Diary* with page numbers following quote.]

victory. Later, he changed the female identification figure and projected it onto Cosima. In her diary, she describes how Richard had the pianist Rubinstein play the prelude and the first scene to Act III, and then writes: "'H. Sachs has married Eva' [. . .] R. then enlarges upon Germany, which, he had been convinced, would acclaim this work, though of course it has been so badly performed—and he becomes agitated in a way that is not good for him. [. . .] 'None of it fits,' he says 'I have married Eva'—I then respond: 'But according to Herwegh you are Sachs and Walther in one, and according to me you are all of them, Tristan and Marke, Lohengrin and Parsifal [. . .] .'" (*Diary*, 623).[26]

II

The effects of the French Revolution and the struggle of the bourgeoisie for their own identity were still felt during Wagner's lifetime. *Die Meistersinger* is replete with constructions of femaleness and maleness essential for the establishment of this bourgeois identity. With his texts, music, and the dramatic action, Wagner created a reservoir of images and sounds still valid today to be stored in the collective consciousness. The collective consciousness, to which political action and representation always refer, constitutes a frame in which certain memories are localized and ordered. One can also conceive of it as a storehouse of images that are connected to one another and to the thoughts and actions of each respective collective. Nonverbal, including musical and visual, cultural practices and rituals also participate in this frame of cultural consciousness, which also affects gender-specific representation.[27] With her beauty, modesty and status as object, Eva Pogner represents "the feminine" in an idealized manner, and thus strengthens the polar construction of dual genderedness, which, in the nineteenth century, was so important both for the formation of bourgeois society as well as for the psychological establishment of patriarchal dominance.

After 1790, female statues and images stood as symbols of freedom, of the republic, of the nation, as well as symbols of cyclic-timeless nature. Wagner's oeuvre can also be considered within the context of this regeneration of acoustic and visual metaphors whose purpose was to further and sustain bourgeois self-awareness. While the male is presented as an individual, replete with wishes, interests, and history (Hans Sachs), the woman is seen as nature personified. From this, one understands why Eva Pogner has so far been taken as a "natural" female being. She stands alone, isolated, in contrast to the fraternal group of like-thinking men. While the men act, the woman functions as an object for which the men must com-

---

26. Entry for 15.02.1881, in: C. Wagner, *Tagebücher*, 4:692.
27. Cf. Silke Wenk, "Geschlechterdifferenz und visuelle Repräsentation des Politischen," *Frauen Kunst Wissenschaft* 27 (1999): 25–42.

pete and which they must court. By representing its opposite, the image of idealized femininity enables the perception and recognition of the male hero and the male group. Wagner was convinced that art should conceal itself and appear as nature. He had a similar approach to the formation of gender roles which he thought should appear "natural."

If the bourgeois male could thus form both his individual and his group male identity against the backdrop of an ahistorical and statuary woman, yet another important message was conveyed. It was of vital importance to be loved; indeed this was even more important than possession of the woman. This is clear if one considers that the man stood higher than the woman in the nineteenth-century hierarchy of values: it was more noble to forsake a woman than to look on as she went over to another man. Sacrificing the woman did not affect a man's self-worth; on the other hand, if a woman were instead to choose a rival, male honor would certainly be injured. Wagner's life-long wish to make a woman align herself to a single man (him), for whom she would live and die, coincided with bourgeois efforts. A woman abandoning a man was equivalent to emasculation and was unacceptable. Elisabeth dies for Tannhäuser, Senta for the Flying Dutchman. Elsa dares to resist this construction a little and pays a high price. After Eva Pogner reveals her love to Hans Sachs, he can then send her on to Walther. This subtheme from *Die Meistersinger* is reminiscent of the Hollywood cult-film *Casablanca* (Rick can return Ilsa to her husband only after he knows that she actually loves him) and is a topos which surfaces time and again in Western culture. It is gender specific because it is always the man who must be loved and who thereafter takes control, and it is the woman who must love with every fiber of her body, but who must then suffer because of it.

This intensification of the bourgeois feminine ideal is continued in Walther's *Preislied*, which plays a central role in the opera.[28] In the first "bar," Stolzing idealizes Eva in paradise; in the second, "das hehrste Weib" is celebrated as the "Muse of Parnassus," and in the closing strophe, "Parnassus and Paradise" are celebrated together. What Hans Mayer misconstrues as "mere addition" is actually the successful synthesis of what the woman, in Wagner's opinion, was supposed to achieve: she had to be both a sexual being as well as someone who could show the way to Parnassus, the seat of the muses in Greek mythology.[29] Wagner thus suc-

---

28. That Walther courts Eva with help of a song was possible only for a man. A woman courting a man with song would have been equated with a siren, and would be associated with coquetry, sensuality, and egoism. The sensual enchantment of the voice would be negatively valued in the case of a woman, but not in the case of Walther, whose song, by means of its mellifluousness, wins the ultimate prize.

29. Hans Mayer, "Parnass und Paradies: Gedanken zu den *Meistersingern von Nürnberg*," in *Programmheft "Die Meistersinger von Nürnberg,"* Munich Opera House (Munich, 1979), 30.

ceeds in deifying art and the artist while simultaneously reducing the woman to a subservient role. This is already evident in the rehearsal of the Preislied (Act III), when Walther says of his ideal woman:

> as her hand wove its leaves round my head:—
> where love hath bound me, here fame hath crowned me;
> I drink from her radiant eyes all joys of paradise, in love's fair dream.

Hans Mayer, who concerned himself throughout his life with Wagner's oeuvre, believed that Wagner simply introduced the two female images of the Madonna and the biblical Eve in order to combine the allegories of Parnassus and Paradise into a representation of art as he conceived it. According to Mayer, Wagner saw the Madonna as an opposite of the biblical Eve just as, earlier in *Tannhäuser,* she had been the opposite of the heathen Venus. Unlike Tannhäuser, Hans Sachs is no longer a "Minnesänger" (minstrel), but rather a middle-class Protestant. Biblical Eve is for him like Venus, the evil Eve, the temptress. Nevertheless, return to paradise is possible, not with Eva's help, but rather despite the harlot. Return is possible thanks to art.[30] Like so many of his colleagues, Hans Mayer ignores Wagner's conviction that the male artist was inspired by the woman. Dieter Borchmeyer is an exception when he albeit respectfully corrects Mayer: "Eva, with fruit from the Tree of Life, is not at all the seductress or the corrupter as Hans Mayer suggests in his otherwise most significant essay of 1979." On the contrary, in the new paradise, she is beloved Muse and Eve at one and the same time. This is why Eva crowns Walther not only with laurel leaves but also with myrtle. The crown is thus "Singer prize and love token, symbol of paradisiacal life and Parnassian art both at once."[31]

Even Peter Wapnewski does not go far enough in his interpretation when he describes Titian's *Madonna*—which Wagner revealed to be his source of inspiration—as "the image of heavenly love which represents as such the extreme successor to earthly love achieved through painful renunciation."[32] But Richard did not really sanctify renunciation, since he hoped all along that Mathilde would leave her husband and come to him.[33] In Venice it became painfully and ultimately clear to him that Mathilde would never be at his disposal. To avoid facing inner devastation, he turned the defeat around and found solace by creating a figure with whom he could identify. That strengthened him internally. Wapnewski's division into heavenly "no

---

30. Ibid., 23–38.
31. Dieter Borchmeyer, *Das Theater Richard Wagners: Idee—Dichtung—Wirkung* (Stuttgart: Reclam, 1982), 226.
32. Peter Wapnewski, *Der traurige Gott: Richard Wagner in seinen Helden* (Munich: Beck, 1978), 105.
33. Cf. Note 8.

longer desiring love" was never Wagner's objective.[34] He sought erotic and spiritual intercourse with a woman, a combination he later found with Cosima.

Jeremy Tambling maintains: "Wagner's entire metaphorical system, both in his essays and in his works for the stage, is based on the juxtaposition of polarized opposites." This is carried over into female sexuality: "I believe the drive in Wagner to be double: between the bourgeois, dignified pose and repression of the sexual in Eva and *Die Meistersinger* generally and the intense production of the sexual woman in Kundry. This duality in Wagner's discourse makes the woman destabilizing throughout."[35] Such an oversimplification, however, does not do justice to the complexity of Wagner's thought and compositions. Tambling overlooks the fact that ambivalences are evident, particularly in the area of sexuality. Since Wagner was convinced that the love between two people came by surprise and was inescapable, he had to concede sexual desire to both the man and the woman. A desiring "femme fragile" ran counter to the nineteenth-century bourgeois norms and also outraged bourgeois women, but Wagner held firm nevertheless.[36] Between the opposite poles of the virtuous and the sexually desiring woman, he also created figures like Brünnhilde, who is both virtuous and desirous. Since Eva combines the biblical and the mundane Eve, to characterize her as asexual is too limiting.

In his first appearance, Walther von Stolzing sings a Lied which is replete with sexual innuendo. It "swells," and "the surge grows" "swollen with new feelings the army of sighs swims to the sea." In this context, Sachs's criticism of Stolzing is clear enough:

Your song has filled them [the Meistersinger] with dark dismay;
And with good cause, for, truth to say,
A song so full of poet's passions
May kindle our daughters in wicked fashion.
But to praise long-lasting married bliss,
We've other words and tunes than this.

It is here that Wagner's criticism of the petit bourgeoisie, often conveyed in his letters to Mathilde Maier, becomes clear. He would, for instance, casti-

---

34. Wapnewski, *Der traurige Gott,* 106.

35. Jeremy Tambling, *Opera and the Culture of Fascism* (Oxford: Clarendon, 1996), 125 and 42.

36. The female author Luise Büchner (1821–1877) wrote outraged after a visit to the *Ring* in Bayreuth: "One gets off course if one [. . .] makes the irreverent attempt to replace moral law with the unbridled passions of nature." Luise Büchner, "Weibliche Betrachtungen über den *Ring des Nibelungen,*" *Die Frau* (1878), reprinted in: *Frau und Musik,* ed. Eva Rieger (Frankfurt/Main: Fischer, 1980), 218.

gate her "bourgeois bigotry" because she refused to move in with him and take care of his household. "Your family could run my household. And then? What would your aunts say to that?—Ah, get away with you!! You are all quite pitiful—the lot of you! Quite pitiful! You must be prepared to take risks with a man like Wagner" (*SL,* 558).[37] Wagner is aware both of the elemental power of sexuality and of its taboo status.

Tambling also overlooks the fact that the music illustrates intentional ambivalences. For instance, Wagner wrote the following about the music for *Der Ring des Nibelungen*: "By the way, only the music will give you insights into many of my more concealed and refined intentions: I sensed this now with surprising certainty."[38] Indeed the music cedes to Eva the ability to desire sexually, and shades her with diverse traits. Nevertheless, she does not have a motif which represents her throughout; she is swallowed up in a representation of woman which consists solely of love. By contrast, the renunciation motif, which is given to Sachs, is orchestrated with the warm and tender sounds of the strings and not, as in the case of Wotan, Elisabeth, Brünnhilde, or King Marke, with the rather more depressing bass clarinet. In this way, Sachs is cast less as someone suffering, and much more as a compassionate and wise human being who, while being aware of everything that happens around him, distances himself from everyday activity and vanity. It would be a little too coy to construct an unresolvable contradiction out of the fact that Wagner identified with Hans Sachs while nevertheless lacking Sachs's nobility in the way he managed his own affairs. Nevertheless, Sachs occupies the historically cultural position of the male as composer and creator. Wagner, who fantasizes himself as Sachs, creates a congruence with his protagonist, who shows the *Volk* where it needs to be in awe and where it needs to subordinate itself. The paradigm of the artist as the embodiment of male authority, as the leading figure and goodly leader of the *Volk,* is never in doubt.

III

Music and femininity are made parallel by Wagner in a manner customary for the nineteenth century.[39] As the theme of the *Preislied,* Eva remains an object; like the music itself, she represents everything that concerns feelings, emotions, and the soul. She is hardly presented as having a life of her

---

37. Letter of 11.05.1863, in: *Richard Wagner an Mathilde Maier,* 93. Cf. his letter to Ferdinand Praeger of May 1857: "Just don't come to me with any of those English notions about self-restraint [...] as far as propriety and bourgeois virtue are concerned!" Richard Wagner, *Sämtliche Briefe,* 8:338.
38. Letter of 02.09.1856 to Franz Müller, in Wagner, *Sämtliche Briefe,* 8:173.
39. Cf. Sigrid Nieberle, *FrauenMusikLiteratur: Deutschsprachige Schriftstellerinnen im 19. Jahrhundert* (Stuttgart, Weimar: Metzler, 1999).

own; her courtship of Sachs is a result of the moment only, and her agreement to flee with Walther is a consequence of her love for him. That she is prepared to do everything for her beloved is, in nineteenth-century terms, no sign of unfeminine (masculine) self-sufficiency but, on the contrary, proof that she abandons her own needs: the only thing that matters is what the beloved wants or does. And the fact that all the motifs that have anything to do with her are derived from the *Preislied* speaks for itself.

An investigation of gender roles can arrive at clear results only if one recognizes that all forms of texts that Wagner left behind (letters, drafts, diary entries, philosophical and literary texts, as well as the music itself) form part of an interconnected discourse. Wagner combines the cultural mold of the female with his own experience; often both coincide. His compositional style of refined simplicity, combined with the multiple references to nature throughout the opera, contribute to the impression that the love between two people is like a force of nature—a conviction that doubtless followed from his love for Mathilde Wesendonck. But the music also conveys the notion that the role of women as servant to male interests was something natural. Thus, Wagner remains faithful to the polarizing ideology of his century. He was suspicious about "educated" women, who, according to the perceptions of his age and according to his own convictions, had lost their femininity and threatened male dominance.[40] Eva's position is similar to that of the *Volk* who, represented and characterized by peasant songs and dances, evidently has a status lower than that of the bourgeois male, who is predestined for dominance. On the other hand, Wagner sought intense relationships with women, discussed literature, music, and contemporary intellectual trends with Cosima, and distanced himself from any sort of primitive demeaning of women. Indeed, Eva sighs: "What trouble I always have with men!" (Act II). She does not allow herself to be debased into a primitive object of male desire; she takes the initiative, wants to flee, reveals her subtle and complex relationship to Sachs, and ultimately achieves what she wants. This seems to be just as convincing a subtext, one which Carolyn Abbate reads in Wagner's female roles, and which in this case often breaks with the norms of gender construction, but which nevertheless never undermines the basic construction of Eva's character.[41]

From his unrealized relationships with women, Wagner experienced the kind of resignation that he projects onto a spiritual plane with Sachs, thereby idealizing himself, but that he was unable to sustain in his own life. Nevertheless, the figure of Sachs holds out promise: a man denies himself a young

---

40. Cf. the conflict between Wagner and the writer Malwida von Meysenbug from 15.09.1873, in Cosima Wagner, *Tagebücher*, 2:727.

41. Carolyn Abbate, "Brünnhilde Walks by Night," in her *Unsung Voices: Opera and Musical Narrative in the Nineteenth Century* (Princeton, N.J.: Princeton UP, 1991), 206–49.

woman who is fond of him because he thinks more of her than of himself—a gesture that Wagner was never willing to require of himself. Love is lifted into a spiritual sphere; like the Marschallin in *Der Rosenkavalier,* an older person forgoes the relationship with the younger one and does not succumb to aggression or self-pity, but overcomes the pain with dignity and stature. Wagner thus transcended his own personal shortcomings and, in so doing, created a masterpiece of extraordinarily composed music and emotional complexity which admittedly remained captive to nineteenth-century gender roles and rather cast its glance backward instead of forward.

—Translated by Nicholas Vazsonyi

Works Cited

Abbate, Carolyn. *Unsung Voices: Opera and Musical Narrative in the Nineteenth Century.* Princeton, N.J.: Princeton University Press, 1991.
Abbate, Carolyn, and Roger Parker, eds. *Analyzing Opera: Verdi and Wagner.* Berkeley: University of California Press, 1989.
Adler, Günter, et al. *Poet Hans Sachs: Leben, Zeit, Werk, Wirkung.* Anhand Zwickauer Quellen. Dresden: Sächsisches Druck- und Verlagshaus, 1997.
Adorno, Theodor W. "Arnold Schoenberg." In his *Prismen. Gesammelte Schriften 10.* Frankfurt/Main: Suhrkamp, 1977.
———. "Culture and Administration." In *The Culture Industry: Selected Essays on Mass Culture,* edited by J. M. Bernstein. London: Routledge, 1991. Originally published as "Kultur und Verwaltung" (1960), in his *Soziologische Schriften I,* edited by Rolf Tiedemann (Frankfurt/Main: Suhrkamp, 1972).
———. "Kultur und Verwaltung" (1960). In his *Soziologische Schriften I.* Edited by Rolf Tiedemann. Frankfurt/Main: Suhrkamp, 1972. In English as "Culture and Administration," in *The Culture Industry: Selected Essays on Mass Culture,* edited by J. M. Bernstein (London: Routledge, 1991).
———. "New Music, Interpretation, Audience." In his *Sound Figures,* translated by R. Livingstone. Stanford, Calif.: Stanford University Press, 1999.
———. "Selbstanzeige des Essaybuches *Versuch über Wagner.*" Edited by Gretel Adorno and Rolf Tiedemann. In his *Gesammelte Schriften,* 13:504. Frankfurt/Main: Suhrkamp, 1971.
———. "Versuch über Wagner." *Gesammelte Schriften.* 13:7–148. Frankfurt/Main: Suhrkamp, 1971. Also: Frankfurt/Main: Suhrkamp, 1974. In English as *In Search of Wagner,* translated by Rodney Livingstone (London: New Left Books, 1981).
———. "Wagner's Aktualität." In *Ob nach Auschwitz noch sich leben lasse: Ein philosophisches Lesebuch,* edited by Rolf Tiedemann. Frankfurt/Main: Suhrkamp, 1997.
Amerongen, Martin von. *Wagner: A Case History.* Translated by Stewart Spencer and Dominic Cakebread. London: Dent, 1983.
Antropp, Dr. "Festlicher Auftakt in Salzburg: *Die Meistersinger* unter Furtwängler in Anwesenheit von Dr. Goebbels." *Völkischer Beobachter,* 25 July 1938.
Attali, Jacques. *Noise: The Political Economy of Music.* Translated by Brian Massumi. Minneapolis: University of Minnesota Press, 1985.
Bakhtin, Mikhail. *Problems of Dostoevsky's Poetics.* Translated by Caryl Emerson. Minneapolis: University of Minnesota Press, 1984.
Barthes, Roland. "The Death of the Author." In his *Image, Music, Text,* translated by Stephen Heath, 142–48. New York: Hill and Wang, 1977.
Barthes, Roland. *S/Z.* Translated by Richard Miller. New York: Hill and Wang, 1974.
Bauer, Erwin. "Die Meistersinger von Nürnberg." *Völkischer Beobachter,* 18 November 1940.
Bauer, Hans-Joachim. *Richard Wagner.* Stuttgart: Reclam, 1992.
Bauer, Yehuda. *Rethinking the Holocaust.* New Haven and London: Yale University Press, 2001.

Beacham, Richard. *The Roman Theatre and Its Audience*. London: Routledge, 1991.
Beer, Max Josef. *Eva Pogner: Ein deutsches Charakter-Frauenbild*. Wien: Gutmann, 1882.
Benjamin, Walter. *Illuminations: Essays and Reflections*. Edited by Hannah Arendt, translated by Harry Zohn. New York: Schocken Books, 1969.
Benz, Richard. *Blätter für deutsche Art und Kunst*. Jena: Eugen Diederichs, 1915.
———. *Die deutsche Romantik: Geschichte einer geistigen Bewegung*. Leipzig: Reclam, 1937.
———. *Geist und Reich: Um die Bestimmung des Deutschen*. 3d ed. Jena: E. Diederichs, 1933.
———. *Märchen-Dichtung der Romantiker: mit einer Vorgeschichte*. Gotha: F. A. Perthes, 1908.
———. *Die Welt der Dichter und die Musik*. 2d ed. Düsseldorf: Diederich, 1949.
Benz, Richard, and Arthur von Schneider. *Die Kunst der deutschen Romantik*. Munich: R. Piper, 1939.
Bergson, Henri. "Laughter," In *Comedy*, edited by Wylie Sypher, 61–190. New York: Doubleday, 1956.
Bermbach, Udo. "Liturgietransfer: Über einen Aspekt des Zusammenhangs von Richard Wagner mit Hitler und dem Dritten Reich." In *Richard Wagner im Dritten Reich*, edited by S. Friedländer and Jörn Rüsen, 40–65. Munich: C. H. Beck, 2000.
———. "'Die Meistersinger von Nürnberg.' Politische Gehalte einer Künstleroper." In *Deutsche Meister—Böse Geister? Nationale Selbstfindung in der Musik*, edited by H. Danuser und H. Münkler, 274–85. Berlin: Edition Argus, 2001.
———. "Die Utopie der Selbstregierung: Zu Richard Wagners 'Die Meistersinger von Nürnberg.'" In his *Wo Macht ganz auf Verbrechen ruht: Politik und Gesellschaft in der Oper*, 238–59. Hamburg: Europäische Verlagsanstalt, 1997.
Bernstein, Michael A. *Foregone Conclusions: Against Apocalyptic History*. Berkeley: University of California Press, 1994.
Bertram, Johannes. *Der Seher von Bayreuth: Deutung des Lebens und Werkes Richard Wagners*. Berlin: Buchmeister Verlag, 1943.
Blau, Herbert. *The Eye of Prey: Subversions of the Postmodern*. Bloomington: Indiana University Press, 1987.
Bloch, Ernst. *Das Prinzip Hoffnung*. Frankfurt/Main: Suhrkamp, 1959.
Bloch, Ernst. "Über Wurzeln des Nazismus" (1939). In his *Gesamtausgabe*. Vol. 11: *Politische Messungen, Pestzeit, Vormärz*. Frankfurt/Main: Suhrkamp, 1970.
Booth, Michael. *Victorian Spectacular Theatre 1850–1910*. Boston: Routledge, 1981.
Borchmeyer, Dieter. "Beckmesser—the Jew in the Brambles?" *Program Book. Bayreuther Festspiele 1996*. 100–109.
———. "Nürnberg als ästhetischer Staat: *Die Meistersinger*—Bild und Gegenbild der Geschichte." In his *Richard Wagner: Ahasvers Wandlungen*. Frankfurt and Leipzig: Insel Verlag, 2002.
———. "Nürnberg als Reich des schönen Scheins: Metamorphosen eines Künstlerdramas." In *Deutsche Meister—Böse Geister? Nationale Selbstfindung in der Musik*, edited by H. Danuser und H. Münkler, 286–302. Berlin: Edition Argus, 2001.
———. *Das Theater Richard Wagners: Idee—Dichtung—Wirkung*. Stuttgart: Reclam, 1982. In English as *Richard Wagner: Theory and Theatre*, translated by Stewart Spencer (Oxford: Clarendon Press, 1991).

Borchmeyer, Dieter, Ami Maayani, and Susanne Vill, eds. *Richard Wagner und die Juden.* Stuttgart, Weimar: Metzler, 2000.

Bordwell, David. *On the History of Film Style.* Cambridge, Mass.: Harvard University Press, 1997.

Boutroux, J.-C. "Souvenirs de Salzbourg." *Le monde musical* 49.5 (1938): 118–19.

Brewster, Sir David. *The Stereoscope: Its History, Theory, and Construction with Its Application to the Fine Arts and Useful Arts and to Education.* London: John Murray, 1856.

Brinkmann, Reinhold. "Lohengrin, Sachs und Mime oder Nationales Pathos und die Pervertierung der Kunst bei Richard Wagner." In *Deutsche Meister—Böse Geister? Nationale Selbstfindung in der Musik,* edited by H. Danuser und H. Münkler, 206–21. Berlin: Edition Argus, 2001.

———. "Wagners Aktualität für den Nationalsozialismus." In *Richard Wagner im Dritten Reich,* edited by S. Friedländer and Jörn Rüsen, 109–41. München: C. H. Beck, 2000.

Broesel, Wilhelm. *Evchen Pogner.* Berlin, Leipzig: Schuster & Loeffler, 1906.

Bryant, Keri. "Mixed Messages: The Role of the Jew in Sixteenth-Century German Fiction." Ph.D. diss., University of Pennsylvania, 1994.

Büchner, Luise. "Weibliche Betrachtungen über den *Ring des Nibelungen,*" *Die Frau* (1878). Reprinted in *Frau und Musik,* edited by Eva Rieger. Frankfurt/Main: Fischer, 1980.

Buck, Paul. *Richard Wagners* Meistersinger. Frankfurt/Main: Lang, 1990.

Bülow, Paul. "Adolf Hitler und der Bayreuther Geistesbezirk." *Zeitschrift für Musik* 100, 7 (1933): 677–80.

———. "Der Führer und das Haus Wahnfried." *Zeitschrift für Musik* 106. 4 (April 1939): 362–65.

———. "Das grosse Hassen: Marxistische Hetze zum Wagner-Jahr," *Völkischer Beobachter,* 1 February 1933.

Calinescu, Matei. *Five Faces of Modernity: Modernism, Avant-Garde, Decadence, Kitsch, Postmodernism.* Durham, N.C.: Duke University Press, 1987.

Carnegy, Patrick. "Stage History." In *Richard Wagner:* Die Meistersinger von Nürnberg, edited by John Warrack, 135–52. Cambridge: Cambridge University Press, 1994.

Castle, Terry. "Phantasmagoria: Spectral Technology and the Metaphorics of Modern Reverie." *Critical Inquiry* 15 (Autumn 1988): 26–61.

Cicora, Mary A. "'Eva im Paradies': An Approach to Wagner's *Meistersinger.*" *German Studies Review* 10.2 (1987): 321–33.

Clauss, Ludwig Ferdinand. *Die nordische Seele: Artung, Prägung, Ausdruck.* Halle: M. Niemeyer, 1923.

———. *Die nordische Seele: Eine Einführung in die Rassenseelenkunde.* Munich: J. F. Lehmann, 1934.

———. *Rasse und Seele: Eine Einführung in die Gegenwart.* München: J. F. Lehmann, 1926.

———. *Rasse und Seele: Eine Einführung in den Sinn der leiblichen Gestalt.* 3d ed. Munich: J. F. Lehmann, 1934.

Corrigan, Robert, ed. *Comedy: Meaning and Form.* 2nd ed. New York: Harper and Row, 1981.

Works Cited

Crary, Jonathan. *Techniques of the Observer: On Vision and Modernity in the Nineteenth Century.* Cambridge, Mass.: MIT Press, 1992.

Csampai, Attila, and Dietmar Holland, eds. *Richard Wagner: "Der fliegende Holländer."* Reinbek bei Hamburg: Rowohlt, 1982.

———. *Richard Wagner: "Die Meistersinger von Nürnberg": Texte, Materialien, Kommentare.* Reinbek bei Hamburg: Rowohlt, 1981.

Dahlhaus, Carl. *Richard Wagners Musikdramen.* Velber: Friedrich, 1971. In English as *Richard Wagner's Music Dramas,* translated by Mary Whittall (Cambridge: Cambridge University Press, 1979).

"Daniel Barenboim and Edward Said: A Conversation." *Raritan* 18.1 (1998): 1–31.

Danuser, Hermann. "Universalität oder Partikularität? Zur Frage antisemitischer Charakterzeichnung in Wagners Werk." In *Richard Wagner und die Juden* edited by Dieter Borchmeyer, Ami Maayani, and Susanne Vill, 79–100. Stuttgart, Weimar: Metzler, 2000.

Danuser, Hermann, and Herfried Münkler, eds. *Deutsche Meister—Böse Geister? Nationale Selbstfindung in der Musik.* In Zusammenarbeit mit der Staatsoper Unter den Linden. Berlin: Edition Argus, 2001.

Debord, Guy. *Society of the Spectacle.* Detroit: Black and Red, 1983.

Derrida, Jacques. *Of Grammatology.* Translated by Gayatri Chakravorty Spivak. Baltimore: Johns Hopkins University Press, 1976.

Deutschmann, Linda. *Triumph of the Will: The Image of the Third Reich.* Wakefield, N.H.: Longwood Academic, 1991.

Diebold, Bernhard. "Der Fall Wagner: Eine Revision." In *Richard Wagner: Ein deutsches Thema: Eine Dokumentation zur Wirkungsgeschichte Richard Wagners 1876–1976.* Edited by Hartmut Zelinsky, 190–92. Frankfurt/Main: Zweitausendeins, 1976.

Ducharte, Pierre. *The Italian Comedy.* Translated by Randolph Weaver. New York: Day, 1929.

"Der Festablauf am 21. März." *Völkischer Beobachter,* 21 March 1933.

Fischer, Jens Malte. *Richard Wagners "Das Judentum in der Musik": Eine kritische Dokumentation als Beitrag zur Geschichte des Antisemitismus.* Frankfurt/Main: Insel, 2000.

———. "Richard Wagners 'Das Judentum in der Musik': Entstehung—Kontext—Wirkung." In *Richard Wagner und die Juden,* edited by Dieter Borchmeyer, Ami Maayani, and Susanne Vill, 35–52. Stuttgart, Weimar: J. B. Metzler, 2000.

Frantz, Constantin. "Offener Brief an Richard Wagner." *Bayreuther Blätter* 1 (1878): 169.

Freud, Sigmund. "Jokes and the Comic." In *Jokes and Their Relation to the Unconscious,* edited and translated by James Strachery, 188–221. New York: Norton and Routledge & Kegan Paul, 1960.

Freytag, Gustav. "Der Streit über das Judenthum in der Musik." *Die Grenzboten* 28 (1869): 336.

Friedländer, Saul. "Bayreuth und der Erlösungsantisemitismus." In *Richard Wagner und die Juden,* edited by Dieter Borchmeyer, Ami Maayani, and Susanne Vill, 8–18. Stuttgart, Weimar: Metzler, 2000.

———. "Hitler und Wagner." In *Richard Wagner im Dritten Reich,* edited by Saul Friedländer and Jörn Rüsen, 165–78. Munich: C. H. Beck, 2000.

———. *Nazi Germany and the Jews.* Vol. 1: *The Years of Persecution, 1933–1939.* New York: Harper Collins, 1997.

Friedländer, Saul, and Jörn Rüsen, eds. *Richard Wagner im Dritten Reich.* Ein Schloß Elmau-Symposium. Munich: C. H. Beck, 2000.

Frye, Northrop. *Anatomy of Criticism.* Princeton, N.J.: Princeton University Press, 1957.

"Der Führer legt den Grundstein zum Nationaldenkmal Richard Wagners." *Völkischer Beobachter,* 7 March 1934.

Geck, Martin. *Zwischen Romantik und Restauration: Musik im Realismus-Diskurs 1848–1871.* Stuttgart: Metzler, 2001.

Geertz, Clifford. *The Interpretation of Cultures.* New York: Basic Books, 1973.

Gilman, Sander L. "Why and How I Study German," *German Quarterly* 42 (1989): 192–204.

Goebbels, Joseph. *Der Angriff: Aufsätze aus der Kampfzeit.* Edited by Hans Schwarz van Berk. 5th ed. Munich: Zentralverlag der NSDAP, 1936.

———. *Das eherne Herz: Reden und Aufsätze aus den Jahren 1941/42.* Munich: F. Eher, 1943.

———. *Goebbels-Reden.* Edited by Helmut Heiber. Dusseldorf: Droste Verlag, 1971.

———. "Richard Wagner und das Kunstempfinden unserer Zeit: Rundfunkrede von Reichsminister Dr. Goebbels," *Völkischer Beobachter,* 8 August 1933.

———. *Signale der neuen Zeit: 25 ausgewählte Reden.* Munich: Zentralverlag der NSDAP, 1934.

Goehr, Lydia. *The Quest for Voice: On Music, Politics, and the Limits of Philosophy.* The 1997 Ernest Bloch Lectures. Oxford: Clarendon, 1998, and Berkeley: University of California Press, 1998.

Gregor-Dellin, Martin. *Richard Wagner: Sein Leben, Sein Werk, Sein Jahrhundert.* Munich: Piper, 1980. In English as *Richard Wagner: His Life, His Work, His Century,* translated by J. Maxwell Brownjohn. New York: Harcourt, 1983.

Grey, Thomas S. "Bodies of Evidence." *Cambridge Opera Journal* 8.2 (1996): 185–97.

———. "Selbstbehauptung oder Fremdmissbrauch? Zur Rezeptionsgeschichte von Wagners 'Meistersingern.'" In *Deutsche Meister—Böse Geister? Nationale Selbstfindung in der Musik,* edited by H. Danuser und H. Münkler, 303–23. Berlin: Edition Argus, 2001.

———. *Wagner's Musical Prose: Texts and Contexts.* Cambridge: Cambridge University Press, 1995.

Grillparzer, Franz. "Grillparzers Grabrede, 29. März 1827." In *Ludwig van Beethoven: In Briefen und Lebensdokumenten,* ed. Reinhold Schimkat, 212–14. Stuttgart: Reclam, 1961.

Grimm, Jürgen. *Molière.* Stuttgart: Metzler, 1984.

Groos, Arthur. "Constructing Nuremberg: Typological and Proleptic Communities in *Die Meistersinger.*" *19th Century Music* 16.1 (1992): 18–34.

Gunning, Tom. "An Aesthetic of Astonishment: Early Film and the (In)Credulous Spectator." In *Viewing Positions: Ways of Seeing Film,* edited by Linda Williams, 114–33. New Brunswick, N.J.: Rutgers University Press, 1995.

———. "The Cinema of Attraction(s)." *Wide Angle* 8.3–4 (1986): 63–70.

Günther, Hans F. K. *Rasse und Stil: Gedanken über ihre Beziehungen im Leben und in der Geistesgeschichte der europäischen Völker, insbesondere des deutschen Volkes.* Munich: J. F. Lehmann, 1926.

———. *Rassenkunde des deutschen Volkes.* 2d ed. Munich: J. F. Lehmann, 1923.
Günther, Hans F. K., and G. C. Wheeler. *The Racial Elements of European History.* Translated by G. C. Wheeler. New York: Dutton and Co., 1928.
Gutman, Robert. *Richard Wagner: The Man, His Mind and His Music.* New York: Harcourt, Brace, 1968.
Habermas, Jürgen. *The Structural Transformation of the Public Sphere: An Inquiry into a Category of Bourgeois Society.* Translated by Thomas Burger. Cambridge, Mass.: MIT Press, 1989.
Hamann, Hermann. *Die literarischen Vorlagen der Kinder- und Hausmärchen und ihre Bearbeitung durch die Brüder Grimm.* Berlin: Mayer & Müller, 1906.
Hanslick, Eduard. *Aus meinem Leben.* Edited by Peter Wapnewski. Kassel: Bärenreiter, 1987.
———. "Dr. Ed. Hanslick über Richard Wagner's 'Meistersinger.'" *Allgemeine musikalische Zeitung* 3.29 (1868): 225.
———. "Die Meistersinger von Richard Wagner." In *Die moderne Oper: Kritiken und Studien,* 292–305. Berlin: Hoffman, 1875. Reprint, Westmead: Gregg International, 1971.
———. *Musikalisches Skizzenbuch.* Vol. 4 of *Die moderne Oper.* Berlin: Allgemeine Verein für Deutsche Literatur, 1888.
———. *Sämtliche Schriften.* Edited by Dietmar Strauß. Cologne and Vienna: Böhlau, 1993.
Hein, Peter. *The Metaphysics of Virtual Reality.* New York: Oxford University Press, 1993.
Heine, Heinrich. *Aus den Memoiren des Herren Schabelewopski* (1822–1826). In his *Werke,* vol. 2, ed. Helmut Holtzhauer, 281–339. Berlin: Aufbau, 1974.
Helmholtz, Hermann von. "Recent Progress in the Theory of Vision (1868)." In his *Selected Writings,* edited by Russell Kahl, 144–222. Middletown, Conn.: Wesleyan University Press, 1971.
———. "Über das Sehen des Menschen (1855)." In *Philosophische Vorträge und Aufsätze,* edited by Herbert Hörz and Siegfried Wollgast, 45–78. Berlin: Akademie-Verlag, 1971.
Hermand, Jost. *Geschichte der Germanistik.* Reinbek bei Hamburg: Rowohlt, 1994.
Herz, Joachim. "Der doch versöhnte Beckmesser." In *Richard Wagner. Die Meistersinger von Nürnberg: Texte, Materialien, Kommentare,* edited by Attila Csampai and Dietmar Holland, 213–15. Reinbek bei Hamburg: Rowohlt, 1981.
Hewitt, Andrew. *Fascist Modernism: Aesthetics, Politics, and the Avant-Garde.* Stanford, Calif.: Stanford University Press, 1993.
Hitler: Sämtliche Aufzeichnungen, 1905—1924. Edited by Eberhard Jäckel and Axel Kuhn. Stuttgart: DVA, 1980.
Hobsbawm, Eric, and Terence Ranger, eds. *The Invention of Tradition.* Cambridge: Cambridge University Press, 1983.
Hoffmann, E.T.A. *Poetische Werke.* Berlin: Walter de Gruyter, 1957.
Hoffmann, Kurt. "Meistersinger-Erlebnis: Ein Bayreuther Stimmungsbild," *Bayreuther Blätter* 60 (1937): 151–52.
Hohendahl, Peter Uwe. "Reworking History: Wagner's German Myth of Nuremberg." In *Re-Reading Wagner,* edited by Reinhold Grimm and Jost Hermand, 39–60. Madison: University of Wisconsin Press, 1993.
Horkheimer, Max, and Theodor W. Adorno. *Dialektik der Aufklärung: Philosophische Fragmente.* Frankfurt/Main: Fischer, 1997.

Hutcheon, Linda. *Irony's Edge: The Theory and Politics of Irony.* London: Routledge, 1994.

Huyssen, Andreas. *After the Great Divide: Modernism, Mass Culture, Postmodernism.* Bloomington: Indiana University Press, 1986.

Jay, Martin. *Downcast Eyes: The Denigration of Vision in Twentieth-Century French Thought.* Berkeley: University of California Press, 1993.

Jens, Walter. "Ehrenrettung eines Kritikers: Sixtus Beckmesser," In *Richard Wagner. Die Meistersinger von Nürnberg: Texte, Materialien, Kommentare,* edited by Attila Csampai and Dietmar Holland, 249–57. Reinbek bei Hamburg: Rowohlt, 1981.

Jouve, Pierre-Jean. "In Memoriam Salzbourg." *La Nouvelle Revue Française* 51.299 (1938): 177–86.

Katz, Jacob. *Richard Wagner: Vorbote des Antisemitismus.* Veröffentlichung des Leo Baeck Instituts. Königstein/Ts.: Jüdischer Verlag Athenäum, 1985. In English as *The Darker Side of Genius: Richard Wagner's Anti-Semitism.* Hanover, N.H.: University Press of New England, 1986.

Kinderman, William. "Hans Sachs's 'Cobbler Song,' *Tristan,* and the 'Bitter Cry of the Resigned Man,'" *Journal of Musicological Research* 13 (1993): 161–84.

Kleinspehn, Thomas. *Der flüchtige Blick: Sehen und Identität in der Kultur der Neuzeit.* Reinbek bei Hamburg: Rowohlt, 1989.

Koepnick, Lutz. *Nothungs Modernität: Wagners Ring und die Poesie der Macht im neunzehnten Jahrhundert.* Munich: Wilhelm Fink, 1994.

———. *Walter Benjamin and the Aesthetics of Power.* Lincoln: University of Nebraska Press, 1999.

Köhler, Joachim. *Wagners Hitler. Der Prophet und sein Vollstrecker.* Munich: Karl Blessing Verlag, 1997. In English as *Wagner's Hitler: The Prophet and His Disciple,* translated by Ronald Taylor (Oxford: Polity Press, 1999, and Malden, Mass.: Blackwell Publishers, 2000).

Komow, Ray. "The Structure of Wagner's 'Assembly of the Mastersingers' Guild,'" *Journal of Musicological Research* 13 (1993): 185–206.

Kramer, Lawrence. *Music and Poetry: The Nineteenth Century and After.* Berkeley: University of California Press, 1984.

———. *Music as Cultural Practice, 1800–1900.* Berkeley: University of California Press, 1990.

Lange, Walter. "Richard Wagner Verkünder deutschen Niederganges und Aufstieges." In *Offizieller Bayreuther Festspielführer,* edited by Karl Grunsky. Bayreuth: Verlag der Hofbuchhandlung Georg Niehrenheim, 1927.

Large, David and William Weber, eds. *Wagnerism in European Culture and Politics.* Ithaca, N.Y.: Cornell University Press, 1984.

Lee, M. Owen. "Wagner's Influence: The First Hundred Years," *Wagner: The Terrible Man and His Truthful Art,* 33–64. The 1998 Larkin-Stuart Lectures. Toronto: University of Toronto Press, 1999.

Levin, David J. "Reading a Staging/Staging a Reading." *Cambridge Opera Journal* 9 (1997): 47–71.

———. "Reading Beckmesser Reading: Anti-Semitism and Aesthetic Practice in 'The Mastersingers of Nuremberg,'" Special Issue on Richard Wagner, edited by David J. Levin and Mark M. Anderson. *New German Critique* 69 (1996): 127–46.

Levin, David J, ed. *Opera through Other Eyes.* Stanford, Calif.: Stanford University Press, 1993.

Listerman, Randall. *Nine Carnival Plays by Hans Sachs.* Ottawa: Dovehouse Editions, 1990.

Lorenz, Alfred. *Das Geheimnis der Form bei Richard Wagner.* Vol 3 of 4. *Der musikalische Aufbau von Richard Wagners "Die Meistersinger von Nürnberg."* Berlin: Max Hesse, 1924–33. Reprint, Tutzing: Hans Schneider, 1966.

MacAloon, John J., ed. *Rite, Drama, Festival, Spectacle: Rehearsals toward a Theory of Cultural Performance.* Philadelphia: Institute for the Study of Human Issues, 1984.

Mack, Dietrich. *Der Bayreuther Inszenierungsstil.* Munich: Prestel-Verlag, 1976.

Magee, Bryan. "Wagner's Theory of Opera." In *Penetrating Wagner's "Ring": An Anthology,* edited by John L. DiGaetani. New York: Da Capo, 1978.

Mann, Thomas. "Bruder Hitler." In his *Essays. Vol. 4. Achtung Europa! 1933–1938,* edited by Hermann Kurzke and Stephan Stachorski, 305–12. Frankfurt/Main: Fischer, 1997.

Mayer, Hans. *Anmerkungen zu Richard Wagner.* Frankfurt/Main: Suhrkamp, 1966.

———. "Parnass und Paradies: Gedanken zu den Meistersingern von Nürnberg." Programmheft *Die Meistersinger von Nürnberg.* Munich: Munich State Opera, 1979.

———. *Richard Wagner in Bayreuth, 1876–1976.* Trans. Jack Zipes. New York: Rizzoli, 1976.

———. *Richard Wagner in Selbstzeugnissen und Bilddokumenten.* Reinbek bei Hamburg: Rowohlt, 1969.

McClatchie, Stephen. *Analyzing Wagner's Operas: Alfred Lorenz and German Nationalist Ideology.* Eastman Studies in Music. Rochester: University of Rochester Press, 1998.

McCormick, John P. *Carl Schmitt's Critique of Liberalism: Against Politics as Technology.* Cambridge: Cambridge University Press, 1997.

McDonald, William E. "Words, Music and Dramatic Development in *Die Meistersinger.*" *19th-Century Music* 1.3 (1978): 246–60.

McGlathery, James. *Wagner's Operas and Desire.* New York: Peter Lang, 1998.

Meinecke, Friedrich. *Die deutsche Katastrophe: Betrachtungen und Erinnerungen.* 5th ed. Wiesbaden: Brockhaus, [1946] 1955.

———. *Weltbürgertum und Nationalstaat.* In his *Werke,* vol. 5, ed. Hans Herzfeld. Munich: Oldenburg, 1962.

Meisel, Martin. *Realizations: Narrative, Pictorial and Theatrical Arts in Nineteenth Century England.* Princeton, N.J.: Princeton University Press, 1983.

Die Meistersinger und Richard Wagner: Die Rezeptionsgeschichte einer Oper von 1868 bis heute. Eine Ausstellung des Germanischen Nationalmuseums in Nürnberg. Edited by Gerhard Bott and Eimar Buck. Cologne: Kopp, 1981.

Millenkovich-Morold, Max von. "Richard Wagner in unserer Zeit." *Zeitschrift für Musik* 105, no.5 (1938): 469–73.

Millington, Barry. "Die Meistersinger von Nürnberg," In *The New Grove Dictionary of Opera,* edited by Stanley Sadie, 3:312–16. London: Macmillan, 1992.

———. "Nuremberg Trial: Is There Anti-Semitism in *Die Meistersinger?*" *Cambridge Opera Journal* 3.3 (1991): 247–60.

———. *Wagner.* Rev. ed. Princeton, N.J.: Princeton University Press, 1992.

Millington, Barry, ed. *The Wagner Compendium: A Guide to Wagner's Life and Music*. London: Thames & Hudson, 1992, and New York: Schirmer, 1992.

Miss., "Alljudas Kampf gegen Richard Wagner." *Völkischer Beobachter*, 29 December 1927.

Montrose, Louis. *The Purpose of Playing*. Chicago: University of Chicago Press, 1996.

Morrow, Mary Sue. *German Music Criticism in the Late Eighteenth Century: Aesthetic Issues in Instrumental Music*. Cambridge: Cambridge University Press, 1997.

Mosse, George L. *The Nationalization of the Masses: Political Symbolism and Mass Movements in Germany from the Napoleonic Wars through the Third Reich*. Ithaca, N.Y.: Cornell University Press, 1975, and New York: H. Fertig, 1975.

Müller, Ulrich, and Peter Wapnewski, eds. *Richard-Wagner-Handbuch*. Stuttgart: Alfred Kröner, 1986. In English as *Wagner Handbook*, translated by John Deathridge. Cambridge, Mass.: Harvard University Press, 1992.

Murphy, Kerry. "Berlioz, Meyerbeer, and the Place of Jewishness in Criticism." In *Berlioz: Past, Present, Future*, edited by Peter Bloom. Rochester, N.Y.: University of Rochester Press, 2002.

"Das nationalsozialistische Reichs-Symphonie-Orchester." *Völkischer Beobachter*, 19 March 1932.

Nieberle, Sigrid. *FrauenMusikLiteratur: Deutschsprachige Schriftstellerinnen im 19. Jahrhundert*. Stuttgart, Weimar: Metzler, 1999.

Nietzsche, Friedrich. *Human All Too Human: A Book for Free Spirits*. Translated by M. Faber. Lincoln: University of Nebraska Press, 1986.

———. *Sämtliche Werke: Kritische Studienausgabe in 15 Bänden*. Edited by Giorgio Colli and Mazzino Montinari. Munich: dtv, 1980.

Nohl, L. "Die Meistersinger in Wien." *Neue Zeitschrift für Musik* 66.11 (11 March 1870): 104.

Overhoff, Kurt. *Die Musikdramen Richard Wagners: Eine thematisch-musikalische Interpretation*. Salzburg: Pustet, 1967.

Petzet, Detta, and Michael Petzet. *Die Richard Wagner-Bühne König Ludwigs II*. Munich: Prestel-Verlag, 1970.

Pleasants, Henry, III, ed. and trans. *Vienna's Golden Years of Music 1850–1900: Eduard Hanslick*. New York: Simon and Schuster, 1950.

Porat, Dina. "'Zum Raum wird hier die Zeit.' Richard Wagners Bedeutung für die nationalsozialistische Führung." In *Richard Wagner und die Juden*, edited by Dieter Borchmeyer, Ami Maayani, and Susanne Vill, 207–20. Stuttgart, Weimar: Metzler, 2000.

Prang, Helmut. *Geschichte des Lustspiels: Von der Antike zur Gegenwart*. Stuttgart: Kröner, 1968.

Pretzsch, Paul, ed. *Cosima Wagner und Houston Stewart Chamberlain im Briefwechsel 1888–1908*. Leipzig: Philipp Reclam Verlag, 1934.

Raabe, Peter. "Wagners Meistersinger in unserer Zeit." In his *Die Musik im dritten Reich: kulturpolitische Reden und Aufsätze*, 68–72. Regensburg: G. Bosse, 1935.

Rasch, Hugo. "Die Festvorstellung in der Staatsoper." *Völkischer Beobachter*, 23 March 1933.

"Die Reichs-Kultur-Kammer eröffnet: Der Führer bei der Feier in der Berliner Philharmonie." *Völkischer Beobachter*, 16 November 1933.

"Reichsminister Dr. Goebbels huldigt Richard Wagner." *Der Angriff*, 7 August 1933.

"Richard-Wagner-Gedächnisfeier in Anwesenheit des Reichskanzlers." *Völkischer Beobachter*, 14 February 1933.

"Richard Wagner Morgenfeier." *Völkischer Beobachter,* 25 February 1932.
Ridder, Klaus, and Hans-Hugo Steinhoff, eds. *Frühe Nürnberger Fastnachtspiele.* Munich: Schöningh, 1998.
Robinson, Paul. *Opera and Ideas: From Mozart to Strauss.* Ithaca, N.Y.: Cornell University Press, 1985 and New York: Harper & Row, 1985.
Roell, Gustav. "Neue Beiträge zu alten Problemen: 3. Die Prügelszene in den *Meistersingern von Nürnberg*: Eine Würdigung des Dramatikers Richard Wagner," *Bayreuther Blätter* 56 (1933): 141–43.
Rose, Paul Lawrence. *Wagner: Race and Revolution.* New Haven, Conn., and London: Yale University Press, 1992.
Rosenberg, Alfred. *Gestaltung der Idee: Reden und Aufsätze von 1933–1935.* Edited by Thilo von Trotha. Munich: F. Eher Nachf., 1943.
———. *Kampf um die Macht: Aufsätze von 1921–1932.* Edited by Thilo von Trotha. Munich: F. Eher Nachf. 1937.
———. *Letzte Aufzeichnungen: Nürnberg 1945–46.* Uelzen: Jomsburg Verlag, 1996.
———. *Der Mythus des 20 Jahrhunderts: Eine Wertung der seelisch-geistigen Gestaltenkämpfe unserer Zeit.* Munich: Hoheneichen-Verlag, 1940.
———. *Das politische Tagebuch Alfred Rosenbergs aus den Jahren 1934–35 und 1939–40.* Edited by Hans-Günther Seraphim. Göttingen: Musterschmidt, 1956.
Sams, Eric. "Eduard Hanslick: The Perfect Anti-Wagnerite." *The Musical Times* 116 (1975): 867–68.
Scheit, Gerhard. *Verborgener Staat, lebendiges Geld: Zur Dramaturgie des Antisemtismus.* Freiburg: ca ira, 1999.
Schiller, Friedrich. *Über das Schöne und die Kunst: Schriften zur Ästhetik.* Munich: dtv, 1984.
Schmidt, Jochen. *Die Geschichte des Genie-Gedankens in der deutschen Literatur, Philosophie und Politik 1750–1945.* 2 vols. Darmstadt: Wissenschaftliche Buchgesellschaft, 1985.
Schmitt, Carl. *The Crisis of Parliamentary Democracy.* Translated by Ellen Kennedy. Cambridge, Mass.: MIT Press, 1986.
Schneider, Andrea. *Die parodierten Musikdramen Richard Wagners: Geschichte und Dokumentation Wagnersche Opernparodien im deutschsprachigen Raum von der Mitte des 19. Jahrhunderts bis zum Ende des Ersten Weltkrieges.* Anif-Salzburg: Müller-Speiser, 1996.
Scholes, Robert. *Semiotics and Interpretation.* New Haven, Conn.: Yale University Press, 1982.
Schopenhauer, Arthur. "Vom Sehn." In *Kritik des Sehens,* edited by Ralf Konersmann, 187–201. Leipzig: Reclam, 1997.
Segal, Erich. *Roman Laughter.* Cambridge, Mass.: Harvard University Press, 1968.
Sheffi, Na'ama. *The Ring of Myths: The Israelis, Wagner and the Nazis.* Translated by Martha Grenzeback. Brighton: Sussex Academic Press, 2001.
Sichard, Emma von. "Feste deutscher Kunst." *Völkischer Beobachter,* 22 May 1930.
Spotts, Frederic. *Bayreuth: A History of the Wagner Festival.* New Haven, Conn.: Yale University Press, 1994.
Stafford, Barbara Maria. *Good Looking: Essays on the Virtue of Images.* Cambridge, Mass.: MIT Press, 1996.
St-g, J. "Der alte Schwindel von Richard Wagners Blutbeimischung," *Völkischer Beobachter,* 12 December 1929.

Stock, Richard Wilhelm. *Richard Wagner und die Stadt der Meistersinger: Den Grossen von Bayreuth Richard und Cosima Wagner zum Gedächtnis in ihrem 125. und 100. Geburtsjahr.* Nuremberg: Verlag Karl Ulrich & Co., 1938.

———. *Richard Wagner und seine Meistersinger: Eine Erinnerungsgabe zu den Bayreuther Kriegsfestspielen 1943.* Nuremberg: Verlag Karl Ulrich, 1943.

Stuckenschmidt, H. H. "Bayreuther *Meistersinger*: Die Eröffnung der Festspiele." *BZ am Mittag*, 22 July 1933.

Tambling, Jeremy. *Opera and the Culture of Fascism*. Oxford: Clarendon, 1996.

Tanner, Michael. "The Tonal Work of Art." In *The Wagner Companion*, edited by Peter Burbidge and Richard Sutton, 140–224. London: Faber, 1979.

———. *Wagner*. Princeton, N.J.: Princeton University Press, 1996.

Taruskin, Richard. "Double Trouble." *The New Republic*, 24 December 2001, 26–34.

Turner, Richard. "Wagner's *Die Meistersinger*: The Conceptual Growth of an Opera." In *Wagner 1976: A Celebration of the Bayreuth Festival*, 83–97. London: The Wagner Society London, 1976.

Turner, Victor. "Frame, Flow, and Reflection: Ritual and Drama as Public Liminality." In *Performance in Postmodern Culture*, edited by Michel Benamou and Charles Caramello, 19–32. Madison, Wisc.: Coda Press, 1977.

Vaget. Hans Rudolf. "*Der Jude im Dorn* oder: Wie antisemitisch sind *Die Meistersinger von Nürnberg?*" *Deutsche Vierteljahrsschrift für Literaturwissenschaft und Gesitesgeschichte* 69.2 (1995): 271–99. In English as "Sixtus Beckmesser—a 'Jew in the Brambles'?" *Opera Quarterly* 12 (1995): 35–45.

———. "The 'Metapolitics' of *Die Meistersinger*: Wagner's Nuremberg as Imagined Community." In *Searching for Common Ground: Diskurse zur deutschen Identität 1750–1871*, edited by Nicholas Vazsonyi, 269–82. Cologne and Weimar: Böhlau, 2000.

———. "Wagner-Kult und nationalsozialistische Herrschaft." In *Richard Wagner im Dritten Reich*, edited by S. Friedländer and Jörn Rüsen, 264–82. Munich: C. H. Beck, 2000.

———. "Wieviel 'Hitler' ist in Wagner? Anmerkungen zu Hitler, Wagner und Thomas Mann." In *Richard Wagner und die Juden,* edited by Dieter Borchmeyer, Ami Maayani, and Susanne Vill, 178–204. Stuttgart, Weimar: Metzler, 2000.

Viereck, Peter. "Hitler and Wagner." *Common Sense* 8 (November 1939): 3–6.

———. *Metapolitics: The Roots of the Nazi Mind*. 3rd ed. New York: Capricorn Books, 1965.

Völsung, Erwin. "Bayreuther Kriegsfestspiele 1943: *Die Meistersinger von Nürnberg.*" *Nationalsozialistische Monatshefte* 14.157 (1943): 405–7.

Voss, Egon. *Die Dirigenten der Bayreuther Festspiele*. Regensburg: G. Bosse, 1976.

———. *Studien zur Instrumentation Richard Wagners*. Regensburg: G. Bosse, 1970.

———. "Wagners 'Meistersinger' als Oper des deutschen Bürgertums." In *Richard Wagner. Die Meistersinger von Nürnberg: Texte, Materialien, Kommentare*, edited by Attila Csampai and Dietmar Holland, 9–31. Reinbek bei Hamburg: Rowohlt, 1981. In English as "Wagner's 'Meistersinger' as an Opera for the German Bourgeoisie," translated by Stewart Spencer, *Wagner* 19 (1991): 39–62.

Wade, Nicholas J., ed. *Brewster and Wheatstone on Vision*. London: Academic Press, 1983.

Wagner, Cosima. *Die Tagebücher.* Edited by Martin Gregor-Dellin and Dietrich Mack. München, Zürich: Piper, 1976. In English as *Cosima Wagner's Diaries,* translated by G. Skelton. New York and London: Harcourt, Brace, Jovanovich, 1977.
Wagner, Nike. *Wagner Theater.* Frankfurt/Main: Insel, 1998.
Wagner, Richard. *Dichtungen und Schriften.* Edited by Dieter Borchmeyer. 10 vols. Frankfurt/Main: Insel, 1983.
———. *Gesammelte Schriften und Dichtungen.* Edited by W. Golther. 10 vols. Leipzig: Deutsches Verlagshaus Bong & Co., 1887–1911.
———. *Mein Leben.* Edited by M. Gregor-Dellin. Munich: List-Verlag, 1976. In English as *My Life,* translated by Andrew Gray, edited by Mary Whittall (Cambridge and New York: Cambridge University Press, 1983).
———. *Die Meistersinger von Nürnberg.* Libretto. Stuttgart: Reclam, 1963.
———. *Die Meistersinger von Nürnberg: Opera in Three Acts.* Libretto, German and English. Translated by Susan Webb. New York: The Metropolitan Opera Guild, 1992.
———. *Prose Works.* Translated by William Ashton Ellis. 8 vols. London: Kegan Paul, 1895. Reprint, Lincoln: University of Nebraska Press, 1995.
———. *Richard Wagner an Mathilde Maier (1862–1878).* Edited by Hans Scholz. Leipzig: Weicher, 1930.
———. *Richard Wagner an Mathilde Wesendon[c]k: Tagebücher und Briefe 1853–1871.* Edited by Wolfgang Golther. Leipzig: Breitkopf und Härtel, [1904], 1914.
———. *Richard Wagner to Mathilde Wesendonck.* Translated by William Ashton Ellis. New York: Vienna House, 1972.
———. *Sämtliche Briefe.* Edited by Hans-Joachim Bauer and Johanner Forner. Leipzig: Deutscher Verlag für Musik, 1991.
———. *Sämtliche Schriften und Dichtungen.* Edited by R. Sternfeld. Leipzig: Breitkopf und Härtel, 1911–16.
———. *Selected Letters of Richard Wagner.* Edited and translated by Stewart Spencer and Barry Millington. New York and London: Norton, 1987.
Walker, Alan. *Franz Liszt.* Volume Two: *The Weimar Years 1848–1861.* New York: Knopf, 1989.
Wapnewski, Peter. *Richard Wagner: Die Szene und ihr Meister.* 2nd ed. Munich: C. H. Beck, 1983.
———. *Der traurige Gott: Richard Wagner in seinen Helden.* Munich: C. H. Beck, 1978.
Warrack, John Hamilton, ed. *Richard Wagner,* Die Meistersinger von Nürnberg. *Cambridge Opera Handbooks.* Cambridge: Cambridge University Press, 1994.
Weiner, Marc A. "Reading the Ideal." *New German Critique* 69 (1996): 53–83.
———. *Richard Wagner and the Anti-Semitic Imagination.* Lincoln: University of Nebraska Press, 1995.
———. "Über Wagner sprechen: Ideologie und Methodenstreit." In *Richard Wagner im Dritten Reich,* edited by Saul Friedländer and Jörn Rüsen, 342–62. Munich: C. H. Beck, 2000.
Wenk, Silke. "Geschlechterdifferenz und visuelle Repräsentation des Politischen." *Frauen Kunst Wissenschaft* 27 (1999): 25–42.
Westernhagen, Curt von. *Richard Wagners Kampf gegen seelische Fremdherrschaft.* München: J. F. Lehmann, 1935.

Wilshire, Bruce. *Role Playing and Identity*. Bloomington: Indiana University Press, 1982.

Wittgenstein, Ludwig. *Bermerkungen über die Philosophie der Psychologie I*. Frankfurt/Main: Fischer, 1984.

———. *The Collected Works of Ludwig Wittgenstein*. Oxford: Blackwell, 1998.

———. *Philosophische Untersuchungen I*. Frankfurt/Main: Suhrkamp, 1971.

———. *Vermischte Bemerkungen: Eine Auswahl aus dem Nachlass*. Edited by H. von Wright. Frankfurt/Main: Suhrkamp, 1994.

Wollen, Peter. "Introduction." In *Visual Display: Culture beyond Appearances*, edited by Lynne Cooke and Peter Wollen, 9–13. Seattle, Wash.: Bay Press, 1995.

Zelinsky, Hartmut. "Die 'Feuerkur' des Richard Wagner oder die 'neue Religion' der 'Erlösung' durch 'Vernichtung.'" In *Musik-Konzepte 5: Richard Wagner: Wie antisemitisch darf ein Künstler sein?*, 79–112. Munich: text und kritik, 1978.

———. *Richard Wagner—ein deutsches Thema: Eine Dokumentation zur Wirkungsgeschichte Richard Wagners 1876–1976*. Frankfurt/Main: Zweitausendeins, 1976.

Zentner, Wilhelm. "Richard Wagner und die Volksbildung: Ansprache gehalten bei der 26. Hauptversammlung des Bayerischen Volksbildungsverband." *Zeitschrift für Musik* 100.7 (1933): 699–701.

Contributors

KLAUS VAN DEN BERG, Assistant Professor of Theater at the University of Tennessee in Knoxville since 1997, teaches theater history, theory, and dramaturgy. In addition to articles in books on August Strindberg, George Tabori, and image theory in contemporary performance, he has published essays and performance criticism. He is currently working on a book on Walter Benjamin's image theory and on performances in the German theater.

DAVID B. DENNIS is Associate Professor of History at Loyola University Chicago. He is the author of *Beethoven and German Politics, 1870–1989* (1996), and several other works on the intersection of German music and politics, including "Beethoven at Large: Reception in Literature, the Arts, Philosophy, and Politics," in the *Cambridge Companion to Beethoven* (2000), and an essay on Brahms's *Requiem*. He is presently working on a book surveying Nazi reception of Western humanities in the *Völkischer Beobachter*.

DIETRICH FISCHER-DIESKAU's legendary forty-five-year international singing career began in 1947 with the Brahms *Requiem,* followed the next year with his operatic debut in Berlin as Posa in Verdi's *Don Carlos*. He is equally well known for his performances of a wide range of operatic roles and his distinctive interpretations of Lieder, especially those of Franz Schubert, preserved on numerous recordings. His recording of Hans Sachs, with Eugen Jochum conducting, is on the Deutsche Grammophon label. Though his singing career ended in 1993, he continues to teach, conduct, and write.

LYDIA GOEHR is Professor of Philosophy at Columbia University. She is the author of *The Imaginary Museum of Musical Works* (1992) and *The Quest for Voice: On Music, Politics, and the Limits of Philosophy* (1998), six essays on Richard Wagner. She is currently writing on music and politics from the perspective of critical theory, and is preparing a book entitled *Unresolved Endings: The Philosophical Problems of Modernist Opera*.

THOMAS S. GREY is Associate Professor of Music at Stanford University. He is author of *Wagner's Musical Prose: Texts and Contexts* (1995) and editor and co-author of the *Cambridge Opera Handbook* on Richard Wagner's *Der fliegende Holländer* (2000). Besides serving as editor for forthcoming volumes on Wagner and the history of opera (also from Cambridge), he is working on a book-length study of music and visual culture in the nineteenth century. From 1999 to 2001 he served as editor-in-chief of the *Journal of the American Musicological Society*.

PETER HÖYNG is Associate Professor of German at the University of Tennessee in Knoxville. He has edited a book on George Tabori (1998), has published numerous articles and book reviews, and has presented at national as well as international conferences. He was recently honored by the University of Tennessee with *The Jefferson Prize*, and his second book on historical plays in eighteenth-century Germany is being published in fall 2002. He is currently working on his third book project: Beethoven's intellectual life in Vienna.

LUTZ KOEPNICK is Associate Professor of German, Film, and Media Studies at Washington University in St. Louis. He is the author of *The Dark Mirror: German Cinema between Hitler and Hollywood* (2002); *Walter Benjamin and the Aesthetics of Power* (1999), for which he received the Modern Language Association's Jean and Aldo Scaglione Prize for Studies in Germanic Languages and Literatures in 2000; and of *Nothungs Modernität: Wagners "Ring" und die Poesie der Politik im neunzehnten Jahrhundert* (1994). His current book project is entitled "Framing Attention: Windows on Modern German Culture."

HARRY KUPFER's international career as an opera stage director has included productions in London, Amsterdam, Vienna, San Francisco, Cologne, Salzburg, Florence, Hamburg, Munich, and Berlin. His Wagner productions in Bayreuth include *Der fliegende Holländer* (1978) and *Der Ring des Nibelungen* (1988). Starting in 1972, he was Opera Director at the Staatsoper in Dresden and, in 1981, became Chief Director at the Komische Oper in Berlin. His productions at the Berlin Staatsoper Unter den Linden include a Wagner-cycle together with Daniel Barenboim.

EVA RIEGER, Professor of Musicology at the University of Bremen from 1991 to 2000, has lived in London, Berlin, and Göttingen, and now resides in Zürich and Vaduz, Liechtenstein, where she works as an independent scholar. She published the letters of the singer Marie Fillunger to Eugenie Schumann in 2002 (*"Mit tausend Küssen Deine Fillu": Briefe der Sängerin Marie Fillunger an Eugenie Schumann 1875–1893*) and is currently working on the biography of Minna Wagner, née Planer, which will be published in 2003.

PETER SCHNEIDER began conducting in 1959 in Salzburg and Heidelberg, becoming Kapellmeister of the Deutsche Oper am Rhein in 1968, followed by posts as Generalmusikdirektor at the opera houses of Bremen (1978) and Mannheim (1980). He has conducted regularly at Bayreuth since 1981, including productions of *Der fliegende Holländer, Lohengrin,* and the *Ring* cycle. He has also conducted at the Staatsoper Vienna, Dresden, Staatsoper and Deutsche Oper in Berlin, as well as in Barcelona, at the San Francisco

Opera, and the Metropolitan Opera in New York. Between 1993 and 1998, he was the chief conductor of the Bayerische Staatsoper in Munich.

HANS RUDOLF VAGET is the Helen and Laura Shedd Professor of German Studies and Comparative Literature at Smith College, where he has been teaching since 1967. He has published widely focusing primarily on Goethe, Wagner, and Thomas Mann, as well as on music history and film. Cofounder and current president of the Goethe Society of North America, recipient in 1994 of the Thomas-Mann-Medaille, he is also one of the chief editors of the new edition of Thomas Mann's works, letters, and diaries. In 2001, he was awarded a Research Prize by the Alexander von Humboldt Foundation.

NICHOLAS VAZSONYI, Associate Professor of German and Director of the German Studies Program at the University of South Carolina, has published extensively on German literature and culture from the eighteenth to the twentieth century. His first book, *Lukács Reads Goethe: From Stalinism to Aestheticism* (1997), was followed by an interdisciplinary and bilingual volume *Searching for Common Ground: Diskurse zur deutschen Identität 1750–1871* (2000). He is currently working on a book concerning what he terms the "Wagner Industry."

Index

Abgesang, 26, 37, 212–13
Adorno, Theodor W., 10, 16–17, 19, 58–61, 65, 67–69, 73–74, 84, 146, 150, 160, 178–79, 190, 192–93, 197, 199, 201
aestheticization: of politics, 60–61, 64, 206–7
aesthetics: musical, 4, 6, 9, 10, 13, 19; politicization of, 16, 18, 64
alazon, 161
Ander, Aloys, 170
Angriff, 103, 109
Anschluss, 110
anti-Semitism, 1, 5, 10, 12, 18–19, 42, 100–4, 106, 115, 119, 135–37, 139–40, 146–47, 150, 153–55, 160–62, 166–68, 175n18, 179–81, 183–85, 187, 189, 191–96, 199–203, 205–6, 208
antiquity, 147, 149, 154, 161
Appia, Adolphe, 151n31
appropriation: of Wagner's works, 9, 13–14, 18, 39, 60, 68, 97, 125, 137–38, 145, 205–7
Aristotle, 161
Arnim, Achim von, 126
audience, 5, 9, 17, 58–65, 67–70, 108, 147, 150–52, 154–62

Bach, Johann Sebastian, 8–9, 25, 27, 30
Bakhtin, Michael, 94
Bakunin, Mikhail, 1, 133
bar form, 9, 175–76
Barenboim, Daniel, 124–25, 136, 139, 141
Barthes, Roland, 148–49
Bayreuth, 15, 95–96, 106, 108–9, 111–12, 194; festival, 63. *See also* Festival Theater, Bayreuth; *Meistersinger*: stagings
Bayreuther Blätter, 101, 105, 114, 166n2
Beaumarchais, Pierre Augustin Caron de, 158

Beethoven, Ludwig van, 1, 9, 25, 59, 182
Bender, Paul, 51
Benjamin, Walter, 96
Benz, Richard, 102
Bergson, Henri, 148, 154, 158, 162–63
Berlioz, Hector, 196
Bischoff, Ludwig, 168n4, 176, 182
Bismarck, Otto von, 14, 117
Bloch, Ernst, 98–99, 145
Bohnen, Michael, 51
bourgeoisie, 25, 27, 63, 92, 97n50, 116, 209, 219, 222
Brendel, Franz, 169
Brentano, Clemens, 126
Brewster, David, 85–87
Bruckner, Anton, 107
Bund Deutscher Mädel, 111

Chamberlain, Houston Stewart, 102
characterization: dramatic, 2, 10, 17; musical, 2, 10, 17
chorale, 8, 12, 28, 211, 213
chromaticism 13, 69, 175–76, 213–15
Clauss, Ludwig Ferdinand, 102
comedy, 18, 19, 123–24, 145–49, 151, 154–56, 158–59, 161–62, 164, 178–79, 203. *See also* humor; laughter
commedia dell'arte, 147, 152–55, 159–60
community, 4n12, 12, 63, 74–81, 90–92, 95, 97, 107–8, 110, 115–16, 155, 157, 208
convention: musical, 73; theatrical, 78, 81, 147–49, 152–53, 155–56, 159, 161–64, 194, 199
counterpoint, 8, 11, 12, 25–27, 29, 35–37
critics: music, 104, 165–67, 188
culture industry, 60, 84, 95

David, King of Israel, 26–27, 31, 130

decadence, 9, 13,
Deinhardstein, Johann Ludwig, 129
desire, 213, 215–16, 218, 222–24
diatonicism, 13, 175, 214
Döll, Heinrich, 81–82, 84, 89–90
Dresden: uprising of 1849, 132–33, 166
Dürer, Albrecht, 13, 99, 104, 114, 130
Dustmann, Luise, 170, 173, 182n33

eiron, 161

Fastnachtspiel, 130, 153–56, 159
Faust, 6, 112
Fechner, Gustav, 75
festival, 91–92, 94–96,
Festival Theater, Bayreuth, 26, 63, 108, 111. See also Bayreuth Festival
Fétis, F.-J., 175
film, 96, 98–99
Franco-Prussian War. See Second Reich
Frantz, Constantin, 207–8
Freud, Sigmund, 59, 90n34, 148, 154n44
Freytag, Gustav, 186
Friedrich, Götz, 16n54, 204
Frye, Northrop, 149, 151, 153, 162

gaze, 77–81, 96
gender, 7, 19–20, 209, 215–16, 219–20, 223–25; musical discourse of, 10–11, 211–12, 215, 223
genius, 41, 59, 64–66, 91, 104, 108–10, 112, 117, 124–26, 141, 201, 206
genre, 123, 145–49, 163–64
German identity. See identity, German
Germanness, 7–8, 10–12, 18, 40, 104, 107, 109, 113–15, 118, 124–25, 130–31, 133, 138, 191, 206. See also identity, German
Gervinus, Georg Gottfried, 126–27, 131
Gesamtkunstwerk, 64, 198
gesture, 78
Gewandhaus, Leipzig, 107
Geyer, Ludwig, 104–5

Goebbels, Joseph, 7–8, 98n1, 99, 102, 109–10, 112, 207
Goethe, Johann Wolfgang von, 6, 18
Goldoni, Carlo, 151, 158
Goliath, 28
grand opera, 11–12, 67, 196, 198
Grillparzer, Franz, 9
Grimm Brothers, 18, 42, 126, 128, 131, 175n18, 188n44, 199–202, 204
Grunsky, Hans Alfred, 206
guild, 12, 25, 46, 205, 212
Günther, Hans F. K., 102
Gutzkow, Karl, 184

Habermas, Jürgen, 92n39, 94
Hampe, Michael, 204
Händel, Georg Friedrich, 9
Hann, Georg, 51
Hanslick, Eduard, 7, 10n35, 19, 42, 63, 146, 150, 165, 167–73, 177–84, 188–89, 195, 203
Hanslick, Karoline, 181–82, 195
Haydn, Joseph, 9, 182
Heine, Heinrich, 134–35, 184n37
Helmholtz, Hermann von, 75, 86–88
Herwegh, Georg, 219
Herz, Joachim, 204
Hiller, Ferdinand, 182
historians' debate (*Historikerstreit*), 190
Hitler, Adolf, 5, 14, 95–96, 99, 101, 104, 107–11, 115, 117–19, 125, 136–38, 145–46, 157, 189–92, 194, 206–7
Hitlerjugend, 111
Hoffmann, E.T.A., 121, 126, 128
Hofmannsthal, Hugo von, 38
holocaust, 18–19, 101, 106, 119, 162, 190–93, 204–5
Horst-Wessel-Lied, 98–99, 109
humor, 146–47, 162, 164, 178–79, 199. See also comedy; laughter

identity, German, 15, 124–6, 134, 140, 200, 202. See also Germanness
improvisation, 5, 9, 28, 174–75, 201
innovation, 91, 122, 124, 138

Index

inspiration, 46, 64, 221
instrumentation, 24–25, 33–35, 37, 54, 211–13, 218, 223

Jank, Christian, 81, 84
Jens, Walter, 204
Jew: caricature of, 10n35, 17, 42, 100n8, 147, 167, 180, 192, 196–97, 199; representation of, 10, 17–18, 103, 105–6, 153, 185–86, 188–89, 193–94, 196–98, 200, 202–3, 205–6
Jewish conspiracy: Wagner's fear of, 19, 103, 106, 136–37, 166–69, 173, 181–83, 195
Jude im Dorn, Der, (Jew in the Brambles). *See* Grimm Brothers

King Marke, 67, 69, 112, 130
Kisch, Salomon Abraham, 181
Krüger, Eduard, 168n4
Kulturindustrie. *See* culture industry

laughter, 147–48, 150, 153, 155, 159–60, 162–63, 199. *See also* comedy; humor
Laussot, Jessie, 217
Leipzig, 27, 107; Gewandhaus, 107
leitmotiv, 19, 25, 27, 60, 214–15
Lessing, Gotthold Ephraim, 147
Levi, Herrmann, 136
Levine, James, 136
Ley, Robert, 112
Liszt, Franz, 13, 133, 178, 215
Lorenz, Alfred, 9, 16, 26–27, 33, 206
Lortzing, Albert, 91, 129, 156
Ludwig II, King of Bavaria, 82, 165, 166n2, 183, 210
Luther, Martin, 28, 125

Machtergreifung (seizure of power), 107
Maier, Mathilde, 222–23
Mann, Thomas, 125, 190–91, 201
Marx, Karl, 1
mastersingers, 8, 13, 25–26, 41–42, 46, 53, 62, 90, 129, 151
Meinecke, Friedrich, 138, 190

Meistersinger von Nürnberg, Die: first draft (1845) of, 123, 132, 152, 159, 181, 215, 217; parodies of, 185–88; prose sketch (1861) of, 132, 170–71, 211, 217; protests against, 184–85;
characters:
David, 10, 28–30, 36, 53, 64, 79–80, 154–55, 160, 162, 172;
Eva Pogner, 2, 7, 10–11, 13, 15, 17, 19, 28, 33–34, 38, 41, 43, 46–47, 53–54, 62, 65, 67, 78, 80–81, 117, 120, 123, 130, 150, 152, 154–57, 159, 161n68, 162, 187, 209–10, 212–15, 217–24;
Hans Sachs, 2, 4n12, 8–10, 13, 16–17, 20, 34–43, 45–46, 49–53, 58, 62–63, 65–68, 70, 73, 78–81, 92, 95, 97, 105, 109–12, 114, 116–20, 130–32, 139, 150, 152–64, 168, 179, 187, 198, 204, 207, 210, 213–15, 217–24;
Magdalene, 28, 53, 79, 155, 160, 162, 212–13;
Sixtus Beckmesser, 5–6, 10, 13, 17–19, 32, 35, 38, 42, 44–45, 49, 53, 63–67, 78–80, 90, 93, 100–101, 103, 105–6, 113n55, 116, 119–20, 123–24, 130, 147, 150, 152–54, 156, 158–63, 165, 167–68, 171–80, 183–90, 192–93, 195–99, 201–6, 208, 211–12;
Walther von Stolzing, 5–11, 17, 26, 28, 30–32, 37, 40–41, 46–47, 49–50, 52, 54, 58, 61–62, 65–70, 73, 78–79, 81, 90–91, 93, 97, 105, 117–9, 122–5, 130, 132–33, 138–39, 150, 152, 156–63, 174–7, 179, 185–88, 198, 200–1, 204, 212–13, 215, 218–20, 222, 224;
Veit Pogner, 7, 10, 13, 17, 31, 33, 37, 42, 46, 63, 130, 150, 153n34, 157, 174;

Meistersinger von Nürnberg, Die: (continued)
sections of:
  cobbler's song (Act II), 35–36, 54, 105, 178–79, 218;
  festival meadow (*Festwiese*, Act III), 33, 38, 42, 50, 55, 76, 79–81, 83–84, 89–97, 111, 114–16, 139, 153–54, 156–58, 162–63, 168, 174, 179, 180, 203–5, 211–12;
  Fliedermonolog (Act II), 34, 41, 53–54, 213, 218;
  Hans Sachs, final monologue ("Verachtet mir die Meister nicht"), 8, 27, 39–40, 46, 54–55, 62, 68–69, 109–14, 118–19, 124, 136, 139, 156–58, 198, 201, 207;
  prize song, (*Preislied*, Act III) 7, 17, 26, 33, 37, 58, 62, 64–69, 107, 157–58, 168, 174, 180, 203–4, 212, 214–15, 220–21, 223–24;
  prelude to Act I, 8, 11, 23–28, 33–34, 98, 105, 179, 211–12;
  prelude to Act III, 36–37, 54, 162, 217, 219;
  quintet (Act III), 38, 162;
  riot scene (Act II), 35–36, 42, 48, 79, 90, 100, 105–6, 114, 154, 158–62, 179, 184, 212;
  serenade (Act II), 30, 33, 35–36, 44, 105–6, 154, 157, 159, 160–61, 163, 168, 178–81, 185, 196–97, 203, 218;
  trial song (Act I "Fanget an!"), 2, 7n22, 46, 54, 64, 66, 69, 78, 157, 160, 163, 168, 174, 175, 177, 179, 199–203, 213, 215, 218;
  "Wach auf" chorus (Act III), 36, 38, 108–10, 207;
  "Wahn" monologue (Act III), 35, 37, 54, 67–68, 80, 114, 179;
  stagings: 1868 Munich, 81–84, 88–89, 173; 1924 Bayreuth, 14, 108; 1925 Bayreuth, 14n51;

1933 Bayreuth, 18, 95, 108–9, 206; 1933 Berlin, 107, 206–7; 1935 Nuremberg, 103, 206; 1951 Bayreuth, 14–15; 1956 Bayreuth, 15; 1960 Leipzig, 204; 1963 Bayreuth, 93, 156n48; 1977 Stockholm, 204; 1979 Berlin Deutsche Oper, 204; 1984 Bayreuth, 204; 1985 Sydney, 204; 1989 Seattle, 204; 1993 Frankfurt, 204; 1994 Stuttgart, 204; 1996 Bayreuth, 204

Mendelssohn-Bartholdy, Felix, 19, 165–68, 181–82, 184, 186–87
metapolitics. *See* Frantz, Constantin
Meyerbeer, Giacomo, 19, 136, 166–68, 181, 184, 186, 196
middle ages, 8–9, 49, 74, 76, 82, 92, 114, 126–27
Minnesota, 123n1
modernity, 12
Molière, Jean Baptiste, 151–52, 158
Mozart, Wolfgang Amadeus, 9, 52, 158, 162, 182, 212
Müller, Johannes, 75
Munich. *See Meistersinger*: stagings
myth, 7–8, 12n46, 46, 73, 108, 132n20, 151, 157, 191, 202

Napoleon I, Bonaparte, 126
national socialism, 8, 99, 101, 103, 106, 110, 112, 114, 116, 119, 190, 205. *See* nazi,
nationalism, 5, 8, 14, 39, 40, 73, 91, 99, 110, 138, 140–41, 150, 156n50, 206
nazi, 8–9, 13, 18, 39–40, 60–61, 68, 76, 95–99, 101–7, 112–14, 117, 125, 137, 140, 142, 145–47, 157, 179, 189, 190, 206–7
Nehl, Christoph, 204
Neue Zeitschrift für Musik, 165, 168n4, 185
Neuenfels, Hans, 204
New German School, 13, 169, 176
Nietzsche, Friedrich, 1, 11, 66, 120, 147n10, 178, 201
Nohl, Ludwig, 185

Novalis, Friedrich von Hardenberg, 126
Nuremberg, 5, 7–8, 12–13, 33, 42, 46, 49, 73–74, 81–82, 84, 91–92, 95–96, 98–99, 103–4, 108, 110, 113–5, 125, 128, 130–31, 138–40, 142, 151, 153–54, 181, 205; Laws, 115, 125, 138; rally. *See* party congress

Paris, 123, 132–35, 196, 211
party congress, Nuremberg, 95–96, 98, 103, 110, 115, 125, 138, 145, 151
pedantry, 42, 53, 65, 67, 91, 120, 124, 138, 147, 168, 178, 189
performance, 1, 6–7, 13–17, 23, 39, 51, 56, 58, 61, 65, 79, 87, 90, 93, 146–47, 152–53, 157–59, 163; ban in Israel, 3, 192
phantasmagoria, 17, 74–76, 84, 91, 95–97
Planer, Minna. *See* Wagner, Minna
Potsdam, Day of (March 21, 1933), 107–8, 207
propaganda, 18, 60, 99, 101, 106, 109–11, 114, 118, 206–7

Quaglio, Angelo II, 81–82, 84

Raabe, Peter, 113, 116
radio, 58–59, 65, 96, 109
rally. *See* party congress
Ranke, Leopold von, 131
Reformation, 114, 125
Reichskulturkammer, 110
Reichsmusikkammer, 105, 113, 116
Reichsparteitag. See party congress
renaissance, German, 73, 75
renunciation, 5, 20, 36, 39, 41–42, 67, 69, 211, 215, 217–18, 220–21, 223–25
revolutions of 1848, 104, 106, 132. *See also* Dresden, uprising of 1849
Riefenstahl, Leni, 76, 95–96, 98–99, 113
Rochaix, François, 204

romanticism, 5, 12–13, 73, 79, 80, 126, 135
Rosenberg, Alfred, 102, 103n21, 109, 112–13, 113n55
Rousseau, Jean-Jacques, 92–95
Rubinstein, Joseph, 136, 219
rules, 78, 122; of mastersingers, 5, 26, 30, 36–37, 41–42, 46, 53, 65, 116, 152, 175

Sachs, Hans, 5, 8, 13, 91, 103, 114, 120, 127, 129, 153–56. *See also Meistersinger*: characters, Hans Sachs
Salzburg Festival, 110–11
Sardou, Victorien, 151
Schiller, Friedrich, 4n11, 12, 80n18, 122, 139, 134, 147, 217–18
Schlesinger, Maurice, 196
Schmitt, Carl, 93
Schopenhauer, Arthur, 85
Schumann, Robert, 182
Scribe, Eugene, 151, 157
Scudo, Pierre, 175
Second Reich, 14, 74, 125, 133, 141
seizure of power (*Machtergreifung*), 107
sexuality, 7, 41, 46, 152, 210, 212–13, 215–16, 220–23
Shakespeare, William, 94, 146n9, 151, 199
Sheridan, Richard, 158
Shostakovich, Dmitri, 189
Shrovetide play. *See* Fastnachtspiel
song contest, 7, 42, 93, 150, 203
spectacle, 76–79–81, 84, 89, 90–93, 95, 96n48
Standhartner, Dr. Joseph, 170–72
stereoscope, 75, 85–90, 96
Stock, Richard, 102–4, 110–11, 114–15
Stollen, 175, 201
Strauss, Richard, 28, 113, 225
Streicher, Julius, 115
Strobel, Otto, 206
style, musical: French, 11; German, 11; Italian, 11, 52, 160–61, 185–86, 197–98

tableau: theatrical, 90, 149, 156–61, 163–64
Tabulatur, 9, 32, 42, 46
Tannhäuser, 40
Tausig, Karl, 136, 173
Third Reich, 14, 17–18, 97–98, 106, 110, 113, 115, 117, 139, 160, 194, 205, 207
thirty years' war, 12
Tietjen, Heinz, 18, 76, 95–96
Titian, 221
tradition, 5, 13, 19, 31, 40, 46, 53, 62, 67–68, 80–81, 91, 129, 147, 152–53, 159, 163–64, 210

Uhlig, Theodor, 168n4, 202
unification of 1871, German. *See* Second Reich
utopia, 13, 39, 91, 145, 151, 157, 207

Venice, 221
Verdi, Giuseppe, 186–87
Vergangenheitsbewältigung, 15, 17
Vienna, 128, 132, 169–71, 173, 184–85, 187
Viereck, Peter, 191
vision, 17, 74, 76–79, 87, 90, 95–96
visuality, 17, 74–76, 85, 90, 95–96
Volk, 5, 11, 55, 62–65, 68–70, 79–81, 89–91, 93, 95–97, 104, 106, 108–9, 111–12, 114–19, 131–32, 134, 139, 152, 154–55, 168, 202, 205, 208, 223–24
Völkischer Beobachter, 103–7, 109, 111, 113

Wackenroder, Heinrich, 13, 126, 129, 131
Wagenseil, Johann Christoph, 30, 128, 175
Wagner, Carl Friedrich, 104
Wagner, Cosima, 40, 102, 136, 140, 156n50, 165, 182, 184–85, 217, 219, 222, 224
Wagner, Minna, 211, 217
Wagner, Richard: *A Communication with my Friends*, 11, 79, 159; *Art and Revolution*, 11, 195; *Artwork of the Future*, 76–77, 195; *fliegende Holländer, Der*, 25, 39, 135, 170, 220; *German Art and German Policy*, 121, 130n14, 166n2; *Judaism in Music*, 12n45, 19, 100n7, 103, 136, 165–67, 169, 172–73, 179–86, 189, 194–95, 197–98, 200, 203–4; *Lohengrin*, 127, 169–70, 173n14, 174, 219–20; *Meistersinger von Nürnberg, Die*. See separate entry; *My Life*, 121, 127–28, 133, 171; *On Conducting*, 28; *On German Art*, 121; *Opera and Drama*, 11, 195, 207; *Parsifal*, 121, 123, 127, 145, 151n31, 219, 222; *Rienzi*, 194; *Ring des Nibelungen, Der*, 38, 39, 49, 127, 145, 151n31, 165, 172, 174, 202–3, 210–11, 222–23; *Tannhäuser*, 127, 146, 169, 220–21, 223; *Tristan und Isolde*, 2–3, 13, 17, 38–40, 67–69, 127, 145, 152, 170–71, 174, 177, 211, 216, 219, 223; *What is German?*, 12n44, 132n21, 166n2
Wagner, Siegfried, 105
Wagner, Wieland, 15, 93, 156n48
Wagner, Wolfgang, 42, 204
Wahn, 4n10, 5, 36–37, 60, 68, 79, 94
Walther von der Vogelweide, 8
Wartburg, 128
Weber, Carl Maria von, 107, 212
Wesendonck, Mathilde, 20, 210–11, 215–17, 221, 224
Westernhagen, Curt von, 103, 108
Wheatstone, Charles, 85–86
Windt, Herbert, 98–99
Wittgenstein, Ludwig, 16, 56–58, 60, 62
Wolf, Hugo, 54
Wolfram von Eschenbach, 52
Wotan, 51–52, 112

Ziegler, Hans Severus, 206
Zurich, 195, 216